Cubs Forever

Memories from the Men Who Lived Them

>>

Bob Vorwald
Photographs by Stephen Green

TRIUMPH
BOOKS

No part of this publication may be reproduced, stored in a retrieval system, or transmitted in any form by any means, electronic, mechanical, photocopying, or otherwise, without the prior written permission of the publisher, Triumph Books, 542 South Dearborn Street, Suite 750, Chicago, Illinois 60605.

Triumph Books and colophon are registered trademarks of Random House, Inc.

Library of Congress Cataloging-in-Publication Data

Vorwald, Bob, 1962-
  Cubs forever : memories from the men who lived them / Bob Vorwald and
Stephen Green.
      p. cm.
  ISBN-13: 978-1-60078-044-8
  ISBN-10: 1-60078-044-X
 1. Chicago Cubs (Baseball team)--History. I. Green, Stephen, 1952-
II. Title.
  GV875.C6V67 2008
  796.357'6477311--dc22

                              2007051772

This book is available in quantity at special discounts for your group or organization. For further information, contact:

Triumph Books
542 South Dearborn Street
Suite 750
Chicago, Illinois 60605
(312) 939-3330
Fax (312) 663-3557

Printed in U.S.A.
ISBN: 978-1-60078-044-8
Design by Wagner | Donovan Design, Inc., Chicago, Illinois

All photos courtesy of Stephen Green Photography unless otherwise indicated.

>>>
Dedicated to Jack Rosenberg
for his inspiration and assistance, to the
men and women of WGN-TV for their
60-year pursuit of excellence, and to
ballplayers everywhere for giving us these
and so many other magical memories.
>>

Contents

Bill Murray puts an exclamation point on his
2004 Opening Day first pitch.

Acknowledgments

>>

This project could not have been conceived and completed without the help of many talented individuals.

Mitch Rogatz, Tom Bast, and the staff of Triumph Books believed in our idea and guided this book to fruition. Tom Ehlmann at WGN-TV gave his approval and full support to *Cubs Forever*, as did John McDonough and Mike Lufrano with the Chicago Cubs. Joe Rios and Katie Marta worked with us at every turn to arrange time and space for interviews at Wrigley Field. Cameraman Jim Tianis shot almost all of the interviews and Terry Bates did a superb job of editing the DVD.

To all the other people who lent a hand, as Jack Brickhouse said in his Hall of Fame induction speech, "You know who you are and you have my undying gratitude." Finally, a huge thank you goes out to each of the interviewees for sharing their time, insight, and treasured memories. ●

Using the long zoom lens of the day, a WGN-TV cameraman captures the action from the back of the left-field bleachers at Wrigley Field.

Introduction

>>

This is a love story.

On April 16, 1948, only eight days after coming on the air for the first time, WGN-TV televised its first Chicago Cubs game, a preseason exhibition contest at Wrigley Field against the Chicago White Sox. Of course, the Cubs lost.

For WGN, the Cubs, their fans, and Wrigley Field, it was love at first sight, the beginning of a unique 60-year romance that continues to this day.

This is not a comprehensive history of the relationship between WGN and the Cubs. It is not an attempt to psychoanalyze how a team that hasn't won a World Series in 100 years has a fan following whose relentless optimism makes Richard Simmons look like a downcast whiner. As John McDonough always says, "Don't try to understand it, just embrace it." This book is a group hug, an attempt to do just that and embrace the amazing relationship between the Chicago Cubs, their fans, and WGN-TV.

Cubs Forever is a reminder of all things good in our world, from Ernie Banks's smile to the quiet grace of Ryne Sandberg; from the unflinching loyalty of Ron Santo to the endless patience of Billy Williams; and from the rosy outlook of Jack Brickhouse to the gregariousness of Harry Caray. The memories and moments of the past 60 years are best told by the men who provided them.

Since 1998, I have been the executive producer of WGN Sports, but my personal love affair with the Cubs goes back to getting hooked while watching games as a seven-year-old fan in 1969. There is a continuing argument in my family as to whether that was my father's greatest gift or if he was just looking to share his pain, but I will always be thankful he included the rest of us in his devotion. I landed a job with WGN in 1982 and have been covering the Cubs in one form or another ever since.

Our goal at WGN-TV for the past 60 years has always been the same: to take you to the ballgame. We have been privileged to work in the greatest television studio in sports in Wrigley Field and have as our viewers the greatest fans in sports.

Jack Brickhouse used to crack "any team can have a bad century." It was funnier 30 years ago than it is now. The breakthroughs of the Red Sox and White Sox, combined with the disappointment of 2003, have definitely added an edge to the genial sunniness that has defined Cubs fans for years. Yet, on each telecast, no matter what the city, we continue to see the daily rekindling of the indestructible love affair between the Cubs and their fans.

The initial key to the success of televised baseball was the vision of Cubs owner P.K. Wrigley. In 1948, television wasn't the guaranteed revenue stream for baseball owners that it is today. It took a leap of faith by Wrigley, and with it, a keen understanding of the team's fan base, to make the collaboration work. WBKB-TV actually was the first television station to broadcast the Cubs, starting in 1946 and joined by WGN-TV two years. WENR made it three stations when they did a slate of games in 1950, but two years later WGN-TV was granted exclusive broadcast rights.

The move to televise all Cubs home games was not well received by Wrigley's fellow owners. "I remember 50 years ago the other owners would call Mr. Wrigley and say, 'Why are you televising your games? You are just diluting your own product,'" recalled Ernie Banks. "And he would say, 'No, I'm not. I am creating fans.' And it grew and grew and grew. He was an amazing man."

"When I came on with the Cubs, WGN was there and Jack Brickhouse was there," Banks continued. "I really didn't think about it all, but years later when I had retired, I would have people come up to me and say, 'I used to rush home from school every day by the seventh inning to see you come to bat.' It was very shocking to me to know that it had expanded all the way around the city. People watched the games and knew who I was. It helped me in a lot of ways to be in Wrigley Field on WGN playing day games."

Longtime WGN sports editor Jack Rosenberg started out at the same time as Banks and echoed his thoughts. "The people we had there and the power of the station, when we first started—who knew it was going to be that big? They told Phil Wrigley in those years to watch out with radio and television, that people wouldn't come if the weather was bad, but he was a prophet and he made a profit."

> *This book is a group hug, an attempt to…embrace the amazing relationship between the Chicago Cubs, their fans, and WGN-TV.*

The emergence of the Cubs as America's team was never more evident than in 1962. The recently launched Telstar communications satellite made it possible to bounce television signals across the Atlantic to Europe. On the much-ballyhooed July 23, 1962, premiere, the plan was to showcase several elements of Americana to an audience across the pond. When the signal came up, national news anchors Walter Cronkite and Chet Huntley informed viewers that a scheduled President Kennedy press conference had not yet started. Instead, the first view of America sent to Europe was something much better: the Cubs and Wrigley Field via WGN-TV.

Pat Pieper informed the crowd over the PA that the game was now being shown in Europe, and as flags waved and the crowd cheered, Jack Brickhouse chimed in with a greeting from Chicago. "Well, we realize that all this doesn't make sense to you folks in Europe, but if we hadn't shown you a bit of our national game on this first trans-Atlantic show,

we'd have never heard the end of it. As a matter of fact, right now our colleagues who are doing the translating are going crazy trying to say *runs, hits,* and *errors* in Swedish and Italian. Anyway, here it is—a brief glimpse of American baseball played in the biggest arena in the world. All the way from Wrigley Field in Chicago to the Colosseum in Rome."

The call letters WGN stand for "World's Greatest Newspaper" in deference to the station's owner, the always-modest *Chicago Tribune*. By the late 1970s, "We Go National" might have been more apropos. The boom in cable and home satellite dishes created a need for programming that was readily satisfied by the Cubs when WGN became available across the country as one of the first "superstations." For many players and fans alike, the chance to see the Cubs each afternoon was sheer delight. "It was outstanding," recalled Cubs shortstop Ivan DeJesus. "When the cable came in, back home in Puerto Rico we had a chance to see the games. It was a nice feeling; my family had a chance to see me play, all of my friends back home."

The combination of national exposure, the arrival of Harry Caray, and the success of the 1984 team created a national phenomenon that was not lost on the new breed of Cubs players. For Jody Davis, it was evident both at home and on the road. "Back when I played, all the games were in the afternoon, so you either watched the Cubs or soap operas. I think we won that battle. It was amazing to me the Cubs fans and our relationship at Wrigley Field, but when we would go on the road, it would be five, six, ten thousand people pulling for us in the road stadiums."

"I was lucky throughout my career," explained Ryne Sandberg. "Every single game I played was on WGN and I knew that people were watching. I knew that my relatives and friends were watching in the state of Washington. I knew that people in Arizona were watching me and I knew that friends on other teams were watching me play, so that was just exposure that was unique to the Chicago Cubs. I was just fortunate to have all those games on TV and have everybody watch me play."

The fact that the Cubs played day baseball truly made them the only game in town on a national scale. Director Arne Harris would cackle to the crew each weekday, "They love us in Vegas, guys. We're the only thing on in the sports books." Cubs baseball was a staple of the Armed Forces Network sports schedule as well, a fact we realized in 1998 when we started soliciting e-mails during the telecast and heard from soldiers around the world and found out that 4:00 AM viewing parties were the norm at the American Embassy in Moscow when the Cubs had a night game during the pennant race that year.

As part of our special that year celebrating Sammy Sosa Day at Wrigley Field, we sent WGN reporter Robert Jordan to Sammy's hometown of San Pedro de Macoris in the Dominican Republic. There was no cell phone connec-tion available, but we were able to cue Jordan through the magic of WGN. Across the street was a small bar that picked up the Cubs on WGN off a satellite dish. One of the patrons stationed himself at the door with a view of the TV and hol-lered out to Jordan each time to tell him he was on the air!

Change has been the one constant of our six decades of Chicago Cubs baseball on WGN. Different camera loca-tions, high-definition television, and shifting game times all make the broadcasts markedly different than they were 60 years ago. But one thing will never change: our passion to do everything possible to provide an outstanding presenta-tion of the games for the great Cubs fans who have made us a part of their family throughout the years. It's been a great ride. The moments, memories, and voices that follow are a wonderful reminder of just how good it can be. ⚾

The legendary Vin Scully with WGN-TV's
Bob Vorwald (left) and Jim Tianis (right).

The Lady

>>>

VIN SCULLY

You don't have to be a Cubs fan to love Wrigley Field. Just ask Hall of Fame broadcaster Vin Scully, long the voice of the Brooklyn and now Los Angeles Dodgers. His eloquent descriptions have graced the airwaves for more than 50 years while doing Dodgers games and also taking his turn handling national broadcasts throughout his career. Scully is the unquestioned dean of baseball announcers, so when he speaks of love for a ballpark, he gets your attention.

Among his many postseason assignments, Scully was the play-by-play man for the 1989 National League playoffs between the San Francisco Giants and the Cubs. As the nation tuned in to NBC to watch the opening of Game 1 at Wrigley Field, Scully's voice delivered a splendid homage to one of his favorite places:

> She stands alone on the corner of Clark and Addison, this dowager queen, dressed in basic black and pearls, 75 years old, proud head held high and not a hair out of place, awaiting yet another date with destiny, another time for Mr. Right.
>
> She dreams as old ladies will of men gone long ago. Joe Tinker. Johnny Evers. Frank Chance. And of those of recent vintage like her man Ernie. And the Lion [Leo Durocher]. And Sweet Billy Williams.
>
> And she thinks wistfully of what might have been [shots of the 1984 playoffs on the screen], and the pain is still fresh and new, and her eyes fill, her lips tremble, and she shakes her head ever so slightly. And then she sighs, pulls her shawl tightly around her frail shoulders, and thinks—this time, this time it will be better.

If you can just imagine Scully's soothing intonation echoing over shots of the Friendly Confines, it is the perfect personification of the Wrigley Field we all love so dearly.

"Not a wrinkle on her, though. She's still in very good shape," Scully said, when asked about the ode to the lady Wrigley. "I do remember sitting in the hotel room and writing that, trying to conjure up in my mind how I could relate Wrigley. Then you start thinking how far back it goes, the oldest ballpark in the National League, and then it was going to be at night, so you think of dark, and then the lights, so you think of pearls. Once in a while you get lucky, and that's what I wrote."

His history with Wrigley Field spans more than 50 years of visits, back to a time when television was in its infancy and the crowds at the park were as sparse as Cubs wins. When the first night game was rained out on 8/8/88, Scully called the first official game the next night on an NBC telecast. He has listened to Pat Pieper and Wayne Messmer, knew Ernie Banks as a shortstop, studied outfielders from Hank Sauer to Sammy Sosa, and watched as the Wrigley neighborhood has been transformed from sleepy to sassy. Through it all, Scully has been one of the great voices in baseball and knows a true gem when he sees it. It takes one to know one.

WRIGLEY FIELD

"I have to tell you in all honesty—and I'm not saying this because of WGN—going to Wrigley Field has always been a treat for me. I can remember in the early days when I would go to Wrigley, there was a full orchestra behind home plate with a male singer and a female singer, and no matter how you felt Sunday morning when you got to the ballpark, you heard that orchestra, it just lifted everything up. I'll always remember a memorable weekend when I was doing *The Game of the Week*. I was doing Friday night, and we did Saturday afternoon in Boston in Fenway Park, Yankees–Red Sox. Then I got on an airplane, flew over to Chicago and the Dodgers-Cubs on Sunday. To spend a weekend at Fenway and Wrigley is to go back in a time capsule. The fans are like nowhere else, and you are aware of them, like you used to be in the old days at Ebbets Field and other places. So Wrigley Field has always had a very warm, warm spot in my heart along with the fans. They've always been very gracious and kind, good-natured kidding and all that stuff."

SINGING THE SEVENTH-INNING STRETCH IN 1998
"I hope people understand, I guess I did it reasonably well, and the Cubs asked me to come back and do it again, and I said no, no, no. This was not an ego trip for me. I didn't stand up and sing 'Take Me Out' so that I could have more exposure, in all honesty. I did it for one reason, and it was in memory of Harry [Caray]. So that's why I did it once and never again. I remember Tommy Lasorda saying to me afterward, 'You were singing, and you said, "Cubbies."' I said, 'Yeah, when in Rome. Did you think I was going to say, "Dodgers"?' It was wonderful, and I enjoyed the experience very much."

WOULD WINNING CHANGE THE CUBS?
"The Brooklyn Dodgers were looked upon as zany and inept, then they changed completely. They got better, and their image changed from Bum to, I guess now, Hollywood. To the fan, to the kid growing up in Chicago, if they [the Cubs] won 10 World Series, I think they would still be the Cubs." —*Vin Scully*

JIMMY FARRELL

Umpires don't get much love from the fans or the players at Wrigley Field, but for more than 25 years, Cubs umpires were blessed with a chief protector of the highest order in Jimmy Farrell. He took care of all their needs in a small, converted barracks that serves as the umpires' room.

Farrell was one of the most beloved faces of Wrigley Field for his ever-present smile, cheery attitude, and kind words for all—just the temperament you need if you are going to minister to the needs of four umpires every day. He retired after the 2007 season, but not before making hundreds of friends throughout baseball.

If he had been a player, Farrell would have been called a late bloomer since he didn't arrive at Wrigley until after he retired for the first time. "I was a school custodian when I retired," said Farrell. "I had nothing to do, and I was driving my wife, Eleanor, crazy at home, so somebody told us to come over here, that they were hiring some people at Wrigley Field. I came down here, and I filled out an application with the girl at the desk. They gave me a small card to fill out, and I put my name, that I was retired, and my phone number. I figured it would end up in the wastepaper basket. Two days later, Dallas Green called me and wanted to know if I wanted the umpires' room job, and I said sure. It was a lucky thing."

"I was green as grass. I didn't know anything about an umpires' room. John Vukovich helped me a lot, introducing me to players and getting autographs from them back when the umpires could get autographs. I went on from there. It's been a great, great run."

One unintended benefit of his new position was a new name. "From the time I went to St. Gabriel's grade school, I was known as 'Bro' Farrell," said Farrell. "When I came here, I put my real name, James Farrell, on the card. So Harry Caray thought my name was James, and he would look down when Arne [Harris] put me on television once in a while and say, 'There's little Jimmy Farrell, what a great little guy, that fella.' Ever since that time, everybody knows me as Jimmy. I never went by Jimmy in my life. The umpires, the players, all the people around here call me Jimmy, all because of Harry Caray."

The umpires' attendant duties start with preparing the day's baseballs by rubbing them down with a special mud from Delaware used by Major League Baseball. After that comes a myriad of tasks with one thing in common:

Umpires' attendant Jimmy Farrell leaves the game ball on the mound for the Cubs starting pitcher.

making the umpires as comfortable as possible. "On a normal day, you get three or four dozen baseballs for the game," Farrell said. "Then you come in and hang up the umpires' equipment, get their shoes ready for them, etc. We want everything ready for them when they come in the door. I made sure the coffee was ready and would get them a little something to eat if they wanted it when they came in. We're here to help them and get them something if they need it. Once the game starts, you take them water, and after the game, have food and the shower all set up for them. You're here for them, whatever they want. I never met a bad umpire since I've been here. They're all great guys, and it's been a great experience for me."

During batting practice, Farrell made the rounds of the dugout and offered his usual dose of cheer. "Of all the friendly people I've met here, he may be the friendliest," offered Len Kasper. His broadcast partner takes it a step further. "The only bad thing about Jimmy is that he worked with umpires, and you know how I feel about umpires," laughed Bob Brenly. "If there was ever a human being on the earth that could get along with umpires, it's Jimmy Farrell."

It's not surprising that Farrell made many friends for life. "Doug Harvey, Ed Vargo, all the guys that retired, I have so many memories from them," he said. "Harry Wendelstedt was another great umpire. He brought me down to his umpiring school once and introduced me to all his students at their graduation. One time the umpires sent us to Las Vegas, all expenses paid. I could go on and on about these guys."

"The umpires love him," said fellow attendant Tom Farinella, who took over Farrell's duties after his retirement. "I've known him for over 30 years and never known anyone to say a bad word about him. His wife, Eleanor, came out every day and sat behind home plate, then met him after the game to go home together. That's just great."

Farrell was known to entertain visitors to the umpires' room during the game, including one of his favorites, Kerry Wood. "I spent a lot of time with Jimmy," said Wood, who gushes when it comes time to talk about Farrell. "There were days where I would sneak back to the umpires' room during the game and just chat. Jimmy is great. I've had great conversations with him. He's a special human being."

The feeling is mutual. Farrell would sometimes leave Wood a message on the mound when he dropped off the game ball, including the *W* he inscribed on the ball before Wood pitched Game 7 against the Marlins. Things didn't work out, but you can't blame Farrell for trying.

Because of Wrigley Field's limited space, the umpires' room is just off the Cubs' clubhouse, and when Farrell watched the game, he stood in the home dugout. Don't ask him to tattle on any of the bench jockeys, although his presence helped mute some of the criticism of the men in blue. "What you hear out there stays out there!" Farrell declared when asked for some dugout dirt. "I did hear some stuff about the umpires, since I was in the dugout, but it was usually in fun. Remember, tomorrow is another day, and they'll be out there shaking hands on the field. In the spur of the moment people say things, but they always forget about it. It doesn't last. Before you know it, they may see each other in a cocktail lounge and buy each other a drink. It's baseball. You can't figure out baseball. Nobody will ever figure out baseball. That's the way it is. You just never know."

FAMILY MATTERS

"The thing I liked most is helping when family members come to town. Families that come here to Chicago have such a good time. I made sure that they were taken care of and got good seats for the game. If it was a day game, they can go out to dinner together after the game. The umpires are all in a better mood when they have their families here. They are away from them most of the year, and I know they miss them terribly."

HANGING OUT WITH THE PLAYERS

"When the clubhouse used to be down the left-field line, guys would leave the dugout and come in here to watch the game, chew the fat, and have a cup of coffee. Billy Buckner was the greatest. We were celebrating our 40th wedding anniversary, and I said to him for fun in the dugout, 'By the way, Bill. We're having an anniversary party in Lisle tonight if you want to stop over.' He said, 'Where's it at?' and I told him the directions to my son's house. I knew that he wasn't going to come and was just BS-ing me. Sure enough, at 8:00 PM the doorbell rang, and there was Bill. He came in and joined us, and we had a great time together."

TODAY'S UMPIRES

"The new kids are coming in now. They're a different breed. They drink a lot of water now and not beer like they used to. They work out in the hotel before they come here or in the room here after the game. They are much more health-conscious than the old-timers were. They're good kids. They have so much pressure on them now with supervisors on them and everything being watched. It's a hard job with travel all the time." —*Jimmy Farrell*

FAVORITE MEMORY

"It was our 61st [wedding] anniversary. Charlie Reliford was here as the chief umpire at the time. He sent me out for something, then while I was gone, called up Jim Hendry to set it up. I came back in, and he told me to get hold of Eleanor. She came down to the umpires' room, then we all went out to home plate together. The umpires had flowers for us and took a picture of us all together. It was the greatest thrill of my life. It was really something."

HARRY CARAY

"I think Harry Caray right now is probably up in heaven with God in the booth doing a baseball game between the angels and the saints, and he is probably saying, 'There's so-and-so.' God will say, 'That's not his name, Harry!' and Harry will say, 'Well, okay, we'll call him Stosh or something then.' If I get there, he'll say, 'There's little Jimmy Farrell from the umpires' room.' I hope that comes true."

RUNNING THE SCOREBOARD: FRED WASHINGTON

It might be impossible to pick one spot as the best seat in the house at Wrigley Field, but if you want to make that list, a good place to start is with Fred Washington's perch in the center-field scoreboard. Washington is a longtime member of the Cubs' scoreboard crew, and nothing escapes his gaze through an open window atop the center-field bleachers.

Washington joined the Cubs in 1984, working with security before joining the grounds crew in 1990 and assuming his current duties. Like most of the grounds crew, he has multiple duties that start long before the game begins. "On a game day, I have to go around, open up the bathrooms, turn the lights on, make sure that they have everything the matrons need to carry them through the day," he explained. "After that, I have a couple of field chores. I'll go out there and do them, and my last chore is the chalk lines. I put the chalk lines down from third base to home, from home to first base. After which I put the chalk lines up, and I come up here to sit here and do the game."

By the time Washington heads upstairs, Brian Helmus, the "chairman of the board," has the team match-ups arranged on the scoreboard and the team flags atop the board hung in order of the standings. With Darryl Wilson on the second level manning the computer to get updates from around both leagues, the scoreboard crew is ready for action, using the system that has been in place almost as long as the scoreboard itself.

"When the Cub game starts, I handle the hits for both teams," said Washington. "I also handle the lowest game on the left side, which is usually the White Sox game and the game above it. We have the whole scoreboard going. We have to keep the crowd informed and everybody else informed as to what's going on in the other games. When Darryl calls down his orders for me, they sound like this. He'll tell me, 'Freddy, in the bottom game, American League side, put two runs in the bottom of the

Fred Washington has worked the scoreboard high above the center-field bleachers since 1990.

third.' We'll keep going until that game is over, at which time we will take down the zeroes and numbers and put up blanks. After the game is over, the public will see all blanks except for the final score, which is placed over by the tenth inning."

Friday afternoon games are the quietest for the scoreboard crew because the Cubs game is almost always the only one in progress. Saturday and Sunday have what the crew calls "a full board," which keeps everyone moving. Washington handles the hits while Helmus posts the runs scored by the Cubs and their opponent. Washington also does the game above the Cubs' on the National League side. No matter what, one of the two has to keep an eye on the game in front of him. "If Darryl calls down to give me some orders to go do this, I'll wait until Brian is sitting there, and then I'll get up and go. He may call something down for Brian, and he may call something down for me at the same time. One of us will move, the other one will sit. When one comes back, we will go and do our chores, then come sit back down."

There are plenty of bleacher volunteers willing to scale the ladder and help out in the scoreboard, but the current crew is doing just fine, thank you. "I'll stick my head out of the window, and this is what I see all day long. 'Can I come up?'" said Washington. "No, you can't. 'Can my girlfriend come up?' No, she can't. This is a lot of fun, this is entertainment, but this is also a job, from my perspective. I can't have people come up here because what are they going to do? Interrupt me, because I have chores to do. The things that I have to do pertain to all of the fans who are out there and also everybody nationally that is looking at this game. So I have to keep myself focused so that everybody gets the right information."

Washington's last assignment of the day is to head to the top of the scoreboard and raise the famous *W* and *L* flags, depending on the outcome of the day's game. He tries to spare the feelings of the commuters when deciding when to post an *L* for the El. "If we lose a game and there is an El train going by, there's a lot of people on that El,

and they're looking up to see which flag I put up," he said. "If the El is going by, I never raise the loss flag. I always stop and wait for it to pass, and then I'll raise it. But if it's a *W* flag, I can't wait for the El to come by. I'll stop and wait for the El to come so I can raise that won flag. I can just imagine people on the El cheering. It just does my heart a world of good because long before I came here, I was a Cubs fan. Long after I leave here, unless it's in a body bag, I'll still be a Cubs fan."

BEST SEAT IN THE HOUSE

"This is the best seat in the house, probably the best job in the world considering that you're a baseball fan and me personally also a Cubs fan. Everything that happens in this ballpark you can see from this viewpoint. There's nothing that you miss." —*Fred Washington*

GIVING BACK

"Some days when I am looking out, I will see a little kid waving at me and watching me. If I get the chance, I like to go down, and I give the kid a baseball I might have around from batting practice. One day I gave one to a little boy who must have been here with a family reunion because he kept looking up at me and waving after I gave him a ball, then his whole family gave me a standing ovation. It doesn't cost anything to be nice. I am just trying to add something to somebody's experience so that they come out here and enjoy it. It might be their first game, it might not be, but it gives me extra joy to watch a kid's face light up. It will stay with them for a long time."

GROUNDS-CREW PRIDE

"We had a family day here on the concourse for all the workers to bring their families in and mingle with the players. They had about 30 people participating in a hula-hoop contest here, and they got me to do it. The last two left were me and Vanessa Dawson, Andre's wife. All the guys at my table were wishing that I would lose because they didn't want the grounds crew to be known as the hula-hoops champions. Vanessa beat me, and they were relieved."

FRIENDS FOR LIFE

"There's a lot of things that go on around here that are really nice. The thing that stands out with me the most is I started here as a worker in 1984, and I've met some people here that will be my lifetime friends. Considering that you are just coming into a job, you would never envision the fact that you're going to meet somebody who has such an impact on your life. But you can meet people here who will be your lifetime friends, and it's the most amazing thing to me. It overshadows even baseball. A lifetime friendship means more to me than a baseball game, a baseball team, because it's the human element of it."

LEE SMITH

Six-foot-six, 250 pounds. A menacing scowl. An excruciatingly slow gait while meandering in from the bullpen with the game in the balance. Add in a fastball in the high 90s, and you have all the ingredients for a great closer—in this case, one Lee Arthur Smith, the most dominant relief pitcher in Cubs history.

It almost didn't happen. The Cubs nearly lost their closer of the future when he was assigned to the bullpen after struggling as a starter. "When I was in the minor leagues and the Cubbies made me a relief pitcher, I packed my bags and went home from Triple A," Smith said. "Billy Williams came to my house, and I can't tell you in public what he said to me, but he convinced me to come back and play baseball. I guess the rest is history. It was frustration. I guess that is the nature of what you go through with the Cubbies and baseball itself, not just the Cubs, I guess. That little round ball has made a lot of grown men cry."

Things clicked for Smith late in 1982, and he broke through in 1983 with a 1.65 ERA, 29 saves, and his first All-Star appearance. The next year, he started a streak of four straight years with 30 or more saves, becoming the first National League reliever to reach that mark, and he always took his time doing it. "Nobody was slower coming to the mound from the bullpen than Lee Smith," said Steve Stone. "You didn't want to face him in the shadows because you really couldn't see the ball all that well."

The Wrigley Field shadows became an extra weapon in Smith's arsenal. The Cubs had added a number of 3:05 PM businessman's special start times, and no one was happier about that than Smith. "Oh man, it was beautiful," he said. "I wish we could have played all our games at 3:05, but some of the games went too long and they had to start them up the next day, I guess. The main reason is when we got in late or coming from the West Coast. I don't know how the guys who played every day did it. It was crazy, but I loved it."

Bob Brenly still winces at having to face Smith in those games. "Let me just say this," he said. "I look forward a lot more to seeing Lee Smith in our booth to sing the seventh-inning stretch than I did to facing him at around 5:30 on some of those matinees. It was just unfair."

Smith was always accused of having a daily siesta in the Sleepy Confines as part of his routine. "Yeah, that's true," he said. "There was nothing better than waking up with a three-run lead. It was refreshing! Yeah, I did, but it was always if nobody saw me in the dugout, they said, 'Smitty's asleep.' But you don't last 18 years in the big leagues sleeping. I'd watch the umpires and the other team, so I did my homework. Occasionally, I'd take a nap, but the clubhouse now is so plush, I'd never wake up. I'd have to hire a guy to wake me up."

His 180 saves and 452 relief appearances are still Cubs records. Smith did his best work at a time when the one-inning closer was still a gleam in Tony La Russa's eye. "I remember one game when Rick Reuschel came back, I pitched four innings in a game in Houston. It was up to the discretion of the scorekeeper whether or not I got a save. I gave up two runs, and the guy said it wasn't an effective three innings. I was like, but I pitched four! I didn't get a save. Back then, it was like the guys who were tossed out to the bullpen were guys that weren't good enough to start.

Lee Smith amassed a Cubs-record 180 saves during his eight seasons with the team.

It was like, 'Let's send him to the bullpen 'til the game is out of hand.'"

Smith loved a good joke as much as anybody. "One time we had an umpire who was friends with a jockey," remembered Jimmy Farrell, the umpires' attendant. "All this jockey wanted to do was take batting practice, so they arranged for him to come to the park and get him in the cage. I'll never forget the look of terror on his face when he was standing there and saw Lee Smith doing that slow walk with a scowl on his face to come and pitch to him! Of course, once he got there, Lee broke up and served him some easy ones."

General manager Jim Frey opted to trade him to Boston for Al Nipper and Calvin Schiraldi after the 1987 season, surprising most Cubs fans, but Smith never slowed down. He pitched in the major leagues for 10 years after the trade in 1987 and retired with 478 career saves, which was a major league record at the time.

CUBS FANS

"They are definitely the best. When I came to the big leagues, I met so many people, and I'd go out into the park. The Cubbies didn't know it at the time, but I was playing basketball with half the Bleacher Bums after the games. You get to know people on a first-name basis, and it's like a family." —*Lee Smith*

WRIGLEY FAMILY

"I would go over to the firehouse a lot. Our parking spot was right there, so I would go hang out with those guys. The chief let me read his newspapers. Yosh Kawano never had a paper for us, so I would spend my quality time there reading the paper and talking to the guys.

"Most of the guys that I still see now, more than my old teammates, are the grounds-crew guys. I still see Rick Fuhs and all of them. They were my guys. I used to try on the 1:20 games to help them out. I had an agreement with the grounds crew because I knew they got time and a half after 4:30, so that's where my slow walk started. It was for

my buddies. I would fuss on the mound and make them come out to fix it. They would say, 'Lee, there's nothing wrong with the mound. Nobody strides where you do.' I'd tell them, 'Just fix it, guys. I have to make sure you get your time and a half.' Of course, I made them buy the beer!"

THE '84 CUBS

"We were never out of a game. We had that confidence and that definitely spills over to the bullpen, and as a closer, I had that confidence."

CLINCHING IN 1984

"Ah, that's a vague memory because [Rick] Sutcliffe had a lot of champagne for us! Just to go out there and be a part of it—wow! As a matter of fact, Steve Trout still comes around and shows me the tapes of us in '84, and people hear me screaming about my 'fro. I'll tell you what, it gives me goose bumps right now just thinking about that. That right there was more than just a team for me; it was like a family. You would never see those guys like one guy out by himself. It would always be the pitchers, or the bullpen guys, or the infielders, outfielders all together. I still see Ryno and Jody and the guys like that, and it's really good. It was more than just a team for me."

THE SAVE RECORD

"I was glad to have it, and I was at the game with Trevor Hoffman of the Padres when he broke my record. The next night he blew a save, though, and I was talking to him and saw this nice plaque. I asked him why it didn't have any writing on it, and he said they were waiting until he retired to fill in the number of career saves. I told him he better not blow another one or they might engrave that thing the next day and show him the door! As a closer, you have to have a thick skin."

BASEBALL TODAY

"I served as the pitching coach for the South African team in the first World Baseball Classic. Obviously, we had a group that had not played that much baseball, and we were trying to teach fundamentals. Those kids had a lot of heart. We had a 17-year-old closer, and we were leading Canada in a close game that could have been a huge upset for us. I went to tell him to go right after those guys, but when I finished, I thought he was going to follow me right off the mound. I said, 'Hey man, one of us has to stay out here!' We lost that game, but it was a great experience."

THE WGN TRUCK

To the first-time observer, the action in the WGN-TV production truck during a game can be an overwhelming sensory experience, with the sight of a wall of monitors and visual effects punctuated by the noise of at least six different conversations being carried on simultaneously. It's like an exquisite ballet combined with a head-on collison between two trucks. For the people who work in that environment, it's just another great day at the ballpark.

The baseball crew members are on-site six hours before the scheduled start of each game at Wrigley Field. Each game day follows a routine of setting up and checking out the equipment, recording elements for the pregame show, a quick break for lunch, then everyone and everything in place for the three-hour-plus roller-coaster ride known as Chicago Cubs baseball on WGN.

What goes on during those three hours is not for the faint of heart. "Let's see, it's controlled chaos, laughter, snarling, and intensity, with hours of boredom punctuated by moments of panic," said Greg Gressle, who supervises the technical setup each day as the engineer-in-charge. "It's a tough thing to run camera on a game for three hours and give your undivided attention and make sure you are right on it at the instance of the bat crack. Believe me, it's not easy."

"The first time I was in a TV truck, the first play I saw was a routine grounder to first, and I was amazed at all the things that happened on that one simple play," said Pete Toma, who runs the replays, handles the business of the game, and guides the announcers in his role as producer.

"If you ask anybody about watching baseball on TV, you usually hear that it's slow and can be boring, but when you see what's happening in here, it's anything but. There are so many different conversations going on at the same time, and each one of us has to listen and talk as a part of several things at the same time."

As director of the telecast, Skip Ellison picks the camera shots that go on the air, and he has to follow the conversation between Len Kasper and Bob Brenly, as well as the action on the field, while giving directions to the rest of the crew. "It's all about trust. I have to trust the camera guys to get the shot, I have to tell Pete to tell me which replay or bit of business we're going to, and I have to trust my technical director to follow my directions. You have great moments, and then there are times when everybody is at each other's throat. What you have to remember is that we are all interested in getting the same great product out, and if we argue, it's because we care. In many ways, it's like a great basketball team. You have to know what moves the other person is going to make. You have to work together. It's remarkable to do that with a different group of people in each city. It's a great feeling when it all comes together."

Marc Brady handles all the graphics for the telecast and manages to roll with the punches while constantly updating the statistical information for each player. "Despite all the noise and how hectic it can get, it is still a pretty smooth machine where everyone knows their job," said Brady. "At the end of the day, when the Cubs have won, you really feel like you were a part of something special."

The truck is not the realm of only Cubs fans. There are a healthy number of White Sox diehards on the crew, which makes for some inventive chatter throughout the season. "As a Sox fan, I can be more objective and tell everybody I see things from the other team's point of view!" laughed Mark Stencel, who works with Brady to build the graphics and statistical information for the telecast. "We all laugh, and I don't dislike the Cubs and would like to see them win just like my team did."

Director Arne Harris and producer Pete Toma put together
another Cubs telecast on WGN-TV.

The legacy of former director Arne Harris and the rest of the WGN pioneers is still strong in the minds of the current crew. "For us, it's about that day's game," said Toma. "We want our viewers to feel like we are taking them to the ballpark. This is not a national show where we're saddled with a story line we have to use or feel the need to educate people about both teams. It's a local broadcast that people can see on a national level."

Toma, Brady, and Ellison are the only crew members, along with Brenly and Kasper, who work on the road telecasts as well. The technical crew is a different set of people in each city, yet the task is the same—take Cubs fans to the ballpark. "It doesn't matter if it's at home or on the road,"said Ellison. "At home, you have a full house. On the road, it's great. I'm a big college football fan, and I always compare the Cubs to any great college program with the loyalty, the love, and the willingness of the fans to travel nationally to see their team play."

MARC BRADY, ASSOCIATE PRODUCER

"The best part of working on the Cubs games is pulling up at Wrigley Field early on a Sunday morning and seeing a line of people around the ballpark, all waiting to get in. It's the most amazing thing in the world. Traveling with the Cubs, you get to see the phenomenon. You pull up in the team bus to the hotel, and you see a father and his son, both in Cub jerseys, there's nothing like that. I traveled with the Bulls, and they were like rock stars when they were good, but the fans for this team want to see the team no matter how it changes from year to year. They are always there.

"The best part about my job is doing baseball for a living and getting paid for it. It's like a marriage—what they take you through, the highs and the lows—but I grew up loving the Cubs and I still do. My favorite moment was being on the field in Atlanta in 2003, when the team was celebrating their first postseason series win since 1908. There were all those Cubs fans there cheering, and it was unbelievable."

WYN GRIFFITHS, CAMERA

"I came to the States from Wales, so I learned about baseball from my wife. She started taking me to games when I moved here. I feel privileged to be able to say that I work with WGN at Wrigley Field. The broadcasts have been going on for 60 years, and there has been so much talent working on these games. I'm a new guy because I have only 15 years in, but this group is special and has a lot of passion to go with experience. Our crew has a lot of fun, but there is a friendly competition to try and get the best shots, which really keeps us fresh.

"One of my favorite days was running the dugout camera the day Kerry Wood struck out 20 Houston Astros. He was my assignment almost the whole game. I remember that he was shaking as he came off the field at the end of the game, and I have to say I was, too."

SKIP ELLISON, DIRECTOR

"Wrigley Field is so unique as a venue because you not only have 40,000 screaming fans every day, you have the neighborhood around the park where we always send a portable camera out before the game to gather some of that flavor. You've got the rooftops, kids on the street playing catch on Waveland Avenue, and so much more. On the field, you have an unbelievable palate to choose from, with the ivy, the scoreboard, the low dugouts, the basket in front of the bleachers, and all the great fans. It's a place like no other in the National League, certainly, and different from Fenway in that you have the neighborhood that is so much a part of things here.

"One of my favorite games was in 2001, when we did the first baseball game in high definition at Wrigley Field. The game ended on a freak play in the ninth inning, with a three-way rundown and Ricky Gutierrez diving in for the winning run. The last two home games of 2007 were also special, with the Cubs winning both to take charge of the division. The crowds were incredible, and the new tradition of singing 'Go Cubs Go' had really taken off."

SCOTT JONES, VIDEOTAPE

"It's fun to come to work, see license plates here from coast to coast, and know that your work makes people happy all over the world. It is cool that with the technology and reach of the superstation, the fun we show can spread so far so fast. Doing day games has always been special, and it still is.

"You could open the doors here in February, and fans would pack the place here. Living in a great city and working on these shows is great. We have a lot of good days together as a crew. When I stop to think about it, there are many things that our crew does together that are totally unspoken because we have been together so long and know how we do our show. That's what I notice when I do a job for a network game or someone other than WGN. There's nothing like that feeling after a good game when we had a good game with lots of runs, and we had a great telecast where everything went well. You are really cranked and pumped up walking away after a game like that."

PETE TOMA, PRODUCER

"No matter where I go, when people find out I'm with WGN, they have a story for me. Flight attendant, waiter, someone who passes me in a garage—it doesn't matter. The crew members who do our games in other cities always want to share how they've watched our games forever and are happy to be a part of our show. It's even more fun to hear how many players say the same thing. I remember meeting Alex Rodriguez at Wrigley in 2003, and he talked about growing up watching baseball on WGN.

"To be a baseball fan and be a part of this is really special. The Kerry Wood game was really something. That whole year in 1998 had so many moments. If you grew up a baseball fan, the number 61 was the number. To see the Roger Maris home-run record broken by Mark McGwire and Sammy Sosa on WGN in the same week is a memory I'll never forget."

JOE PAUSBACK, CAMERA

"You come here to work, and that's almost an honor. People have no issue coming up to us and say, 'Hey cameraman, put me on TV.' There's an immediate bond, and I love that. I've been at it for 23 years, and I'll never get tired of it. It's great. WGN is part of their lives. We are this great local telecast that people get to watch around the world. That makes for a special feel.

"My favorite shot was on Sammy Sosa's 60th homer in 1999. I was running the high home camera, and when he hit it, I knew he crushed it. You watch the outfielder and the fans to get help finding the ball, and on this one, I had it dead center in my shot as it came down and landed in the bushes in center field. Arne Harris said to me, 'You got that one right in the crosshairs, Pausy,' and I was excited that I did. Having my shot of that historic home run go on the air live and nailing it is a great feeling."

GREG GRESSLE, ENGINEER-IN-CHARGE

"It doesn't get old. When I go up to the booth and I look around at Wrigley and the rooftops and the neighborhood and the ivy, there's almost a smell or a texture to that view. It gives you the chills. You can feel the ghosts of Cubs past. You know you are somewhere really special. Being on WGN, you know your work is being seen all over the world.

"I remember that crazy weekend in 1998 when Sammy Sosa hit four home runs and broke the Maris record. I'm really proud of the night in 2001 when we did our first game in high definition. It was amazing and blew me away with the clarity of the picture. I remember vividly the day Arne Harris died and I don't know for the life of me how we did the game, but I am really happy with what we did. I got stuck up on the roof one day adjusting the overhead camera and laughed when my mother called me from Florida to say she saw me when they showed it on the air. What great memories, and I will always have them. I've loved the whole experience."

FRANK LEONE, AUDIO

"I'm a Cubs fan from grade school and grew up watching this team on WGN. I started in '94, and these are some of the best times I've ever had, getting the chance to work here. Sometime during the morning after we set up, I try to make time every day to sit in the stands for a few minutes and soak it in. I watch the grounds crew set up and the first players come out to warm up.

"The Cubs on WGN has always been different from other baseball. It's so clean, you get the fans involved, shots of the lakefront, and I'm proud to be a part of it."

LONNIE THOMAS, CAMERA

"The crew got word at the end of the 2005 season that with the expansion of the bleachers, the Cubs were going to tear down the green shack that houses the center-field camera. We had all spent so many days in there that we didn't want to see it thrown out, so we got permission from the Cubs to take it apart and haul it away. The team left town on a Thursday to finish the year on the road, and after that game we had until the next day at 5:00 PM to take it apart.

"Jim Tianis, his cousin Andy, and I got it down and outside, but the truck we had arranged to come and pick it up was a no-show. We went across the street to a U-Haul place and told them our problem. There was a rental truck sitting in front that was still running, and after we showed the guy on duty there our WGN IDs, he gave us the truck to use—no credit cards, IDs, rental papers, or anything! He was a former Bleacher Bum and happy to help us out. He pointed at the truck in front and said, 'Take that one. Just don't turn it off because there is no way it will start up again.' We loaded the shack and took it to my house, where I rebuilt it. We also did get the truck back in one piece."

STEVE CASEY, VIDEOTAPE

"I've been a Cubs fan ever since I got my tonsils removed as a kid. Maybe the pain associated with that somehow worked in tandem with the pain of rooting for this team.

It's always been my dream to be a part of this since I was in grade school. It's gone by way too fast, and whether the Cubs win or lose, I still can't believe I get paid to work on the broadcasts. Working at Wrigley Field is like seeing a beautiful painting that is different every day. I would watch every game, even if there was only a single camera on the game. My goal was always to work on the WGN crew, and to be able to work with Arne Harris, Harry Caray, and others still blows me away.

"I've been lucky to be a part of so many wonderful games, but one of my favorites was in 1989, when the Cubs came back from a 9–0 deficit to beat Houston here, 10–9. I was in the tape room running a one-inch machine, and to be honest with you, we got so caught up in the comeback that the quality of my work wasn't that great. There may have been a few replays missed because we were jumping up and down and high-fiving instead of listening to Arne tell us to roll our machines!"

MARK STENCEL, GRAPHICS

"Life in the truck is more than just organized chaos. At one time a few years ago, we had three different people named Mark working in the truck, but there was no confusion with names. You always knew which Mark you were talking to and about what because everyone knew their roles so well. It was always important to Arne [Harris] that we show how much fun it is to be at Wrigley Field, and I think we've done a good job of keeping that tradition alive.

"I like being able to impart a good graphic with interesting information, then see the play unfold in a way that exactly illustrates that statistic. Being a part of the Kerry Wood game is a great memory. From the very beginning of the game, I could just tell it was something special, and I got Wood to sign the scorecard I kept during that game."

BOB ALBRECHT, CAMERA

"This is a soap opera that we bring into people's homes every day, but it's live. They become so attached to it, just like a soap. Every day I come to work, I never know what is

Rey Sanchez, Rick Wilkins, and Jose Hernandez check out the replay on the WGN-TV third-base dugout camera.

going to happen, and it never ceases to amaze me that game after game I see something I've never seen before. When I get out of bed in the morning, I look forward to being here. We bring the fans into the telecast, and that's different from other shows I see and work on around the country. I love to show a fan who's into the game and doesn't know he's on TV. The big thing that has changed is the minute we show that guy, his cell phone rings a minute later with his friends calling to tell him he's on WGN.

"My favorite shot was a few years ago on a Sunday afternoon, and the Braves were in town. There was an older gentleman at the game with his son. The father was obviously recovering from a stroke, but as I watched him, he was so into the game that Arne told me to just stay with him the whole time. It was so touching to watch him wave the Cub runners home on a double and to see the joy on his face.

"I remember running camera when Pete Rose tied Ty Cobb's hit record in 1985 and seeing all the flashbulbs going off in his next at-bat when he tried to get the hit to break the record.

"I was running camera on top of the scoreboard for the first night game in 1988, then when the weather turned, I went inside the scoreboard and shot through an open slot for the rest of the telecast."

DAVE GRUNDTVIG, AUDIO

"The people are a big part of what makes this ballpark so unique, which is why it truly is the Friendly Confines. That aura that captivates you walking into the park is because of the people. It's great to work on these games where there is more than just the game itself, it's almost a lifestyle.

"I loved working with Harry Caray. When we started doing night games, Harry had a hard time seeing his score-card, so we got him a brass banker's lamp. He always used a desk mike on a stand and didn't wear a headset the way most announcers do. One day we were coming back from a break and his audio wasn't right—it sounded like he was talking off in the distance. We didn't know what was going

on until he started laughing at what he had done. He was talking into the lamp, which he had grabbed by mistake instead of the microphone. Harry said, 'Folks, if you could only see what a fool I am.' We just loved him, and he was unique."

MIKE CLAY, CAMERA

"For me, I had watched games on WGN and was overwhelmed at the chance to work for Arne Harris. I had heard so much about him that I couldn't believe I was getting the chance to work on his crew. I was so nervous, and even though I knew baseball, I didn't know about televised baseball, but he took me through what to do and what my responsibilities were. I didn't want to let him down. When I would hear him say, 'Nice shot, Mike,' that meant everything to me. This is a great crew, and we work well together, push each other, and know this ballpark."

KEN LYLES, VIDEOTAPE

"When I walk into Wrigley Field, I still have this overwhelming sense that this is where baseball is played, as opposed to many places where there are many events that happen to include baseball. I grew up here, and it's really nice to be around so many guys I looked up to as a kid. Ron Santo is here with radio, Billy Williams is still around the team, Fergie Jenkins was the pitching coach, and they are all approachable. That's great.

"When I think of games we have done, the last game of the 2001 season stands out since we did it right after Arne Harris died the night before. [The tragedy of] 9/11 was still fresh, my dad had just passed, and that was just such a tough time, but I'm proud of that game. It's hard to pinpoint a game I love best because what I'll always remember is working with a great group of people who pushed each other to be better each and every day."

MIKE AIELLO, AUDIO

"From a crew aspect, everybody is in a good mood when we show up. We want to be there, we like being there, and we like working with each other, and that's what is so unique and shows up on the air. What makes our games so special are the shots of the park and our fans. That makes our viewers feel like they are part of the experience so they can get more than just watching the pitch.

"I have some favorite moments, including the one everybody tells you about the night game when Harry grabbed the lamp and started talking into it instead of the microphone. The one I really love is also about Harry. I used to have really long hair, and on my first day working in booth, he turned around and said, 'Hey kid, who the hell is your barber?'"

DERREK LEE

Baseball, like politics, often makes for strange bedfellows. In the 2003 National League Championship Series, Derrek Lee was at the center of the Cubs demise, delivering key hits in both Games 6 and 7 to lead the Marlins to the World Series. Several years later, Lee is probably the most popular Cubs player and one of the faces of the franchise, following in the footsteps of Banks, Santo, Williams, Sandberg, Dawson, Grace, and Sosa. Lee has earned that distinction with a rare combination of power at the plate, uncommon grace on the field, and an inspiring commitment to excellence that is clearly evident to the fans he has won over since coming to the Cubs.

Lee dreams of again dancing on the Wrigley Field infield in celebration of a championship, only this time he wants to do it in a Cubs uniform. "I don't know if I want to remind everybody," he said. "That playoff series was probably the most fun I have ever had playing baseball just because it was such a great series and there was so much excitement in the city. It was a lot of fun to play in."

If anything positive came out of the 2003 loss, it was Lee's firsthand experience with the Cubs faithful at Wrigley Field. It made a strong impression and put the city at the top of his list when the Marlins began to break up their team that winter after their championship season. "Playing here, especially in the playoffs on the opposing team, you could just see the excitement of the fans and how much they had a passion for this team. Chicago was one of the places I always wanted to play just for that reason, having a sellout every day and the excitement in this park." On November 25, 2003, Lee was acquired from the Marlins in exchange for Hee Seop Choi and Michael Nannini.

Lee was a notoriously slow starter, but even as he struggled in his first month as a Cub, he was becoming a fan favorite, which helped ease his transition. "They want to root for you," he said. "If you're doing bad or they don't like the way you're playing, they're going to get on you. But they want to root for you, that's the basis of it. They want to root for you. So if you give them something to cheer about, they're going to cheer you, and that's the great thing about it." He has given them plenty to cheer about, winning the batting title in 2005 and earning All-Star honors in two of the last three seasons.

Bob Brenly watches Lee every day and sees a player in the mold of another Cubs leader from 20 years back. "Derrek is very serious about his business; he's serious about how players on his own team and players on the other team view his actions on the field," Brenly said. "In a way he reminds me a lot of Andre Dawson, who played the game with a lot of class, never wanted to show up a teammate or an opponent, respected the game, respected the fans for spending their hard-earned money to come out here and watch him perform. He felt that every day they should get everything he had: because they took the time and they spent their money to come out and watch, I'm going to give them everything I have. Derrek Lee is the same kind of player as Andre Dawson."

The Cubs' Gold Glove–winning first baseman has a big fan in an old Cubs first baseman. "He's terrific," said Mark Grace, who knows a thing or two about digging out throws at first. "He's so much better than I ever was, all around. Yeah, I was a good fielder, but he's got the power and the average. He's fabulous."

In 2006, Lee's daughter Jada was diagnosed with Leber's Congenital Amaurosis (LCA), an inherited form

Hellman had been in charge of the visitors' clubhouse at Wrigley before moving across the diamond to larger digs with more permanent residents. "The big difference with the visitors' clubhouse is you have different people coming in every few days," he said. "If you get somebody you don't like, you know they are going to be gone soon. For the most part, 99 percent of the people over all the years I've been doing this have been just awesome.

"You don't necessarily take care of the stars more than you take care of the kids, but you try to take care of everybody the same way,"

—Otis Hellman

"On a normal home game, like a day game at 1:20, we get there by 6:30 AM and start breakfast," explained Hellman. "I cook breakfast for the guys and set up, cut fruit up, pass out the wash—just have the clubhouse ready for the guys when they show up. As they show up, we feed them, we cook for them to order, whatever. Then as they go out onto the field, we straighten up the clubhouse and wash the clothes and get ready for the next time they come in. We cater to their needs, and like I tell them in spring training, we want them to be ready to play the game and we want them to stay focused on that. We'll take care of the rest of the business for them. Our job is there to take care of the players, and that's what we do."

For their part, the players know how well they are treated by Hellman and his staff. "Otis is unbelievable," said Derrek Lee. "You know, it is our home here most of the time, so Otis is like our keeper. I wouldn't make it without Otis. He does a great job, and he's a good friend now."

"Otis takes a lot of crap from the guys, but he's one of the best," said Kerry Wood, who admits to doling out his fair share of the aforementioned crap. "You don't find guys in this game who are genuinely there for the play-

ers, genuinely want great things for everybody. They work hard. People don't understand what these guys do in the clubhouse. They make our job so much easier. We don't worry about doing anything other than winning baseball games. They don't get any credit, and they do a lot of work that goes unseen."

Hellman travels with the team throughout the season, organizing the transport of equipment, luggage, and other essentials. "People ask me what's the best part of the job, and I say traveling. And they ask me what's the worst part of the job and I say traveling, because you are not home with your family and stuff, so that takes its toll on that, but myself, my wife, and my kids know that's my job and that's what I have to do, so grow with it and live with it."

Along with juggling a myriad of duties, Hellman also has to juggle personalities. "You don't necessarily take care of the stars more than you take care of the kids, but you try to take care of everybody the same way," he said. "Of course, you look out for the veterans. You understand their needs and what they need, try to take care of them and get things done without saying. All the guys are great, they really are, but the longer you are with them, the closer you become."

The duties of batboy are not mentioned anywhere in Hellman's job description, but he gladly took his turn handling the lumber for a stretch in 2005 when the Cubs needed him. "We won a few in a row," laughed Hellman, who earned high praise for his speedy bat retrieval and willingness to go along with the fun. "I had fun with it."

"Otis is a beauty," said Bob Brenly. "This guy is in a good mood every day. I don't think he's ever been in a bad mood. The best part about Otis is that he can take some heckling. He's a willing participant, and he takes his share every day, not only from the players, but from anybody that walks through that clubhouse. They know that they can stick Otis with a little zinger, and he'll appreciate it."

Another thing he will appreciate is the chance to enjoy the Friendly Confines with a cold one in his hand, but not any time soon. "This is my 25th year with the Cubs, and I've never seen a game yet," said Hellman. "I've never been a

Clubhouse manager Tom Hellman adds the number to a Cubs road jersey.

fan in Wrigley. I'm waiting for that day when I retire when I can sit back and have a beer and a hot dog and watch the ballgame and not have to worry about work. That, I hope, is a long way in the future."

GETTING STARTED

"Most of us start out as a ballboy or batboy or something like that as a kid in high school, which I did. I was a senior, and I was a ballboy in Cincinnati. I worked my way up. I was assistant equipment manager for the Reds and was at spring training with them all the time. I sent out résumés a couple of times. When the Tribune bought the Cubs, they evaluated their front office and staff the first year and let a couple of people go, and I took one of those people's places as the visiting clubhouse manager."

TAILORING UNIFORMS

"At spring training, Majestic [Athletic Uniforms] comes out there and I measure everybody and I tell the guys, 'Tell 'em exactly what you want.' Guys still come back and want to tighten it here or loosen it there, so it's an ongoing process. They gain and lose weight during the year. Some of them gain and some of them lose, so you order the early pants and the late pants for them. Some are the fatter pants and some are the skinnier pants as the season wears on! Depends on what they spend their meal money on, I guess."

ASSIGNING NUMBERS

"The first thing you do is to have a uniform ready for new players the next day. If it's a star player and that number is open, you either give them that number or, like when we got Nomar [Garciaparra] a few year ago, we gave him 8 the first day because Michael Barrett already had 5. Then he talked to Michael and they worked out a little switch, and Nomar got to be No. 5. I'm just the guy that does the change. The middle man gets nothing in those transactions. For the most part, you give a veteran their number. A couple guys wanted 31 this year, but we're holding on to that out of respect for Greg Maddux."

FEEDING THE PLAYERS

"[In] the visitors' clubhouse you get three or four main meals, and that's what you give the teams that come through over and over. The home side for a nine- or 10-game homestand, that's a little more work. I work with a lot of restaurants now that I call up, and they're good about working with me. I try to have a nicer meal for the night games because you know they won't be going out to dinner after the game. We do a little lighter fare for the day games."

WORKING WITH THE MANAGER

"When we get new managers, I tell them how I do things and ask them what they want out of us. Like Lou [Piniella], he just said, 'You take care of business inside and I'll take care of it outside.' It's awesome. He just wants to win, and that's what the bottom line is. We all want to win."

RANDY HUNDLEY

For three decades after Gabby Hartnett retired, the Cubs searched for a reliable catcher to handle their pitching staff. They found their man in 1966 when they acquired Randy Hundley from San Francisco, along with future 20-game winner Bill Hands.

Hundley was available because the Giants were not enamored with his unique style of catching. He used only his mitt hand to catch, while keeping his exposed throwing hand tucked behind his back, a style he learned from his father. Randy had been a good pitcher and shortstop as a young player but yearned to have even more action, so he asked his dad to teach him to catch.

"We start out of the house and he stops me at the front door and says, 'I'm going to teach you to be a catcher, and you're going to be a one-handed catcher.' He points his finger right between my eyes, and I can still see that big finger pointing down on me. He says, 'If I ever see you put that bare hand up to catch the ball, I'm going to come and personally take you out of the game.' I played games right here in Wrigley Field worried about my dad seeing me get

Former catcher Randy Hundley is right at home
watching things behind the plate.

that hand too close to the mitt. Knock on wood, I never missed a ballgame because I had a foul hit my right hand. Back then, a lot of guys would come to me–Tom Haller, Tim McCarver, a number of guys–and ask me, 'What's this one-handed catching stuff?' It extended a lot of guys' careers. Nobody catches two-handed now."

Hundley made his name as a Gold Glove–winning defensive catcher, but he had some pop in his bat, hitting 19 homers in 1966, his first year with the Cubs. For his first four years in Chicago, he was a stalwart behind the plate, catching at least 149 games, including a mind-boggling major league record 160 games in 1968. Like many of the Cubs, he wore down in 1969 after catching 151 games that year.

How did he do it? "I don't know, to be honest with you," Hundley said. "Quite frankly, I'm paying for it now. I had no idea that it was going to take such a toll on my body, but it has. Johnny Bench was very wise. He looked at me and the way I walked after getting out of the game, and he said, 'I'm not going to be in this game forever and have to walk like him, for cryin' out loud.' I didn't want anybody to take my job. Leo [Durocher] would call me, and he'd say, 'How do you feel?' I'd say, 'Stiff. Look at me. How do you think I feel?' He said, 'Aw, you're all right. You're in the game.' I said, 'Okay, you know what you've got, so I'll go do it if that's what you want.'"

Ron Santo saw Hundley's dilemma firsthand. "In our era, there were one-year contracts, and you stayed away from the trainers," he said. "Randy was just always in there."

Regardless of his condition, the Cubs starters knew they were in good hands with Hundley calling the game. "I think Randy had his theory about getting hitters out. I think all the pitchers had their theories, too," said Ferguson Jenkins, who won 20 games six straight years on Hundley's watch. "You have to agree because of the fact that we're out there every fourth day. No two pitchers are alike. What Randy had to know were the little idiosyncrasies we all had about approaching, setting the hitter up, working him in the count, and trying to get him out as best we could. That was a plus, knowing the hitters along with Randy knowing them, as well."

Hundley's iron-man streak ended when he hurt his left knee in 1970. He was injured again in 1971 and played only 82 games those two years. He came back in 1972 and was happy to be behind the plate when both Burt Hooton and Milt Pappas threw no-hitters that year. "I did not catch either of [Ken] Holtzman's no-hitters," Hundley said. "In 1969, I was dehydrated and did not play that day. In 1971, I had slit the tendon on my toe and watched at home on the TV." He was traded to the Twins in 1974, spent the following season with the Padres, then returned to the Cubs for two limited seasons before retiring in 1977.

"Quite frankly, I'm paying for it now. I had no idea it would take such a toll on my body."

—Randy Hundley

In 1982, Hundley held the first Major League Baseball fantasy camp, making it possible for middle-aged baseball lovers to fly to Arizona and play baseball in a Cubs uniform all week while receiving coaching and mingling with ex-Cubs players. Many imitators followed, but none has captured the spirit and success of the original. "I thought going to Arizona just like you're going to spring training would be the thing to do," Hundley explained when asked about the genesis of his camp. "The wonderful thing about it is that everybody who goes has the same emotions that a big-league player has when they go to their first big-league spring training or they get traded to another ballclub. All those emotions are the same and are the wonderful part about it."

ROUGH FIRST VISIT TO WRIGLEY

"I had no idea. You know, when I came in with San Francisco, I'll never forget running from foul line to center field to loosen up. That was the only time I ran because the bleacher fans were all over my case about being a Giant. I only took one lap and went and hid somewhere."

MEMORABLE HOME RUN

"One day at Wrigley, I was up in the ninth against Tug McGraw of the Mets. I just knew he was going to try and get a fastball by me, so I was ready for it and cranked a home run to win the game. Well, when I came around to third base, the grounds crew had already put the base away. Pete Reiser, our third-base coach, grabbed me and held me at third for a few minutes until they brought a base back out because he was worried they might call me out for not touching the base." —*Randy Hundley*

FOCUSING ON THE GAME

"I get asked about so many milestones now, but at the time, we never focused on anything like that. It was about winning and how were we doing in the race. I hit for the cycle at Wrigley once in 1966, and I got it by getting a single in my last at-bat. When I got to first base, I had no idea why the fans were cheering until my coach told me what was going on. I felt foolish for not knowing, but I guess I'm lucky I knew what the cycle was!" (The Cubs won the game, 9–8, in 11 innings, then Hundley caught the second game of the day's doubleheader as well.)

DREAMING UP THE FANTASY CAMP

"I'm sitting in sociology, and I had just started my junior year in high school. I'm bored to death, and I'm sitting sideways, looking out the window daydreaming. It's the middle of February, and I'm reading about guys going to spring training, and I remember how much I idolized ballplayers. They had a chance to go to spring training, and I'm saying, 'Why are these men going to spring training? I ought to be going to spring training.' While I'm going through that thought process, there comes a knock on the door, and they said, 'There's somebody here to see Randy Hundley.'

I thought, 'Well, great, I get to get out of this dumb class.' I'm walking down and I see this silhouette of a huge man, I have no idea who he is. As I approach him, he reaches to shake my hand, and he says, 'Randy, I'm Tim Murchison, and I'm a scout for the San Francisco Giants.' Now, can you imagine what a thrill that would be, just starting out to be a junior in high school and having to play my junior year in baseball and my senior year and a scout knows me? When we had the opportunity to do the fantasy camp, I just figured that every other red-blooded American male had the same dreams of being a big-league ballplayer."

THE 1984 TEAM

"At the fantasy camp, we have incorporated the '84 club into the '69 club, so to speak, and those guys are absolutely wonderful. I love being around them, and I think they love being with us and hearing some of the things that went on when we were playing and likewise with them. It's really been a wonderful transition."

THE GROUNDS CREW: RICK FUHS

The Wrigley Field press box is packed with media of all types on a daily basis, but tucked away in the last row is a vital, but virtually unnoticed, part of the Cubs game-day operation. Balls, strikes, and outs, as well as the batters' numbers, are controlled by groundskeeper Rick Fuhs some 500 feet away from the famed Wrigley scoreboard.

The weathered green box that Fuhs uses to post the counts is the original machinery that came with the scoreboard when it was installed in 1937. The system is designed with a relay from the press box that uses eyelets to uncover numbers for either a ball or strike on each pitch. A light touch of the button in the press box results in an instantaneous adjustment to the board, a feat that has fans marveling to this day.

"I'm in the fifth row of the press area, all the way in the back corner," Fuhs explained. "The panel I work

High above the action on the field, Rick Fuhs runs the scoring box that displays the balls, strikes, and outs on the Wrigley Field scoreboard.

off is from 1937. It's that old. It's real easy to operate and the relay is really quick, so once I hit a button, simultaneously it sends the signal out to the scoreboard and flips the number. It's an eyelet, and the signal flips the eyelet for the number one, two, three, and so on. I've been doing it since 1989, and everybody says I beat the umpire at times. The main thing is that the quickness of the machine I work off is unbelievable. You touch the button and it's up there, so a lot of credit should go to who invented it."

Fuhs got the chance to thank the designer in person in June 2007, when the Cubs hosted 90-year-old Curt Hubertz at a game. Hubertz, an electrical engineer, had worked with his father to design the original scoreboard and the ball/strike system that Fuhs operates to this day. "It was really neat to meet him and talk to him," marveled Fuhs. "He even brought some spare parts for the board that he had at home and gave them to Mike Dour, who is our electrician at the park. If you look at the box I work on, you can see his name engraved on it."

One of the fun things to do at Wrigley is try to watch the umpire's call then glance at the scoreboard to see if your eyes can beat the fastest fingers in the West. "I try to just watch the umpire," Fuhs said. "I get a good feel for what he's going to call just by his movements. If he moves his foot to the right, he's calling a strike. If he stands there still, I'll put a ball up there a split second later than a strike. You get accustomed to how the umpire's going to call it. Sometimes they will cross you up. There are a couple guys, Tim McClelland for one, who are hard to read. It makes it a little hard to post a ball or strike. The key is to get it right."

Like everyone on the Wrigley Field grounds crew, Fuhs has a raft of other duties before hustling up to the press box before the first pitch. "On a typical day, first we have to set up the field for batting practice, so we'll get here early, around 8:00 in the morning," he said. "I cut the infield grass, and Roger [Baird], the head groundskeeper, cuts the outfield. We have guys watering the infield. Then, after we set up the field for batting practice, we do a lot of minor work on the lines, cut the grass to specifications. After batting practice, we get the field ready for the game.

"After the game, we have to get ready for the next day. It's a constant process, including fixing the clay areas where the holes are. The players dig holes in the home-plate area, for instance, so we have to fix it, sweep it out, put new clay in there, tap the new clay in, and level it out. The mound is the same thing. They dig up some holes there. It's a constant process of fixing the holes, putting new clay in, manicuring it, leveling it out, watering it—it's a constant job."

STARTING OUT

"My friends worked here, and they needed some help. Back then you swept the garbage in the stands. So they had a big series, I think St. Louis was in town, and they wanted some extra help. Well, I wound up working around the clock that night because there was a big crowd here, about 40,000. Then the boss kept me on, and I kept working here for a couple years. Then they put me on full time in 1981."

WORKING THE INFIELD

"Everybody is different. The pitchers like the infield grass a little higher. They like the clay in front of home plate a little looser and wet so the ball doesn't hop out of there. The hitters like it harder. They want that ball rushing through the infield and the grass cut shorter. Usually the pitchers win that battle. There's enough negatives for a pitcher here as it is if the wind is blowing out, so we have to give them a little positive. A guy like Greg Maddux always complimented us on the mound, and he complimented me on fixing the front of home plate. I always kept it really loose for him." —Rick Fuhs

FAVORITE DAYS

"I love Opening Day. It's fun to see the season start and how excited the fans are. Another favorite day of mine is July 4. I've always liked that day. Another one is when the White Sox come to play here. It's very electric with the Cubs trying to beat them and the Sox trying to beat us. It's great for baseball, and I look forward to those series, especially at Wrigley Field."

QUIET TIME

"In the morning when I come here, I like to sit on the warning track out there and have a cup of coffee and look at the ivy. It's a fun thing to sit and look at it and look at the field early in the morning when no one is in the park. Sometimes I'm the only one here."

TRIMMING THE IVY

"It gets trimmed when the team leaves. We try to trim it right before they're coming back, like two or three days out. First of all, you like to keep it pretty much straight at the top. You follow a brick line to keep it as straight as possible. You go around the doors and keep it straight. At the numbers you round them off. There's a lot of work involved because you start on the left-field wall over at the left-field pole and go all the way to the right-field pole, and it takes about two days to trim. You have to keep it watered. You don't want it to dry out, and in the fall we pick some seeds and we plant them to try and start out some plants."

RUNNING THE SCOREBOARD

"The key is to stay focused and not get distracted. I'm in the last row up there, so there are times when people are standing up in front of me not aware that I'm behind them looking at the umpire. You just try to stay focused and not make any mistakes. And root for the Cubs. I would love to start the other team out on 0–1 or 0–2. Unfortunately, I can't. I just sit up there and try to keep an even keel."

WRIGLEY FIELD

"I do have a special attachment. We get goose bumps on Opening Day coming out here. We're out here every day trying to manicure this field to our best capabilities, making it perfect for the way the Cub players like it."

FERGIE JENKINS

Cubs fans rightfully mourn the Brock-for-Broglio trade as a dark moment in franchise history, but they might be better off celebrating the 1966 deal with the Phillies that brought Ferguson Jenkins to the team in exchange for Larry Jackson and Bob Buhl.

Jenkins had been a reliever with the Phillies, but Leo Durocher saw something in his new right-hander and gave him a shot. "I was very young, 21 years old, going to be 22 that winter after the trade," Jenkins said. "I just think that every player wants to make a mark. I got my opportunity early in the '67 season. Leo let me start. I won some ballgames. I did really well, and it just continued to flow. I put that string of games together."

Jenkins quickly became the ace of the staff and in 1967 reeled off the first of a still-astounding six-straight 20-win seasons. Often lost in the statistics is the fact that Jenkins completed at least 20 games in each of those seasons.

He was dependable in every regard and ready to go every fourth day. In 1968, Jenkins won 20 games, even though he lost five 1–0 contests. In 1969, he started 43 games and won 21, then followed up with 39 starts and 22 wins in 1970.

The key to Jenkins's success was his ability to throw strikes. He did lead the league in home runs allowed five different times as a Cub, but the majority of those were solo shots off a man who refused to give in, even with the wind blowing out at home. "I used to come right at hitters, I didn't walk anybody," Jenkins said. "I didn't try to walk anybody, and I think that was a part of my game I enjoyed more than anything else, challenging the hitter, making him put the ball in play. I gave up some home runs here and

Fergie Jenkins won 20 games six seasons in a row for the Cubs from 1967 to 1972.

on the road, but I think when a hitter came to the plate, he knew I wasn't going to try and pitch around him. I was coming right after him."

Think about the pitching in today's game, with so many starters adhering to the "five-and-fly" philosophy, and then look at Jenkins's numbers during his 1971 Cy Young season. He went 24–13 with a 2.77 ERA, pitched 30–count 'em, 30–complete games, struck out 263 hitters, and walked only 37.

Jenkins's durability may not get the recognition it deserves, but the men behind him still admire his willingness to take the ball for nine innings. "You know, every now and then your arm hurts you, but Fergie never said a word about it," said Glenn Beckert. "He always took the ball and pitched. It's remarkable that six years in a row he won 20 games. I think that is something that will stick around for a while because now they pull the pitcher out in the sixth inning and here come the relievers. As far as Fergie goes, he definitely deserves to be in the Hall of Fame. I'm glad he's there."

For a young Ken Holtzman, watching Jenkins work was a daily education. "He had the greatest control, command of his pitches that I ever saw," said Holtzman. "Not the greatest stuff, but he could throw them anywhere he wanted at any time. He knew how to change speeds. He was a very intelligent pitcher. He did his homework."

Like the rest of his teammates, Ron Santo always felt the Cubs were at their best with Jenkins on the mound, and Santo admired how Jenkins was able to think his way through the order. "He had a game plan," said Santo. "Fergie was a guy, wind blowing out, wind blowing in, he stayed with the game plan, and that's why he was the pitcher he was. He had a good fastball, unbelievable slider. He hid the ball well. He was 6'4", all arms and legs–he was dynamite. He could put that ball on the outside part of the plate every time."

Jenkins was a superb all-around athlete who could help himself with the bat and holds the career home run record for Cubs pitchers with 13. His game went beyond baseball: he played with the Harlem Globetrotters for two off-seasons, from 1967 to 1969.

Randy Hundley caught Jenkins during his peak years, and they were terrific battery mates. However, just like an old married couple, Hundley said that they bickered from time to time. "Fergie was a little difficult at times, in that he would shake you off and eventually come back to the same pitch you had initially called," complained Hundley, good-naturedly. "Sometimes it gets a little frustrating because you don't know if he's only doing that in order to get the hitter to think a little bit more. After you go through five pitches and you have to give a sixth pitch, it makes for a long time."

The Cubs gave up on Jenkins and shipped him to Texas after a subpar season in 1973, but he rebounded to win 25 games for the Rangers that year. He spent eight seasons in the American League with Texas and Boston, becoming a rare pitcher with more than 100 wins in each league. Jenkins returned to Wrigley Field for two final seasons with the Cubs in 1982–1983 and finished his career with 284 wins and 49 shutouts. He was the first pitcher to retire with more than 3,000 strikeouts and fewer than 1,000 walks. The only other player to match that also wore No. 31 with the Cubs–Greg Maddux.

Fergie was elected to the Hall of Fame in 1991 and served as the Cubs' pitching coach for two seasons in 1995–1996. He established the Ferguson Jenkins Foundation in 1997 and has raised money for a wide variety of charities including the Red Cross, Boys and Girls Clubs, the Make-a-Wish Foundation, and cancer research.

THE FANS' LOVE AFFAIR

"Well, it's something that probably started in the '60s when I came here. We had very low crowds, and then we started winning. In '67, '68, the crowds got really big, and I think it might have been '69 when we drew a million people. I just think the fans started to understand that the organization was going to try to win and maybe try to win a pennant, and '69 was really great, not a Cinderella story, because we were in first place April 15 and we stayed there until September 10. The Mets got strong and overtook us, and unfortunately we just didn't win that year.

Fergie Jenkins totaled more than 3,000 strikeouts while allowing fewer than 1,000 walks in his Hall of Fame career.

"I think it's a neighborhood stadium. You had to park adjacent to the fire station. Fans had a chance to really intermingle with us because we walked through the crowds either coming into the ballpark or leaving. I think that was a big plus for the ballplayers and the fans back in those early days."

THE 1969 TEAM

"I had some good ballplayers behind me: Santo, Kessinger, Beckert, Banks, Williams, you name the guys. When I pitched, they played hard for me. I think that's a plus. I went out there to try to win every game I pitched in, and these guys really played hard. This was a small ballpark back then. The only other small ballpark was Crosley Field. When teams came in here, the wind blew out or across or whatever, guys were looking to pad their averages or pad their home-run totals. We had Kenny Holtzman, Billy Hands, [Rich] Nye, myself, and [Dick] Selma; we tried to shut 'em down. That was our job."

LEO DUROCHER

"We had a tough manager in Leo Durocher. A lot of times he'd give you the ball and say, 'Don't look for help. We're resting the bullpen.' That was my job to go out there and try to hold the team to very few runs. He'd let me hit a lot of times in the seventh or eighth inning, maybe to push the runner around with a bunt or maybe even swing the bat to stay in the ballgame, so I enjoyed that part of it. It was kind of a confidence level that he had for you and you had in your team. So I played to win every time I went out there. I didn't look forward to losing. I wanted to win."

TAKING THE BALL

"Well, Leo had a theory on guys he wanted to play. He would put the starting lineup on the door as we left the clubhouse. So if you had a problem with not being able to play the next day, you had to go to Leo to let him know. The starting lineup was always Kessinger, Beckert, Williams, Santo, Banks, Hundley, whoever else was in the outfield, then the open spot

for the pitcher. When it was your turn to pitch, your name was slotted in. We only had four starting pitchers in the '60s and '70s, so pretty much you knew who was starting when and what ballclub you were going to play against."

FAVORITE GAME

"It might have been in '67 when we went into first place for the first time in quite a few seasons. The crowd stayed because I think the Cardinals were playing the Mets, and the Mets ended up beating the Cardinals. I think about 40,000 people stayed here for the outcome of that game. We beat Cincinnati that afternoon, and they put our *W* flag up. The crowd was pretty happy. It was the first time in quite a few years the Cubs had gone into first place. Winning 20 games here was a lot of fun for me, just playing with some great teammates." —*Fergie Jenkins*

HALL OF FAME TEAMMATES

"Billy Williams was a player who you knew was going to be in the lineup regardless of the circumstance. Bad back, neck, foul ball off the foot, he was going to be there. Similarly, Ernie Banks at first base. I mean guys that want to play, they want to play. Ron Santo ought to be in the Hall of Fame. He went out there diligently, day after day after day to play third base. I had a chance to play with Ryne Sandberg, too, in his rookie year, '82, and again in '83. You can tell the intensity of certain people, how they approach the game, how they like to play, their enthusiasm. They're at the ballpark early, and they want to go out and produce and they want to perform. This is the reason they get that opportunity to get elected to the Hall of Fame, because they are a different cut of a different player. They enjoy what they do. They put the numbers up, regardless of whether they're hurt or not. You've got to play through injuries. Every player has to. I think that's a plus."

WGN cameraman Jim Tianis shoots the action from atop the Wrigley Field scoreboard.

DAY BASEBALL

"I enjoyed that part of pitching in day baseball. I just think that if you love and enjoy where you play, you produce. If you don't like where you're at, it's time to move on."

THE SCOREBOARD CAMERA: JIM TIANIS

In addition to being the perfectly framed centerpiece of the country's most beautiful ballpark, the Wrigley Field scoreboard hosts one of the most spectacular views in baseball when Jim Tianis turns on his camera during each Cubs telecast on WGN. Tianis, along with a host of other WGN cameramen, has been making the trek up to the top of the board since WGN started using the shot in 1987.

So you want to share in the glamour and shoot the game from the scoreboard? No problem, but get ready for a climb that would make a mountain goat envious. "First you cover the national anthem down on the field with that same camera," said Tianis. "You make the trek via the dugout, through the stands out to the bleachers, through the crowd, up the stairs all the way to the back, and underneath the scoreboard. Once you get underneath, there is a trap door, and you walk up this ladder with camera, tripod, and backpack into the scoreboard, close the trap door, then you've got three more flights of stairs to go up until you get to another trap door. You walk up that trap door and you are on top of the scoreboard. You're about as high as you can get at Wrigley Field because you're even with the roof. It's a pretty incredible view."

The view is spectacular, but the tight space is not for the faint of heart. "The top of the scoreboard is pretty confined. There's lots of poles and wires and all kinds of stuff," said Tianis. "If you're not used to the height, it's almost like a diving board. You're kind of in the middle of nowhere. There's nothing around you other than the buildings, so you are up there. Looking straight down on the center-field bleachers, you can see so many things. You can see the city, you can see the lake. Obviously, you see all the baseball players, you can see all that's going on on the field."

Once in position, it's time to shoot the action and remember your role as part of the broadcast team. "During the broadcast, it can get crazy," Tianis admitted. "On the headsets on one side you're listening to Len and Bob, on the other side you're listening to the director, the producer, the other cameramen. There's things going on on the field continually. Depending on the position you're in, you have responsibilities, so it's a little bit like an orchestra. Everyone has their part. Everyone contributes. There's plenty of overlap and people cover for each other, but you're constantly searching, you're constantly looking for stuff. You've got all these different things happening to cover, and in the meantime, you're constantly listening to Len and Bob to try to find that next shot. You don't want the director to have to ask you for the next shot. You want to listen to what's going on and try and find it yourself. Sometimes you get really lucky and you find some really cool stuff."

One of Tianis's favorite shots made local news for several days afterward in 1989. "There was an Andre Dawson home run hit onto Waveland Avenue, and there happened to be a U.S. postman delivering the mail along with a bunch of the ballhawks. They all went after the ball, and he was in the middle of delivering the mail and that was it. He hopped the fence to get the baseball and came up with it. I think he got into a bit of trouble, but that's Wrigley Field. It only happens here."

To capture the fun and excitement at Wrigley requires a cameraman to be in touch with his inner child, something Tianis has no trouble channeling, while some members of the crew joke that he might not be getting enough oxygen on his perch. "My favorite moment when I'm up on the scoreboard is the national anthem because I get to pretend that I'm royalty. Everyone turns and looks at the flag, and I've got 40,000 people that just turn and look at me. Yeah, it's a lot of fun."

WRIGLEY FIELD

"Every part about this place I love. It's hard to pick a favorite spot. Doing camera in the dugouts is fantastic. You're right on the players, you have an interchange with them, you talk with them. It's a great angle. The top of the scoreboard looking down on everybody and just the vantage point up there. I guess if I was going to pick a place it would be the bleachers, just because the energy in the bleachers is so amazing. The energy in the Wrigley Field bleachers is unrivaled in sports. You can't find…it's a living breathing thing, you can't even explain it. It's always changing. Yeah, I would say the bleachers are my favorite spot here."

BEING A CUBS FAN

"To be a Cubs fan, you live your life. People live their lives the way Cubs fans live their lives. You're an optimist. You wake up every day, you go to work, you do what you do, you think that things are going to go well. It's just the way you are, it's just the way Cubs fans are. You constantly think that they're going to win, that they're going to do well, and if there's a bad day, you wipe that off the slate and start fresh, and what better place to start fresh than Wrigley Field? Every single day to come here and work here and again, to be a Cubs fan is to be an optimist. You cannot live your life and think, 'Oh, tomorrow is going to be horrible. Next week is going to be horrible.' You are optimistic, that's the way Cubs fans are. That's why the Cubs have such an attraction, have such a pull on people. It's the same thing as living, you know?" —*Jim Tianis*

MEMORABLE GAME AS A FAN

"The Cubs-Phillies crazy 23–22 game [in 1979]. I remember going with my brother. We were actually at the game, sitting in the bleachers. Halfway through the game, he said, 'That's it, we're done.' They had gone down again for the fifth time. So we went home, and I remember passing Alberto's Pizzeria on Morse Avenue as we left the Morse El. We stopped in and looked up at the window there, and sure enough, the Cubs had taken the lead or tied it, and I was like, 'You see? Why did we leave?' By the time we got home, the Phillies had taken the lead again. I remember watching the end of that game and just being in awe of the sheer amount of home runs that were hit."

WORKING FOR WGN

"Unbelievable. Growing up, watching the Cubs, and then getting the opportunity to work for WGN, it was insanity; it was fantasy. I couldn't believe that they actually asked me to work at Wrigley Field during the summertime with all these names I grew up with—Arne Harris, Joe Cornejo. The first time they called me to do Cubs baseball was in 1989. The Cubs were going into the playoffs, and I was a cameraman, and they called and asked me if I could do videotape. I said sure, yeah, even though I couldn't do videotape. I'm not going to say no. I showed up, was in the videotape room, had no idea what I was doing, faked my way through a couple of hours, and luckily someone walked in and said, 'Hey, we have an extra videotape guy. Aren't you a cameraman? Why don't you go out and do camera, and he'll do videotape.' 'Yeah, okay.' I've been there ever since."

WHAT MAKES A GOOD CAMERAMAN?

"To be a good cameraman, you just have to have a passion for baseball. You have to love the game. If you don't love the game, you're not going to be looking for those little nuances and those little things.

"I don't have a favorite shot, but my favorite play to cover in baseball is a bases-loaded triple. In a bases-loaded triple, everything is happening. I would say it's the coolest play you could cover as far as a baseball broadcast. You've got three guys scoring, a guy sliding into third, and you've got the guy fielding the ball and the cutoff man at third, and you've seen all of that in one play, probably in 15 seconds."

Mark Grace gets the best view in the house of the Sammy Sosa home-run hop.

ARNE HARRIS

"I think the greatest thing about Arne Harris was that he was probably the greatest Cubs fan I've ever met. Working for the greatest Cubs fan in the world was a blast because no matter what they did, he was into it. How could you not want to give everything you have for someone who was so into the game? He never turned it off. The Cubs would be down 10, and he'd say, 'Ten runs won't win this game.' The Cubs would be down 11 runs: 'Ah, 11 runs won't win this game, kid. We'll come back.'

"Arne used to say there are stories on the field, there are stories in the dugout, there are stories outside of Wrigley, and that can only happen here because most of our cameras can see outside the ballpark. There's always something going on, and it's our job to find it."

HARRY CARAY

"We had a blast working with Harry. Working with Harry Caray was like working with Michael Jordan or anyone who, when you show up to work, that day could be history. Something could happen that day that could change everything, or everyone would be discussing, or it would be on the news, it could be a controversy—you just didn't know what was going to happen. Working with Harry or with Arne, having that mix was incredible because Harry was as much a part of the Cubs as Wrigley. He really tied himself into the team. He was just an amazing guy to listen to. I mean, if you have to listen to a guy every day, three hours a day, Harry was a good guy to listen to because he would just keep you on your toes. Yes, he was unorthodox, but he made it a blast. He made baseball fun at Wrigley Field." ●

Hank Sauer, Ernie Banks, and
Monte Irvin pose in 1956.
(Photo courtesy of Getty Images)

The Heroes

ERNIE BANKS

His teams had a losing record in 13 of his first 14 seasons, and he never played in the postseason. Yet through it all, Ernie Banks was a consistent All-Star on the field and the Cubs' greatest ambassador off it. No one embodies the unbreakable spirit of the Cubs fans more than the greatest player in franchise history.

After growing up in the Dallas area, Banks got his professional start with the Kansas City Monarchs in the Negro Leagues. The legendary Buck O'Neil signed him for the Cubs, and in 1953, Banks broke the color line with the team along with Gene Baker, who had been signed from the Monarchs a few years earlier and was in the Cubs' minor league system. Banks wore No. 14, played shortstop, and quickly wowed both teammates and fans with his powerful swing.

In his second full season in 1955, Banks pounded 44 home runs, five of which were grand slams. After hitting "only" 28 in 1956, Banks went on a tear, hitting 43, 47, 45, and 41 round-trippers the next four seasons. His 1958 campaign was one to behold—47 homers and 129 RBIs en route to the MVP, followed by 45 and 143 in 1959 as he became the first player to repeat as the National League's Most Valuable Player. The Cubs were fifth both years, but as the saying went, without Banks, they might have been fifth in Triple A. Banks didn't miss a game either year.

Long before Ripken, A-Rod, and Nomar, Banks broke new ground as a power-hitting shortstop and won a Gold Glove at the position in 1960. Through second-division finishes, the "College of Coaches," and many forgettable Cubs teams, Banks remained the shining light of the organization. He credited his home park with giving his career a boost. "I think that there were a lot of players who say, 'Boy, I wish I had played at Wrigley Field,' so I was very fortunate to have played there," said Banks. "Playing day games all the time you could come home to your family. It's the ideal place to play sports."

In 1962 Banks made the move to first base but continued his steady presence in the middle of the Cubs lineup, averaging 25 homers each year for the rest of the decade. His last big year was in 1969, with 23 homers and 106 runs batted in. In 1970 he became the first Cub and only the ninth player at the time to reach the 500-home-run plateau. He retired in 1971 after 14 All-Star appearances, the most of any Cubs player.

Banks was a great player, but he was an even better teammate. "I remember a lot of funny things from him," said Glenn Beckert. "Ernie would say to me, 'Let's play two. We gotta play two today.' I remember one Opening Day it started to snow, a drizzling snow around the seventh inning, and Ernie was saying, 'Aw, Beck, we're gonna play two!' I said, 'Ernie, you had better have another second baseman because I'm not playing two today.' It was cold and the wind was coming off Lake Michigan, but that was Ernie. There was never a bad day for baseball here with Ernie."

"He was great to deal with," said WGN sports editor Jack Rosenberg. "He's the franchise, when you look at it. Super guy—wherever he went, he was like the Pied Piper. People would follow him, but he always had time for everybody."

Banks was a first-ballot Hall of Famer in 1977, and in his acceptance speech, he made it clear that his path to greatness owed a great deal to his family, teammates, and the Cubs organization. "This is certainly, and will always be, the happiest day of my life," he told the crowd at Cooperstown. "I once read that a person's success is not only dependent on the talent that God gave him, but also upon the people who believed in him. This is certainly true as it concerns my own personal baseball career. Sure, I was the one who played the games, but if it had not been for the people who believed in me and gave me the encouragement, there would be no games and I would not be here today. This great honor and recognition belongs to those people." In 1982, Banks's No. 14 was the first Cubs jersey to be retired. He was named to Major League Baseball's All-Century team in 1999.

The Cubs don't have a mascot. They don't need one when the living persona of the franchise is still so visible. "He attends the Cubs Convention; he's still a big part of our organization," said John McDonough. "I'm not sure every franchise has this, but Ernie Banks is synonymous with the Chicago Cubs. Ernie Banks is a brand. Mr. Cub is a brand. 'Let's play two!' is a brand. That electric smile that he has is a perfect, perfect backdrop to what this ballpark is all about."

In 2007, the Cubs announced plans to build a statue of Banks that will stand outside Wrigley Field near the Harry Caray statue. No tribute could be more well-deserved, and Mr. Cub was excited that his bronze likeness would greet fans coming to the park he had christened "the Friendly Confines." "Tell everybody to make sure they bring a cloth and keep my statue clean," Banks joked. "I want it to look good for a long time."

BEING SO OPTIMISTIC

"It comes from the way I was raised, coming from a large family of 12 as the second child. I was an introvert when I was quite young, then I got into baseball and the Cubs just kind of brought my whole life out. I trained a lot with Buck O'Neil with the Kansas City Monarchs, and that's where it really began. To be around him and listen to him and to his stories, with all his positiveness, it really set that into my life. Then I came to Wrigley Field, and to be around Jack Brickhouse and Vince Lloyd and Lou Boudreau, all the people broadcasting and the players, it became a big part of my life to be very positive about things. Unfortunately, we didn't win when I was playing for the Cubs, but enthusiasm and being positive was something that was embedded in my life."

MR. CUB

"There was a writer named Jim Enright who used to write for the *Chicago American*. He just told me one day, 'You're Mr. Cub.' I said I didn't believe in all that. He said, 'Well, you are.' And I said, if you do that, then every year you should have somebody else on the team who had done well and achieved something be 'Mr. Cub.' He said, 'No, you're Mr. Cub.' We did a book titled *Mr. Cub*, and it stayed with me. It's a big part of my life because everywhere I go there's always somebody who refers to me, 'There's Mr. Cub.' It's very special because not many players who played for a team get named after that team. With the Cardinals, Stan Musial is not Mr. Cardinal. There's no Mr. Giant. It is very special."

NAMING "THE FRIENDLY CONFINES"

"We were on the road for about two weeks, and I was sitting with Jerry Kendall, who played with the Cubs. We were sitting on the plane, and after you are on the road for a while when you lose a lot of games, you get down a bit. So I said, 'We're getting back to the Friendly Confines.' The writers were right there, and it kind of stuck. It became a big thing with the team, with the philosophy of the organization, with the Cub culture, and the people who come out there. It's a friendly place, and we just tied in with the atmosphere of Wrigley Field. It's friendly, it's family, it's fun. It's all of that. It's a wonderful place to play. It's a very special place." —*Ernie Banks*

TODAY'S PLAYERS

"I still like to watch the game and love to get the chance to talk with the players today. I was in Anaheim a few years ago when they were playing the Mariners and was introduced to Ichiro [Suzuki]. The first thing he said to me was, 'Let's play two!'"

Mr. Cub's smile reflects his always positive attitude.

THE ERNIE BANKS STATUE

"It's a wonderful honor, and I'm so grateful to everyone involved with the Cub organization who made the decision to honor me. I didn't get the chance to play in the World Series, so this is my World Series. The statue at Wrigley Field is something that does everything for my whole life. I'm so thrilled about it and very happy because it is a truly wonderful thing."

WHEN THE CUBS WIN

"Winning is an amazing phenomenon. It's gonna be very very special and will actually uplift the image of the game of baseball in the world if the Cubs win. In 2003, when we came close, it was amazing how all of that spread across the United States. A lot of opposing teams were pulling for the Cubs to get into the World Series."

BILLY WILLIAMS

Quiet. Dependable. Steady. Billy Williams was called many things during his Hall of Fame career, but the one that needs to be at the top of that list is "great." The six-time All-Star from Whistler, Alabama, was a reliable presence in the Cubs lineup for 14 years, but his incredible numbers are often overlooked.

Consistency was his hallmark. From 1962 until 1971, he appeared in a National League–record 1,117 consecutive games (later broken by Steve Garvey, as if we didn't have enough reasons to despise him). The 1961 NL Rookie of the Year also hit at least 20 homers 13 years in a row, ending his career with 426 home runs.

Williams had a monster season in 1970 with 205 hits, a .322 average, 42 homers, 129 RBIs, and 137 runs scored, but finished second to Johnny Bench in the MVP voting. Williams won the National League batting title in 1972 with a .333 average, added 37 homers and 122 RBIs, but lost the MVP vote to Bench again that year.

What was the secret of his sweet swing? "I had the traits of a quick bat, and it allowed me to wait on the ball better than the average guy," said Williams. "I followed the ball in the hitting area longer than most players. When I did that, it allowed me to keep my balance. From that point, I just saw the ball, and my quickness just got to the baseball. When I was in Triple A, the writers said I hit the ball out of the catcher's mitt."

While Williams provided highlights each day for WGN, he used the television broadcasts as a tool to make sure his sweet swing stayed on track. Long before sophisticated video rooms were the norm in every clubhouse, he was checking out the mechanics of his work at the plate. "I used the cameras on the third-base side to make sure my hands weren't too low," he said. "The center-field camera I would use to make sure I wasn't too far from home plate. The camera at first base I used to check out my stance and make sure I wasn't too wide."

Ron Santo played with Williams for several years in the minors and became a Cubs regular in 1960, one year before Williams came up for good. For years afterward, Santo watched from the on-deck circle as Williams punished National League pitchers. "Billy was one of the sweetest-swinging left-handed hitters I've ever seen," Santo said. "He had such quick hands, a lot like Ernie [Banks]. You know, Billy was quiet, but he spoke his mind. He was a leader. He wasn't a guy to just sit back."

Even the most loquacious Cub took note of Williams's demeanor. "I learned a lot from Billy," said Ernie Banks. "He likes to fish, and he'd say, 'See what happens to a fish when he opens his mouth? He gets caught. I don't want to talk. I just want to play.' I learned from that."

Williams is justifiably proud of the turnaround his team provided for the Cubs franchise, even though they were unable to make the postseason. "You had a group of guys playing with the Chicago Cubs—Banks, Santo, Kessinger, Beckert—and we were here a long time. We were together for about 10 years. It was just so exciting because early on, there were only 5,000 people out here. I tell the guys now they didn't open the upper deck until the weekend, and they don't believe me because

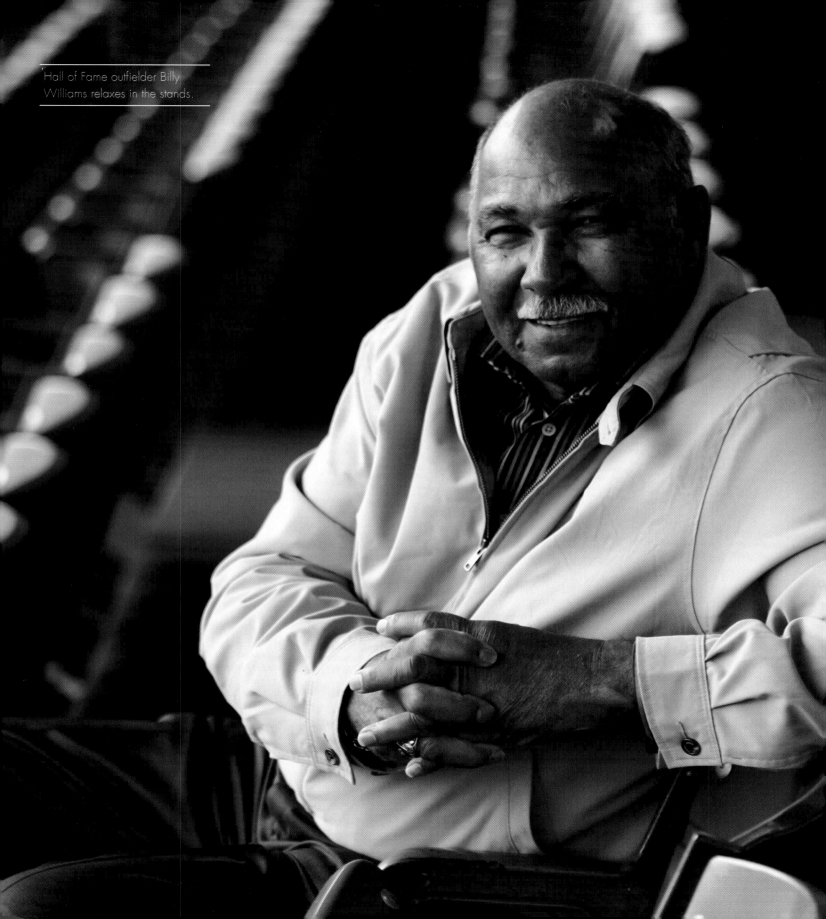

Hall of Fame outfielder Billy Williams relaxes in the stands.

they see the crowds now. I think it's because of the fellows who played in the '60s, because we catered to the fans, we came out and showed them a good time at the ballpark."

In 1975 Williams was traded for Manny Trillo and spent his final two years in Oakland, then retired after the 1976 season. After being snubbed in five straight elections, the baseball writers finally saw the light and elected him to the Hall of Fame in 1987. His No. 26 was retired by the Cubs that same year and still flies atop the right-field foul pole. Williams has remained with the team as a special assistant and is always a popular presence in the dugout and around the batting cage before games.

CUBS FANS

"We used to have a lot of fun. We played a lot of good games here and we enjoyed the fans. It was just a great time of my life. The fans would be lined up. You'd get a chance to talk to the fans and have a ball. When I was playing left field, I would turn around and talk to the people and just enjoy them, the Bleacher Bums. [Jim] Hickman did the same thing. Santo did the same thing. It was just the contact, the closeness we had with the fans. When you play together so long, you become friends, and I think that carried over to the friends we had sitting in the stands to watch us play the game of baseball. As I meet people now who are 45, 50 years old, they come up to me and thank me for the time, for the joy they had during those summers of the '60s and early '70s."

WRIGLEY FIELD

"It's a great place when you sit here and think about the history of ballparks. You think about Babe Ruth pointing and hitting a home run. You think about Ernie Banks's 500th home run. There's a lot of history. Gabby Hartnett's home run. You can sit in Wrigley Field and visualize that. Jack Brickhouse saying 'Hey Hey!' and Harry Caray sitting up there. You can visualize that in Wrigley Field, but most parks you can't."

HIS CONSECUTIVE-GAMES STREAK

"I really am proud of that. Number one, it means you were good enough to be in the lineup every day. The second thing is that you were consistent enough that the manager always thought you were going to help the ballclub that particular day. I went through three stages. First, I was afraid somebody would take my job in left field. The second stage was being aware of the numbers. I knew Stan Musial had the National League record, and I thought I could pass it and get to 1,000. The third stage was that I wanted to be in the lineup to help my team win, and I would be letting them down if I didn't. If I was in the lineup, I knew I would do something to help my team win."

BILLY WILLIAMS DAY, JUNE 29, 1969

"I had hurt my foot the week before and had to work hard so I didn't miss the game. When I got to the ballpark, there were 10,000–15,000 people waiting to get in. It was a doubleheader with the Cardinals, and they tell me they turned away another 10,000–15,000. The first game I got a base hit and wound up scoring the winning run. For the ceremony I had my mother here. I told her to make sure not to faint. During the ceremony, they ran out the car, they ran out the boat, the guys were standing around. It was a great time. It was great. I had a lot of fun. In the second game I got a single, double, triple, and I needed a home run for the cycle that day. Going up to the plate, I knew what I had to do, and the fans knew it because they were chanting my name. That would have really topped it off, but I struck out. As I headed back for the bench, they gave me a standing ovation, and I always said I was the only guy who got a standing ovation for striking out. We won both games, though, and went into first place. By the time I got home and hit the Barcalounger they gave me, I was dead asleep. I'll tell you, it was a beautiful day."

1971 OPENING DAY WALK-OFF HOMER

"We were playing the Cardinals on Opening Day, and two guys who were always real competitors, Bob Gibson and Fergie Jenkins, got into a duel out here. It was like those guys were really working. They didn't throw too many pitches, and even though we went to 10 innings, the game only lasted one hour and 58 minutes. It was cold out there and the temperature started to drop. Bob Gibson threw me a slider inside, and I made good contact with it. I didn't know the ball was going out of the ballpark. I was running down to first base saying, 'Get up, get up, get up!' This is what you say when you hit a ball. The ball went into the stands, and we won it. That was some kind of exciting."

HAVING NO. 26 RETIRED

"When that flag went up, you know you think about the time you came to Chicago, you think about the time you put on a Cub uniform. You think about going out every day and performing for these fans of Chicago, just enjoying the game of baseball. When you see that flag going up, it was really beautiful. When you think about it, that flag will be up as long as Wrigley Field is here. My grandkids have seen that flag. They come out and watch that flag and take pictures. My great-grandkids will come out sometime because I know they are going to be baseball fans, and I know the flag is going to be there."

HIS CUBS CAREER

"You think about it all the time. My wife and I talk about it. A little kid coming up from Alabama playing the game of baseball, getting signed to play professional baseball. All of a sudden, you get a chance to play with the Chicago Cubs, play with Ernie Banks, and spend so many nice summers here in Chicago. It's been a great ride." —*Billy Williams*

RON SANTO

If the frustration of the Cubs during the past 50 years has a face, it belongs to Ron Santo, the greatest third baseman in the team's history and now the team's radio voice. Santo doesn't just wear his emotions on his sleeve. He wears them on his face, in his heart, and makes no apologies for his inability to hide them.

"I had that passion," said Santo. "I believe our whole ballcub in that era had that kind of passion. I kind of carried my feelings on my sleeve so I reacted to a lot of things that a lot of ballplayers might not react to. But that was my personality, and that's what brought out the best in me."

Santo was the premier third baseman of his time in the National League and was selected as an All-Star eight times. While he didn't have the postseason showcase that marked Brooks Robinson's career, Santo won five Gold Gloves and was clearly the finest fielder at his position in the National League. His career numbers include a robust 337 homers and 1,290 RBIs as a Cub.

His excellence came despite very trying circumstances. Santo played his entire career with juvenile diabetes, a condition he hid from everyone until his public announcement on Ron Santo Day at Wrigley Field on August 28, 1971. In 1973 his mother and stepfather were killed in an automobile crash on their way to spring training. Through it all, he was always a man on a mission once he stepped across the white lines.

The Cubs captain set a tone that his teammates not only welcomed but followed as well. "He was hard-nosed," remembered Glenn Beckert. "We all were. Ronnie let it out. He didn't keep anything inside. What he felt came right out. We were all sort of upset to lose. Nobody liked to lose on that team. He was our captain and was, 'This is what we've got to do.'"

When Ken Holtzman took the mound, he welcomed both Santo's fielding and his intensity. "Ronnie was the emotional leader of the team," he said. "He was super intense. He was the one who could fire up the other players. He

Ron Santo has all the tools on hand for a successful broadcast, including a great sense of humor.

was a great competitor. He had a fierce desire to win, a fierce desire to excel, and he's another guy I still count as a close friend."

Santo's passion was never more evident than when he began jumping for joy and clicking his heels after Cubs wins in 1969. The team clubhouse was in the left-field corner, and the day wasn't complete for the fans until they could roar with approval as Santo put the exclamation point on the win during his jog to the clubhouse.

The heel click started by accident after a comeback win in June. With the Cubs down a run in the ninth, Jim Hickman homered to win the game against the Cardinals, and Santo was in heaven. "When he came around, I was pounding him on his head I was so excited," explained Santo. "I ran down the left-field line. I don't even remember doing it, that's how excited I was. I went up in the air and I clicked my heels one time, and we went into the clubhouse and it was just wonderful. I got home—I always turned on WGN-TV to watch the highlights—and the first thing, even before the news came on, was me clicking my heels. And I said, 'I did that?' I couldn't believe it. The next day I came into the clubhouse, and Leo came down to me and he said, 'Can you continue to click your heels?' And I said, 'Well, what do you mean?' And he said, 'Well, after a win, if you could still do that, that would be great.' It was so exciting that year, the way we started off, 11–1, and the excitement, and I said, 'Well, I think so.' He didn't realize I had a cleat cut in one of my ankles from where I clicked my heels! From that moment on, just at home, I would go up and click my heels after a win. And then they were all waiting for me after the game to go down there. Then I used to take Berteau [Street], and I'd see kids come along my car and be clicking their heels. It was fantastic."

The joy of '69 faded painfully in September of that year, and the Cubs were unable to make any more progress in the next four seasons. In 1974 Santo was traded across town to the White Sox for three players, including pitcher Steve Stone. After a miserable season, which included a lengthy stint at second base, Santo retired.

In 1990 Santo returned to the Cubs, this time as a radio broadcaster for WGN Radio. After the station narrowed its choices to Santo and Bob Brenly, Jack Rosenberg convinced the management to hire both of them to join Thom Brennaman. Santo's first day in the booth was anything but an auspicious debut. "Ronnie was there early, and he worked diligently on filling out this perfect scorecard," laughed Brenly, who can't tell this story often enough. "Right before we went on the air, Ron spilled his coffee, and the first thing our audience heard from the new radio team was Ron saying, 'Oh shit!' on the air."

As a broadcaster, Santo has replaced Harry Caray as a living symbol of the Cubs. While Ernie Banks will forever be "Mr. Cub," Santo has now grown to be "Father Cub" to the faithful followers across the nation. He returns their adulation in spades, signing hundreds of autographs each day at Wrigley Field and in the team hotel and broadcast booth when the team is on the road. Santo works tirelessly for the Juvenile Diabetes Research Fund, and his efforts have helped raise millions of dollars for the cause.

In 2003 the Cubs retired his No. 10, and it now hangs with Banks's banner from the left-field foul pole.

THE MAGIC OF 1969

"Our team related to the fans and wanted to relate to the fans. We signed autographs. We talked to everybody. We were like family. WGN-TV, WGN Radio, it was family. We were all one. The fans were just unbelievable. In '69, we drew a million seven for the first time. It's always been a wonderful relationship, but when you think about it, if we had won in '69, what would it have been like? I mean, you would think we did because people still remember us from that era and still relate to us. Now it's the young kids coming up. Most Cubs fans, they don't lose their allegiance. They might move out of town, but they're still there rooting for the Cubs.

"I think we all knew that was our year. Things changed. We didn't get it done, there's no doubt about it. The Knicks won. The Jets won. The Mets won. God lived in New York that year. There is no doubt in my mind."

BEING HARD-NOSED

"A lot of people and a lot of fans thought that, on the field, I was a mean guy and I didn't care about anybody. Off the field, I was completely different, but on the field it was all business. I had a very dear friend of mine who passed away, Don Drysdale. We became friends after four years, but it didn't change our relationship at the plate. He still knocked me on my fanny! I remember him saying—he was pitching the next day and he turned to me and said—'Just remember one thing. When I walk across those white lines, nobody is my friend.' And I said that's just the way I like it. That's just the way it was. I played the game I felt, and when I talk about me, I mean I'm talking about my team. There was more than me as a leader. Billy Williams, everybody was a leader. Hundley, Kessinger, Beckert, you know, everybody was a leader, and that's the passion we had for the game, and I think the fans realized that."

LOVE AFFAIR WITH CUBS FANS

"I was told very young by my mother, 'Always treat people the way you want to be treated.' I've always done that. I've never not said I couldn't sign. If I can't sign, I tell them why. If I walk down the street and somebody says, 'There goes Ron Santo,' I turn around and say hi, have a conversation, because that's what it's all about. It doesn't take much time to stop and make somebody happy. I love it. I just really love being around people."

WRIGLEY FIELD

"When I came up in 1960, 26 years old, we opened in Pittsburgh with a doubleheader, and I had a great series there. Then I got here to Wrigley Field, and I'd seen it on TV, but I'd never been here, and I got in the locker room and got dressed. I was walking out and Ernie was walking with me. We were walking down and I was looking, and the park was empty. I swear I was walking on air. There was this feeling that I'd never had before and the electricity, the atmosphere, and nobody in the stands! That's how I

felt. Anytime we go on the road and the season goes on, you get tired. As soon as you get back and you walk on this field, you are up here. It moves you to another level. The fans, they are just something. I take a lot to heart. The Cubbies are my first love. I just love 'em.

"This is baseball. These fans stand from the first inning, whatever is on the line, and that's telling you how good they are. They know this game, and it's wonderful."

RETIRING NO. 10

"That was the biggest day of my life because Billy Williams and Ernie Banks were up there. I had thought, 'God, I would love to have that.' You never talk about it, but I'd love to have that. Then I got called into a room a few weeks before with John McDonough, Andy MacPhail, and Dennis FitzSimons, but I had no idea what for. Then Andy took a flag out with the No. 10 on it and said, 'No one will wear this number here again.' I had tears I was so excited. The wonderful thing about the ceremony was that we had already clinched. I didn't want my day to interfere with them winning it. Forget my day, let's win and then do it. John McDonough had such a wonderful ceremony. It was heart-wrenching and it was so beautiful. When I got to the mike, I didn't know what I was going to say, but it just came out. What I said at the end was, 'This is my Hall of Fame; that flag right there is my Hall of Fame.'"

RYNE SANDBERG

Philadelphia Hall of Fame third baseman Mike Schmidt feasted on the Cubs during his career, but for all the agony he inflicted on the North Side faithful, we can be thankful for one thing. Schmidt's dominance made a minor league infielder named Ryne Sandberg expendable, a fact that Dallas Green was quick to exploit when he nabbed Sandberg, along with veteran shortstop Larry Bowa, in a trade after the 1981 season.

Despite starting off that season with a 1-for-32 slump, Sandberg rebounded to hit .271 as a rookie and showed that he had the tools to become a solid starter for the team. He followed up in 1983 by hitting .261 with 37 steals, while moving to second base when the Cubs brought in Ron Cey to play third.

Jim Frey was hired as the Cubs manager in 1984, and one of his first projects was to work with his second baseman on becoming more aggressive offensively. "Jim Frey identified Sandberg as a strong guy, an outstanding contact hitter, obviously. But he also had the strength and ability to hit the ball out of the ballpark if he turned on it," said the *Chicago Tribune*'s Fred Mitchell, who was covering the Cubs that spring training in Mesa, Arizona. "Frey encouraged him to do that. He said if you get a pitch in the zone, turn on it and go for the power."

The Cubs skipper remembers Sandberg as one of his favorite players but shies away from taking credit for his radical improvement. "In sports, everybody talks about coaches in changing this and changing that," explained Frey. "I've always thought that the mind is the biggest thing from making people from being good players to great players. It's not a physical thing to me. So I tried to work on him from the standpoint that I thought he had a chance to be the best player in the National League. I wanted him to start thinking about that and accepting the responsibility that goes with it. I said those words to a lot of players over the years, but Sandberg got it! Thank God he got it because he got it just in time to help us win. I'm very proud of him."

Frey's message hit home. Sandberg took his game to new heights, easily winning the National League Most Valuable Player award with a dream season in 1984 (.314, 36 doubles, 19 triples, 19 homers, 84 RBIs, 32 steals, and a league-leading 114 runs scored), launching a decade of dominance as the preeminent second baseman in baseball.

In 1987 Andre Dawson joined the Cubs and found a soul mate in the reserved yet ultra professional Sandberg. "I studied players on occasion, and Ryno was the type that you could learn things from," said Dawson. "I had 10 years in already, and there were still things that I learned from him out on the playing field and in the clubhouse. You have to admire a guy like that because this is what you as a front-office hierarchy dream about with your ballplayers. I knew coming over here what my makeup was, and when you have a guy like Ryno, who was one of the most popular players on the ballclub, in the mix, you know it's going to make for a good clubhouse presence."

Sandberg and Dawson led a young club to another NL East crown in 1989 but were denied a spot in the World Series by the San Francisco Giants. In 1990 Sandberg had his best statistical year when he hit 40 home runs and drove in 100, while stealing 25 bases. More than just a star player, Ryno was beloved by Cubs fans for being the personification of a true ballplayer—hard working, team-first, never flashy, but always steady.

A 10-time All-Star, Sandberg won nine Gold Gloves and set a major league record for career fielding percentage by a second baseman (.989). Sandberg's abrupt retirement came as a shock in 1994, but his return to the game in 1996–1997 did not, and neither did his endless enthusiasm, smooth stroke, or ability to flag down almost anything hit to the right side of the infield. Even in retirement, Ryno managed to hit one last grand slam. His 2005 Hall of Fame induction speech touched a nerve across baseball with his eloquent demand for renewed respect for the game. To all of us who were privileged to watch him compete each day, it was a message that obviously came from the heart.

PLAYING AT WRIGLEY FIELD

"It is alone, especially in the National League. The American League has Fenway Park—same era, same type of feel. In the National League, there was nothing like Wrigley Field. The opposing players would come in and play, whether they were from Montreal or Pittsburgh or places that weren't too exciting an atmosphere to play. These opposing players enjoyed coming to play at Wrigley Field. We talked about it out there at second base. 'This is baseball. This is the atmosphere.' Players enjoyed that. If they were fortunate to have a chance to be traded to the Cubs, they were all

Third base coach Don Zimmer extends a hand after Ryne Sandberg homers off Bruce Sutter in 1984.

for that. Wrigley Field was that one thing that set this team apart from any other team."

GOING TO WRIGLEY AS A FAN

"I have a new appreciation about Wrigley Field and what goes on there. For all those years, I was out in the heat of the moment, focused on baseball, and playing the game. Now, going as a fan, and being part of that—the buzz that you hear from blocks away, two hours before the game, I recognize that now because I'm walking in with the fans. It's the place to be. Everybody wants to be there. I want to be there. I understand that. To go there and watch the game, there are so many great seats. I would say that they are all great seats if you're in the ballpark and you have a ticket. Once you're there, you're somewhat close to the field, and it's just a great atmosphere to watch a game."

BEING HARRY CARAY'S FAVORITE

"I really don't know why. The only conversations I really had with Harry were about baseball because I don't think he liked, or it was not his part, to get close to players. He traveled with us every day on the flights or the buses, whatever it may be, but the only time I would talk to him would be during the pregame, during batting practice. He would come down and ask me about who was pitching that day and how I had done, just baseball talk. He was just getting some information that he would share over the broadcast, to get some insight on the game. We both came over here the same year, in '82. He came over here, and I was a rookie. His last year was my last year in 1997. We shared all those years together and all those games and all those seasons of all the good and the bad, so we had that in common." **—Ryne Sandberg**

THE CHANGES IN 1984

"In '82 and '83, if it wasn't a weekend game or a holiday, fans could come up and get pretty good seats right behind the dugout. In '84 the Cubs put together a team that was very likeable by the fans. We just had everything going and were playing good baseball, and everything fell into place. With Harry doing his thing on TV and now coming up with the nicknames like the 'Daily Double,' the 'Sarge,' and the Jody Davis song, you know he really got that working and really got caught up in that season. It really got things snowballing, and all of a sudden, we saw a couple of people on the rooftops across the street for the first time. 'Look at those people, they're up on the rooftops looking in!' So now today with the hundreds of people who are on the rooftops, I saw that whole thing start. It was the 1984 season that started all that."

FROM HIS HALL OF FAME INDUCTION SPEECH

"The fourth major league game I ever saw in person, I was in uniform. Yes, I was in awe. I was in awe every time I walked on to the field. That's respect. I was taught you never, ever disrespect your opponent or your teammates or your organization or your manager and never, ever your uniform. Make a great play, act like you've done it before; get a big hit, look for the third-base coach and get ready to run the bases; hit a home run, put your head down, drop the bat, run around the bases, because the name on the front is a lot more important than the name on the back. That's respect.

"A lot of people say this honor validates my career, but I didn't work hard for validation. I didn't play the game right because I saw a reward at the end of the tunnel. I played it right because that's what you're supposed to do: play it right and with respect. If this validates anything, it's that learning how to bunt and hit and run and turning two is more important than knowing where to find the little red light at the dugout camera."

They don't get any classier than these two—Andre Dawson and Ryne Sandberg laugh it up while at spring training.

PRAISE FOR HIS HALL OF FAME SPEECH

"It did surprise me. It was just myself reflecting on how I was brought up, the players that influenced me as I came up, the Larry Bowas, the Bill Buckners, the managers—Dallas Green, Jim Frey, and Don Zimmer. That's the way baseball was. Hustling was mandatory. Having respect for the game was mandatory, and it was expected. I just remembered that. After I retired, I just remember watching some games and seeing a lack of that. I had a hard time relating to that. It was fortunate that I had the chance to go into the Hall of Fame to say those things. I knew that it was center stage, and I knew that it was my chance to try and help the game and try and give something back to the game. I was very happy about it."

HIS FLAG FLYING AT WRIGLEY

"I am in awe of that. It's incredible. I was there for Ernie Banks and I was there for Billy Williams. I had games to play that day. I was in uniform. Just to watch that and to have that happen is really a tremendous honor. That day was incredible. The Cubs were fantastic. It's one of the first things I do now when I walk into Wrigley is make sure that it's up there and just try and see if it's real or not every now and then." ●

Vince Lloyd and Jack Brickhouse call the action during the first Telstar broadcast sent to Europe in 1962.

Chip Caray and Steve Stone fill some time during a rain delay at Wrigley Field.

Lloyd Petit, Jack Brickhouse, Harry Caray, and Jack Rosenberg relax at Wrigley Field after an early-season game.

The Voices

> >

JACK BRICKHOUSE

For the first 34 seasons of Cubs baseball on WGN-TV, the face and voice of the Chicago Cubs games belonged to an optimistic, never-say-die announcer from Peoria named Jack Brickhouse. His remarkable career would include stints broadcasting the White Sox, Bears, college sports, wrestling, and many other events, but it was Cubs baseball that was Jack's calling card.

One of his biggest fans was his alter ego on the field, Ernie Banks. They shared a passion for the Cubs and an unshakable belief that better days were always just around the corner. "He was a part of the team and a part of the city," Banks said. "He was very big in helping my career develop and being the kind of person I am today."

Jack Rosenberg, Brickhouse's longtime friend and colleague, always marveled at Brick's resilience and patience. "I always felt that when Jack Brickhouse looked at the Cubs on the field, he never saw a loser. He looked at the world through rose-colored glasses."

One play that sums up how Brickhouse looked at the Cubs came in 1972 at Pittsburgh. The Cubs usually struggled at Three Rivers Stadium, and this day was no different. With no one out and Pirates runners at first and second, Jack launched into a soliloquy about his baseball philosophy, and some magic followed his request:

Hundley hit into a triple play [earlier in the year] so the Cubs have a triple play coming from somebody, so what do you say they collect it now to get this inning over with and get after them in the eighth? Okay, so I'm a dreamer, but that's what this game is all about. You always have to dream the impossible dream until it becomes the possible dream in sports, and that's what makes sports so great.

Ground ball, Santo steps on third. Over to second for two. *Throw that ball! It's a triple play! A triple play! They pulled it off!* Oh brother! The impossible dream just became the possible dream! How about that!

Brickhouse was always quick to point out that he was a broadcaster, not just a sports announcer. He covered political conventions and interviewed several presidents. On a trip to Rome, he tape-recorded an audience with Pope Paul VI at the Vatican. He could do anything and made a career out of doing just that. "You name it and I've done it," he said. "Including reading the funnies to the kiddies on Sunday morning, emceed *Barn Dances,* did a man on the street for six years, fires and parades and catastrophes and wars. You name it and I've done it."

One of Brick's proudest moments came in March 1981, when he was able to convince the newly elected president, Ronald Reagan, to take time out in the Oval Office to talk some Cubs baseball in a one-on-one interview for WGN. Jack Rosenberg accompanied Brickhouse to the White House and remembered it well. "I always produced the spring training shows that kicked off the television season, and Jack hosted them for many years. I said, 'Why don't we try to get President Reagan because he did Cubs baseball on ticker tape in Des Moines, Iowa?' Well, one thing led to another, and three weeks later Jack and I were sitting in the White House doing President Reagan. People shook their heads in the industry that we could do it, and the president could not have been nicer. I remember before the interview started one of his aides said to me, 'Mr. Rosenberg, just so you know it, Mr. Brickhouse will have exactly two minutes for the interview because President Reagan has an ambassador waiting in the next room.' I said, 'With all due respect, sir, if you can

"The trains, the planes, the cabs, the buses—they have carried me millions of miles through the years to get me to where I most wanted to be—the ballgame." —Jack Brickhouse

get two old sports announcers to hold it to two minutes, God bless you.' He really liked that. During the interview, President Reagan said, 'You know, Jack, I don't know if the Cubs are ever going to win, but in my heart I always hope that they will.'"

When it came time to bow out in 1981 after more than 5,000 baseball telecasts, it was only fitting that Brickhouse's last game be at Wrigley Field. Of course, the Cubs lost 2–1 to the Phillies. His sign-off was a reflection of his style—simple, graceful, and full of love for the game. "I think there is a line in Bob Hope's theme song that describes not only baseball, but also our business, our broadcasting business: 'You may have been a headache, but you never were a bore. Thanks for the memories.'"

ON "HEY, HEY!"

"About the second year we were televising, Hank Sauer hit one, and I guess I yelled that. I had been doing it without realizing it. The crew superimposed 'Hey, hey!' on the monitor in the booth, and we all cracked up on it and decided to leave it in." —Jack Brickhouse

THE DREAM JOB
"I guess one of the rewarding things about a job like mine has been the marvelous, marvelous opportunity to be on the scene for some of these truly great moments."

THE GRIND OF THE SEASON
"There are times when you are hungover, and you don't want to work. You had a fight with your wife, you had a battle with the front office. A lot of things can happen. You just plain don't feel good. You're exhausted. You're tired. It's a lousy game, you had a fight with the manager, but I think professionalism takes over."

HALL OF FAME SPEECH
Nothing can summarize Brickhouse's career better than his eloquent Hall of Fame speech, delivered at his induction in August 1983. Rosenberg wrote the speech, and Brickhouse delivered it brilliantly. On his day in the sun, Brick stepped up to the microphone and hit one out of the park:

I stand this day on what I consider the hallowed baseball ground of Cooperstown.

I feel at this moment like a man who is 60'6" tall.

On a clear day in this quaint central New York village, you can hear and see and feel the echoes of baseball's storied past.

The atmosphere to me is breathless and humbling.

It has been my privilege to broadcast the exploits of the Chicago Cubs and the Chicago White Sox for 40 years or more. There in Wrigley Field and Comiskey Park, I have experienced the joy and the heartbreak—probably more of the latter than the former—but Chicago and its beautifully loyal fans have had a resiliency which has kindled a perpetual flame of hope.

In the fantasy of my dreams, I have imagined myself as the announcer for a Cubs–White Sox World Series—a Series that would last seven games, with the final game going into extra innings before being suspended of darkness at Wrigley Field.

Even as I accept this award, my life as a baseball broadcaster flashes before me. The drum beats on. The cities change. The boundaries change. The stadia change. The faces change. The announcers change. But the game remains essentially the same. Nine men on a side, three strikes and you're out. It's a contradiction, baseball is. It can be the simplest of games, yet it can be the most involved. It is the game I love.

The trains, the planes, the cabs, the buses—they have carried me millions of miles through the years to get me where I most wanted to be—the ballgame. A reporter once told me that even if I didn't make it to Cooperstown, my suitcase probably would. Fortunately for me, we arrived together.

Mr. Cub, Ernie Banks, and Mr. WGN, Jack Brickhouse, laugh it up in the Cubs dugout.

And I knew I was in the right place almost immediately. I saw a blur. That had to be Brooks Robinson going to his left. I saw a clutch base hit. That had to be George Kell. I saw a majestic high kick on the mound. That had to be Juan Marichal. I saw a quiet, firm image in the dugout. That had to be Walter Alston. I saw a typewriter, or was it a Video Display Terminal? That had to be Sy Burick. For a boy from Peoria to have his name intertwined with theirs, well…only in America.

It is with the deepest sincerity that I thank my company–the WGN Continental Broadcasting Company in Chicago–for believing in the entertainment value of baseball on radio and television and for believing in me. You will pardon my pride if I insist that our call letters, WGN, are the most respected in the nation. Countless people at WGN and elsewhere have brought me to this broadcasting pinnacle today. You know who you are, and you have my undying gratitude.

Here on a memorable afternoon in Cooperstown, my heart tells me that I have traveled the 90 feet from third to home and scored standing up. Thank you very much.

JACK ROSENBERG

"He was a hale fellow well met." While Jack Rosenberg delighted in using this description for scores of athletes and broadcasters through the years, the phrase best fits him. As the WGN sports editor for 45 years, Rosey's quiet guidance helped build a sports department like no other in the United States as he oversaw coverage of the White Sox, Bulls, Blackhawks, Bears, Notre Dame, Big Ten, and a myriad of other events.

Rosenberg left his job as an award-winning newspaperman in Peoria, Illinois, and joined WGN in 1954, not long after turning down a job with the *Chicago Tribune*. Though he had no experience in television, Jack Brickhouse convinced

him that a bright future lay ahead for him at channel 9 in Chicago. "I had turned down Arch Ward, the legendary sports editor at the *Tribune,* when he offered me $95 a week," remembered Rosenberg. "I told him I was supporting my mother and needed another $10. Then I came back to town and spent the whole day with Brickhouse and accepted a job at WGN for only $85 a week!"

They would become lifelong friends and travel the country together for the next three decades along with the WGN team, including their close friends Lou Boudreau and Vince Lloyd.

During Cubs telecasts, Rosenberg could always be found in the booth next to his pal Brickhouse, Rosey's typewriter clattering softly in the background to furnish information and anecdotes while Brick called the games. Brickhouse was fond of telling visitors, "If I ever said anything funny, it's because Rosenberg wrote it for me." Sometimes, you just had to be there, such as the day in 1977 when the Cubs were getting pounded badly and turned to outfielder Larry Biittner for mop-up duty on the mound. Rosey dutifully typed a line for Brickhouse, who was immediately rendered helpless with a case of the giggles. The note read, "B-i-i-t-t-n-e-r p-i-i-t-c-h-i-n-g."

One of Rosenberg's proudest moments came in 1983 when Brickhouse asked him to author his Hall of Fame induction speech. He convinced Brickhouse that a short speech would be memorable and was honored to be on hand when his old friend brought down the house with his remarks.

After Brickhouse retired, Rosenberg continued to oversee the television broadcasts, easing Harry Caray's transition to the North Side. Rosenberg's next project was a shift to WGN Radio, where he was instrumental in setting up the Cubs Radio Network. He was called back to duty on the television side in 1987. Caray had suffered a stroke and missed the beginning of the season. Rosenberg was vital in helping to line up the all-star replacement announcers, and when Caray returned to work in May, it was with the stipulation that Jack Rosenberg come back and travel with him for the rest of the season.

One of Rosey's last projects was to convince his bosses at the radio station to add Ron Santo to the broadcast team in 1990, a decision for which he laughingly professes to take neither credit nor blame.

THE CUBS MYSTIQUE

"I think the building blocks for the Cubs are the fact that their loyal fans stick behind them win or lose. There was a certain something about the Cubs that separated them from any other team, and it came home in particular in 1969. To this day, that team probably has to be the most captivating losing team in the history of sports. There's nothing like it because the players on that team gave of themselves. I used to watch them stand by the brick wall on the field and sign autograph after autograph and accommodate everyone and smile at them. There was no rushing off to the clubhouse. It stuck with them. They became big men in their own right. I always thought it was a privilege to be around the '69 Cubs."

THE MAGIC OF WRIGLEY FIELD

"I think the atmosphere and the environment at Wrigley Field have done wonders. There is a question whether people go to see the team play or go to see the ivy on the walls. The general atmosphere of that place is incredible. Unless you have actually been there, you would not realize what I am saying. I know people who have written us through the years from all over the world, and they don't say they are coming to see the Cubs win or lose, they want to see Wrigley Field. There has to be something to it. There was something about Wrigley Field that separated it from any other place in the world.

"I don't know if anyone really has it in their vocabulary to tell you what separates it. It's very difficult to do because other cities are justifiably proud of their franchises as well, and you have some great fans all over America. There is just an intangible there that no one could ever reasonably describe. Wrigley Field on a sunny day in June has to be one of the most fantastic places in the world."

THE IMPACT OF WGN

"There's nothing like it. The station and the ball team were hand in hand. It was an incredible relationship that continues to this day. The thing that I was told and I am still told even at my age, people will come up to me and say, 'You know when I was a kid…' and I know exactly what they are going to say. 'I would run home from school and get home midafternoon and you guys would be in the fourth or fifth or sixth inning, and we'd watch the rest of the game.' And they always say, 'You guys were part of our lives.' I don't know if there is anything more flattering than to have people come up repeatedly and say that."

JACK BRICKHOUSE

"He was my great friend. He had tremendous energy. In the seventh inning of the second game of a doubleheader, he appeared to be as fresh as he was in the first inning of the first game. Many of us might have been hoping that the second game would wind up, but Jack was still his usual energetic self. He brought a lot to the table. He had time for everyone. He helped a lot of broadcasters get started. To this day I have worn this watch, which is his. He ushered at my wedding to my lovely wife, Mayora. When I broke the glass, Jack had never been to a Jewish wedding before, and he jumped about three feet in the air. He said he thought someone was taking a shot at him!"

THE WGN SPORTS DEPARTMENT

"We had a very unique setup where we came down the road together. Jack, Vince, Lou, Arne, later Harry. Our lives were intertwined. We had the weddings, the births, the graduations, the bar mitzvahs, the funerals; we were always together. We would travel up and down and across this great country. It was incredible. We had friendships there that you would not expect to get in the workplace. We had 'em, and I think that the general public knew that. When they talk about the family atmosphere at the Tribune and at WGN television and radio, we all had a hand in it." —*Jack Rosenberg*

THE WGN LEGACY

"As I look back now, I feel I am fortunate to have been part of WGN television. I got here in the embryonic stages of television. It is well established that we went on the air in 1948. The thing that I like about being here early on was that we could take chances and go out and do things. Everything was new. You didn't have any inhibitions about 'try this' or 'try that.' If it failed, you did it again. I can't tell you what a thrill it's been for me to be a part of it. Sixty years is a tremendous milestone for this or any industry. I had 45 of those, and I am very proud of that."

HARRY CARAY

As a producer for WGN, every time I walk into the broadcast booth at Wrigley Field, I try to give silent thanks to Harry Caray. So much of the amazing interest in the Cubs and WGN is due to his popularity. When I sit in the booth, I can still hear Harry's voice calling out in the ninth inning, "What a ballgame! Don't you wish you were here?" He was larger than life and left us a blueprint for baseball we try to follow each and every day.

Harry was the total personification of Wrigley Field. Big crowds, cold beer, good baseball—it's what they were both all about. Rarely has any sport seen such a perfect match between an announcer and his surroundings. The secret of his success was no secret at all. His passion matched that of his audience. You could turn on the game and within 30 seconds know how things were going just by the sound of his voice.

When Steve Stone signed on as Caray's partner in 1983, the first commandment was to be genuine. "Harry told me very early in my career, 'Don't try to affect a style,'" said Stone. "Because if you try to force it, fans at home are going to know that you're not being genuine. He said that's the kiss of death. Two things to always remember: One, always be yourself and be genuine. Two, when you look into that camera and when you speak into that microphone, tell the truth. Because if you don't, the fan at home is going

to know that. The easiest way to lose all of your credibility or all of the cachet that you've built up is to start telling the fan other than what their eyes are telling them with the pictures. And I always tried to understand that."

Spring training didn't really start until Harry arrived in Mesa, Arizona, each year on March 1, his adopted birthday. Forget any action on the fields, the throngs would drop everything to go and surround his limousine. One year he popped out, muttered something about being out the night before, and announced, "Does anybody here need a blood transfusion? I've got a pint in each eye."

One of my favorite rituals at Wrigley Field in the mid-'80s occurred in the middle innings each day. Harry would do the first three innings of the game on television, then switch to call the game on WGN Radio for the middle three. At that time, the press box was on a mezzanine level that now houses the luxury suites. Fans seated in the back half of the lower deck terrace didn't have the greatest view of the game, but they did have a front-row view to the sight of Harry ducking into the bathroom for a quick bit of business between innings. The response never varied: there would be a cheer of recognition as Harry bounced out of the TV booth, followed by breathless silence for a minute or so while he emptied his Hall of Fame bladder, and finally a huge roar as he emerged from a successful rendezvous with the men's room and headed back to the booth. Only Harry could get a full ovation just for going to the can.

He preached to us that baseball is fun, that life is to be enjoyed, and that there is a friend around every corner. When I have a few minutes before one of our home games, I like to go stand by his statue outside the ballpark at Clark and Sheffield. There are always throngs of fans nearby taking photos, meeting up before the game, or just gawking. Seeing their faces is an important reminder of how lucky we are to be part of the team that carries on the values he espoused.

Thanks, Harry. You are with us on every telecast, and we do our best to bring your spirit of fun and passion for the Cubs to our viewers every day.

"All right! Let me hear ya—good and loud! A one, a two, a three…"

To celebrate Harry Caray's 50th anniversary behind the mike in 1994, WGN-TV produced a special program, *When Harry Met Baseball,* a celebration of Harry's half century behind the mike.

On May 5, 1994, Harry sat down with Bob Costas at home plate in an empty Wrigley Field for a leng thy interview that would be the body of the special. Years later, his voice rings as distinctive and true as ever.

STYLE OF ANNOUNCING

"I don't know whether the style is different from other announcers, but I think if fans like me at all, it's because they can envision themselves doing the game exactly the way I do it. When the big hitter hits a home run, boy, you're ecstatic. When the big hitter strikes out with the bases loaded and you lose the ballgame, you're despondent. When it's a boring game, you let them know that it's boring. And I think that there's a sense of integrity and honesty there in telling the people exactly what you see and feel. I think that, if there's any difference at all, number one, I don't think there is a bad announcer in the game—they are all outstanding and good. Some may be more interesting than others because of their style, and style is personality or whatever your personality might be. I'm a people guy. Everywhere I go, I look for people to talk to. I do that for a couple reasons, and I think you can understand it. Not only do I go to bars because I like to drink, and I do like to drink, but I go to bars because who do you see there? Baseball fans. You find out firsthand what they like and what they don't like. You can't learn that any other way, unless you have an occasion to talk to the true fans, and when you go to restaurants and bars as much as I do, that's who you talk to, the true fan."

THE APPEAL OF THE CHICAGO CUBS

"The ballclub's appeal is, number one, day baseball. I don't know whether Mr. Phil Wrigley was just a great visionary or whether he was just lucky, but having day baseball is the appeal of the Cubs because generation after generation

after generation, the kids get off the El, they come here, they see the ballgame, they get back on the El, and they're home by 5:30 or 6:00 PM. Can you imagine the youngsters and their enthusiasm telling their parents about the great plays that Sandberg made and the great hit of Grace, and Sosa hit a home run, 'Oh Dad, oh Mom!' And they grow up to be parents, too, and the same things happen year after year after year, generation after generation after generation—that's the appeal of the Chicago Cubs. Now, of course, with the Superstation, this appeal goes all over the nation and the islands. The only game you can see during the day in California is our game, and it's 11:00 AM out there. We don't take fans away from the Dodgers or Angels, but we develop a rooting interest. When the Cubs are there to play the Dodgers, a lot of fans maybe who would not ordinarily go to the ballpark say, 'Hey, let's go see the Cubs play the Dodgers.'"

GETTING CLOSE IN 1984

"You're making me want to cry [laughs]. It was a big disappointment. Nobody could have figured that the Cubs would lose three straight in San Diego. And if it hadn't been for a guy named Steve Garvey, they never would have lost three straight! Garvey was just Superman. In one game, he drove in five of the seven runs, all after two were out. In other words, if they could have gotten Garvey out any one of three different times, instead of the other team making seven runs, they wouldn't have made any. That's how great the name 'Steve Garvey' is. What you just talked about—that's what makes this such a great game. There's no form sheet in baseball. Nothing ever happens that's supposed to happen."

COMING BACK FROM A STROKE IN 1987

"You've just described the greatest despondency a man can go through, when all of a sudden he finds he can't move his right leg, when all of a sudden he finds he can't move his right hand, and he finds he cannot talk coherently. I mean, if they had told me I was going to die in the next 15 minutes,

Harry Caray talks with Bob Costas during the
1994 taping of *When Harry Met Baseball*.

I'd have been very happy. But I didn't die. Then my wife, Dutchie, began to bring in box after box after box, and I had nothing to do but read this mail. We stopped counting at 75,000 pieces of mail, and we must have had 50 more boxes from all over the country. People I didn't realize ever heard me because, as I said earlier, I never think who is listening. I just do my job, and I began to realize that I did mean something to people, that people did get enjoyment from what I did, that people did love what I stood for. I don't know if it was that important so far as my recovery, but who knows the mental aspect of anything? I know it made me think that I wanted to get well and I wanted to get back to work, and I did. Now I can move my right hand and I can move my right leg, but I still talk incoherently, but you can't have everything!"

"CUBS WIN!"

"That's like asking me where the home-run call came from. I don't know. When the ball is hit, you know, 'It might be.' You see the left fielder moving back and you know, 'It could be.' Then it lands in the bleachers, 'It is.' It seems to me the only call because I didn't let the play finish and then call it, which is the easy way to do it because you never make a mistake. Many is the time I thought it was a home run. I'd get, 'It might be, it could be, *whoop*, he caught the ball.' When the game is over, you either win or you lose. You don't like to say, 'Cubs lost.' Everybody knows you got beat. But when you win, it's an ecstatic moment. You develop things, you don't contrive. 'Holy Cow'—the only reason I had is to make sure I didn't use any profanity. 'That wouldn't be a home run in a phone booth'—I've used that all my life. We're all a little bit creatures of habit.

"Anything you contrive in our business is bad. The only thing you do is be your natural self. What you see is what you get when it's me. You may like it, you may dislike it, you may think it's corny, you might think it's mashy—whatever. I say it the way I'm accustomed to saying it. I say it as simply as I can put it. You mentioned ballplay-

ers. Why, sure a ballplayer might be a little angry when he finds out I talked about his error, but the scorer said it was an error. What are you going to do about it?"

BASEBALL FANS ARE THE UNSUNG HEROES

"Absolutely. The fan is the guy that the owners should cater to. The players should cater to them. The players ought to look 'em up and encourage the fan to ask for an autograph. These people make it all possible. I don't care what the contract is, I don't care how much they hit, I don't care how much money they're paid. If that fan isn't sitting in that seat, the game won't be around very long." **—Harry Caray**

THE CONSTANT ATTENTION FROM THE FANS

"It's a small price to pay for something you like. I like the fact that people like me. They make it very clear. I'm not being immodest. It's quite obvious that people seem to like me. Whatever the reason, I'm grateful that they do. I go out of my way to shake hands with people who sit in the handicapped section because there but for the grace of God go I. For a little orphan boy from very humble origins, I'm kind of proud of my own life, and I'm proud of my relationship with these fans who I think the world of. There's no fan that's more loyal than the Chicago Cubs fan. Believe it."

STEVE STONE

Steve Stone's connection to the Cubs and Wrigley Field goes back more than 30 years, beginning with his trade to the Cubs in a deal that sent Ron Santo to the White Sox. Stone went 23–20 in three years with the Cubs before returning to the Sox, then heading off to Baltimore, where he flourished with a 25–7 record en route to the 1980 Cy Young Award.

Elbow problems pushed Stone into the broadcast booth in 1982, where he cut his teeth working on ABC's *Monday Night Baseball.* The next year WGN-TV grabbed

Harry Caray makes sure to take good care of President Ronald Reagan, his broadcast partner for a few innings in 1988.

Steve Stone watches another game unfold from the WGN-TV booth.

him, pairing him with Harry Caray for a daily version of *The Odd Couple* that would run for the next 15 highly entertaining seasons. They were a different duo–Harry, the always-excited and sometimes-frustrated voice of the fan, and Stone, the first-guessing, analytical teacher in the booth. "The one thing Harry left with me from the beginning was, 'You have to know, Steve, when to let the game speak for itself and when we have to speak for the game,'" said Stone. "Most broadcasters have no conception of what that means. He said, 'I'm going to help you to understand when to do that. That and remember, when they're bad down there, we have to be real good up here.'"

One of Stone's greatest feats was holding the telecasts together while hosting a parade of celebrities in the booth following Caray's stroke in 1987. Stone's partners included Bill Murray, Tom Bosley, George Will, Jim Belushi, Brent Musburger, Ernie Harwell, and Pat Summerall. "I loved it," laughed Stone, "but I loved it a lot more when Harry finally came back to the booth."

After Harry's death in 1998, Stone was paired with another Caray–Harry's grandson, Chip. The two were kindred spirits and hit it off immediately, even though they had barely met before Opening Day that year. "I think Steve broadcast the way he pitched," offered Chip Caray. "When he first came up he had a blazing fastball and could throw it right past people. When he got hurt and hurt his arm, he had to start to think his way through the lineup. Whether that was a conscious decision or not of his to broadcast that way I don't know, but he had an unbelievable ability to look two or three innings ahead. He knows the game inside and out. He knows the people, and he knows the personalities. He made it very easy for me as a broadcaster because my job was to steer the ship, and he would tell me where it was going to go. I'd tee it up for him, and he'd hit it 300 yards down the middle every time. We had a lot of chemistry and a lot of fun."

No matter who his partner was, Stone excelled at teaching the game and setting up the situation with what used to be called *first-guessing*. "What I tried to do was give the man at home the options because in baseball there are no right and wrong moves," he explained. "Nothing is really black and white. What it is is shades of gray. If you make the move and it works out, it was a good move. If you make the move and it doesn't work out, it was a bad move. But for every move there are two or three possibilities. I would lay out the possibilities beforehand, and I would lay out what I would do. Then whoever was managing did what he did, which is what he was paid to do, and sometimes it worked out and all these other possibilities went away, and sometimes what I said happened, and the fan at home would say, 'That was interesting.'"

After leaving following the 2000 season to pursue a career in competition consulting, Stone returned to the Cubs' broadcast booth in 2003. The following season was marred by conflicts between Stone, Dusty Baker, and several players on the team. At the conclusion of the season, Stone resigned of his own accord and spent the next two years calling games for ESPN. He remains a fixture on sports radio in Chicago and is a familiar presence at most Cubs home games.

THE CUBS FAITHFUL

"I think one of the reasons why the Cubs fans have had the patience that they've had is that they always enjoy themselves when they come to Wrigley Field and watch a baseball game. And I think they get hooked on looking at this continuing soap opera on a daily basis, knowing that one day it's going to come to an end, one day they are going to win the World Series, and you can't really leave for an extended period of time because if you're not there, if you've invested all this time into this one team, this one city, this one ballpark, and you happen to miss when the day comes when this team wins it all, you're going to say, 'Well what did I do? How many years did I waste?' And that's one of the reasons for the infatuation and all that is the Chicago Cubs and WGN bringing it to you."

The number-one sports team in America smiles before the season:
(front) Arne Harris, Jack Rosenberg, (back) Lou Boudreau, Harry Caray, Steve Stone.

PITCHING FOR THE CUBS

"I was there for three years as a player, and the Cubs—I know this is going to surprise a lot of people—but they weren't particularly good at that point. I like to refer to them as the Golden Years of '74, '75, and '76. But in reality, when you have Carmen Fanzone at third, and you have Dave Rosello at short, Rob Sperring at second, and Pete LaCock at first, your closer is Oscar Zamora, and you've got George Mitterwald behind the plate, and occasionally you fill in with some other guys, and you look out in the outfield and you see Rick Monday and some other guys and you don't know their names—so you had a feeling you weren't going to win it. However, in '75, when we had first place secured by June 15, you went, okay, here it's the miracle. Then reality sets in, and by June 25, you're just down. It was fun to me, I really enjoyed it, but we weren't drawing big crowds in those days."

SPOTTING TENDENCIES

"I would watch a guy take a lead off a base, and the first three times he led off, his front foot would be parallel. And then I would watch and he would turn his front foot out just a little bit, and I'd say, 'I think he's getting ready to run.' To me, that was a tell, and I would look for tells around the field. Most of my career I wasn't particularly good, but I had to be observant. For a short period of time I was good, but sometimes I was the 11th man on an 11-man staff, and you have to be observant. I used to watch the shortstop come in and smooth the dirt in front of his position, but when he went back to his position, he would move over by the third-base line. I knew that they were either going inside on a right-hander or away on a left-hander, and he was expecting a ball in the hole. So I'd say, 'You know, they've just closed up the hole between short and third,' and the ball would get there. Some of that stuff just was observance, and some of it was just a feeling that I had."

FIRST-GUESSING

"I just wanted to give the fan the idea to think along with the manager, let him make a decision as to what he thought should happen at this time, because the beauty of baseball and watching it at home—not necessarily at the ballpark, although that's part of it, too—is managing along with the manager. Everybody believes they can manage. That's what is so wonderful about baseball. And all I was doing was to give the fans options and let them understand that there are other ways to do every move you make. There are other things you can do. Let's figure out why he's going to do what he's going to do. After the fact, and I've heard a lot of broadcasters do that, 'Well, of course he was going to do that.' Well, if you're so sure he was going to do that, mention it before that, then let us know how sure you are because hindsight is always 100 percent."

FAVORITE SERIES

"The favorite series I have was the 2003 season with the season coming down to a precious few games, and because of a rainout, the Cardinals were coming in for a five-game series here. I believe that the Cardinals came in believing that they were a better team than the Cubs and that they were going to run by them and they were going to win. I mean, that's what had happened many years before, and they had every intention that that's what would happen this year. Those games were some of the most tense, most hard-fought, most dramatic, most twisted and turned games I could ever remember. But at the end of that series, the Cubs took four of five, and with the Cardinals coming in thinking they were a better team, they left town knowing they weren't. And for the Cubs, they went on to win the division. That five-game series, if you were to take it from the first inning, watch every inning, could make a series in itself because I can't remember anything as dramatic. And I can't remember any other series, sitting back when the series was over, and literally not being able to get up out of my chair. I was just absolutely rung out with emotion, and I thought that in a nonplaying situation, I had never been involved in anything over a five-game series over four days that was as dramatic as those five."

LASTING MEMORY

"The last game that I did here was for WGN. It was a very disappointing season in 2004. Rather than go into how we got to this certain point, I just remember the last day standing up for the seventh inning and the entire ballpark started to chant 'Stoney.' I was standing up there, and it was frustrating because that team should have been in the playoffs that year, they should have been one of the final eight, not one of the 22 that went home. The acknowledgment of the fans for what I would like to think was my entire body of work and for what happened in 2004 was something that brought a tear to my eye."

WGN AND THE CUBS

"Most of my broadcast career was shaped by Harry Caray right in this beautiful ballpark, right on WGN television. I remember Jim Dowdle [Tribune Broadcasting president] telling me when he hired me, 'If you want to do this just as a passing fancy, we're not the place to go because we do 150 games a year. If you want to make a career out of this, working with Harry, doing it 150 times a year in front of the whole country, it's the best place for you to be.' Probably nobody ever gave me any better advice than that because it's held me in good stead today. The lessons I took from it, the experiences I had in this ballpark, the opportunity WGN gave me, the partners I got to work with. It's just something that is very much a part of my history and is very much a part of who I am today." —*Steve Stone*

ARNE HARRIS

For 40 years, he was Chicago's version of the Wizard of Oz. You could say the name "Arne" and almost everyone in Chicago would know you were talking about Arne Harris, director of the Cubs telecasts on WGN. At the same time, no one had the faintest notion of what he looked like, because

Arne was the man behind the scenes, sitting in front of a bank of monitors, and calling out the shots.

During a typical telecast, the director sits in a production truck outside the ballpark, looks at the various camera shots, and picks the pictures that go on the air to tell the story of the game. Arne took it much further and did more than just show the action on the field. He made Wrigley Field and the Cubs fans the stars of every show.

Harris took Steve Stone under his wing in 1983, and Stone took immediate notice of the style that was different from the network telecasts he had done years before. "He understood somewhat innately that this is a unique experience for everybody, not only at the ballpark, but watching at home, and what he tried to bring to the screen every day was the stories that went on beyond the field," said Stone. "Like if he had an older gentleman eating an ice cream cone, he would go back to him in the second inning and it would be a big ice cream cone. He might have a youngster sitting next to him, and now in the fourth inning, he might have the same ice cream cone, but now it was dripping down the thing and now the youngster was taking a little bite. And he would go back to him again, and it would be part of the continuing saga of what Wrigley Field was all about."

"Arne was so astute as a producer/director that he would give us things. 'Hey, have you ever considered why is he doing this?'" Stone added. "Unlike some people who don't understand the game, Arne knew baseball backward and forward and had done so many Cub games that he had a feeling also for what was going to happen."

He loved the spotlight. Arne started at WGN in 1956 along with director Bill Friedkin (*The French Connection*) and former network czar Fred Silverman and delighted in saying that he had the best gig of the three. Not long after, he was lured away from WGN to hit the road as the public address announcer for the Harlem Globetrotters. His favorite story with the Trotters was going through an airport with the players and "somebody said the little guy in the middle must be the dribbler, so that's what they called me for about five years was 'the Dribbler.'"

WGN-TV director Arne Harris called the shots from the production truck for more than 40 seasons.

Several years later, Arne returned to his first loves, baseball and WGN, and stayed for more than 40 years of service. It was his voice in Jack Brickhouse's ear, his eyes picking the hat shots in the crowd, and his quips that had Harry Caray laughing on the air.

One story he loved to bring up was about the time he was visiting Caray in Palm Springs, California, and Harry had taken him to Frank Sinatra's house. As the night progressed, the group ended up singing around a piano, and Arne always let us know that the Chairman said he had a great voice.

Thousands of fans made their way through the WGN production truck through the years, and Arne treated them all like kings. He would chat up the visitors while still directing the game and would remind everyone as they left, "Hey, remember, if we win today, you have to come back here tomorrow, okay?" He rarely knew anyone's name, but he could talk with them like old friends.

One of his great loves was his white pants, which he wore every day all summer, beginning promptly on Memorial Day and ending on Labor Day. Stone used to say the only place Harris could get them was barbershop or ice cream truck supply stores, but Arne didn't care. In 2001, a camera crew staked out his parking spot to await his arrival at Wrigley Field, anticipating the pants' first appearance of the year. On *The Leadoff Man* that day, we aired the footage of the white pants emerging from the car and added the Bee Gees' "Stayin' Alive" to accompany the shot of Arne's white pants as he walked to the production truck.

I'll never forget the last game Arne worked at the end of 2001. It was a next-to-last game of the year on a Saturday afternoon at Wrigley Field, filled with typical end-of-the-year nuttiness. Journeyman Julian Tavarez flirted with the ugliest no-hitter in Wrigley history, Sammy Sosa hit an inside-the-park home run, and the Cubs won an ugly 13–2 game. In the truck, we were laughing all day, but never more so than when the topic of autobiographies came up. Arne opined that he would call his *Never Take the Blame: The Arne Harris Story* and had everyone in stitches for the rest of the day.

That night, Arne and his wife, Arlene, met Chip Caray for dinner downtown. While waiting to be seated, Arne suddenly collapsed and died almost immediately. There was nothing his friends could do except say good-bye, offer condolences to his family, and try to figure out how to handle the last game of the season the next day.

We quickly decided the only thing to do was turn our game the next day into a three-hour memorial for Arne. Some of the crew met me at the WGN studios, where we spent the night going through tapes and culling some of Arne's greatest moments. Chip was magnificent during the game, opening with a personal message of loss and then deftly keeping tabs on the game while interviewing an A-list of guests who came to our booth or called on the phone to pay tribute to Arne.

Sammy Sosa was without a doubt Arne's favorite player with the Cubs during those last few years. Arne always felt that no matter how the team was doing, our fans would stay tuned to see if Sammy would hit a home run. In the eighth inning of our Arne Harris tribute game, Sammy cranked one out to left and, upon returning to the dugout, made his usual beeline to our camera there. This time, instead of tapping his chest and blowing a kiss, he said, "That one was for you, Arne." It was a great gesture by Sammy and meant the world to Arne's family watching at home.

As I told people later, Arne's death was an awful thing that happened in the best possible way. I like to think he would have enjoyed the televised Irish wake we threw him in that last game. It was one of the best games we have ever done.

On September 10, 2000, Arne was the guest conductor for the seventh-inning stretch. He was always tickled to get a moment in the limelight and he offered up his thoughts on the Cubs on both our *Leadoff Man* show and in the booth with Chip and Steve after singing "Take Me Out to the Ballgame."

WRIGLEY FIELD

"Wrigley Field is still Wrigley Field. There's still people, and there's still kids, and there's still pretty gals, and there's

Jack Rosenberg, Jack Brickhouse, Arne Harris, and Jim West have their scorecards filled out and are ready to go at Wrigley Field.

still rooftops, and there's still boats, so no matter what the score is, it's still fun to come to Wrigley Field.

"I've always felt that Wrigley Field might be the number one attraction in Chicago, particularly in the summertime, obviously. Over the years, even with teams that haven't done well, we've always had the one superstar. Ernie, when things weren't going well, Andre Dawson when things weren't going well, and Sammy now. I think as long as you've got somebody that you can focus on and have fun with, people are going to enjoy the game. Believe me, I've walked out of that truck many times when we've lost two games, and feeling low and saying, "Boy, I'm going to walk by some people and somebody is going to punch me out," and they're happy because they saw Ernie hit a home run. You forget that so many people come out here just to enjoy themselves. Some people plan a trip out here for months, maybe even years in advance. I mean everybody wants the Cubs to win, but if you can't win, at least have a good time, and most of the people who come to this ballpark have a good time."

FAVORITES

"Certainly baseball is my favorite sport. The Bulls with the run they had of eight years where they were winning championships was great, and of course, you can't beat guys like Michael [Jordan] and Scottie Pippen, Dennis Rodman–those were some strange personalities.

"Here at Wrigley, I've been lucky. Broadcasters and players, I can't think of a bad guy I've dealt with. Some of the things that stand out over the years, Ernie's 500th–that's the first real big occasion I dealt with. Certainly Kerry's 20 strikeouts the one game was brilliant. Kenny Holtzman pitching two no-hitters as a Cub, you can't beat that. Maybe the single most impressive thing I can think of is Sammy's streak the last three years. He's going to have 180 home runs in three years. That's unbelievable to me."

A CUBS WORLD SERIES

"It would be great for me. Boy, you've never seen anything. If the Cubs ever win it, it would shut down Chicago. That would be it. The Bears celebration was great, the Bulls celebration was great, and if the White Sox win it, I'm sure it will be great, but throw it out the window. If the Cubs win it, look out, world!"

THE CENTER-FIELD CAMERA

"The key to televising Major League Baseball, the one thing that changed baseball television completely, was the center-field camera. I'll give you an example. When I first started doing the games, we didn't have the center-field camera. Then we got it at home and people loved it, but we didn't have it on the road, so every time we went to do a road game you would see the pitcher/batter shot from behind the screen. We got mail and phone calls from people saying that the coverage on the road is terrible compared to the home coverage, and that was because of the center-field shot."

IT'S ALWAYS ABOUT BASEBALL

"Anybody who says football is our national pastime is wrong. No other sport can play six months every day and draw 25,000 to 30,000 fans a game. What if the Cubs played only 16 Sundays a year—what do you think they would draw in this place? So how can you compare football to baseball? Baseball is about entertainment and there is nothing like a ballgame at Wrigley Field. How can you not like this place? The full ballpark, the stands, the rooftops, the lake—what a sight!" —*Arne Harris*

LEN KASPER

"This is the best play-by-play job in sports, and I look forward to being a daily part of the lives of the best fans in baseball." With those words in November 2004, Len Kasper stepped in to fill some of the biggest shoes in broadcasting when he accepted the position as the television voice of the Chicago Cubs.

The WGN-TV announcing team of
Len Kasper and Bob Brenly.

Working for one of the nation's most visible franchises is nothing new for Kasper, who spent several years covering the Green Bay Packers for WTMJ Radio in Milwaukee, Wisconsin, while doing fill-in work on Milwaukee Brewers TV games. He landed his first full-time television job in Florida calling the Marlins games, where he experienced the joy of seeing his team win a pennant at Wrigley Field. Yes, he was on the wrong side in 2003, but it's a frame of reference he hopes to be able to draw upon sometime soon. Two years later, he joined Bob Brenly in the broadcast booth and was a bit overwhelmed in his first days as the voice of the Cubs. "I think I would have told you that I had somewhat of a handle on the Chicago Cubs, but I'm not sure I really did," said Kasper. "You have to experience it, in my opinion, to understand what it's all about. I've gotten totally caught up in Cubdom and everything about the Chicago Cubs and their long history going back to 1876. When I come to the park every day, I try to learn something new about this franchise."

Growing up in central Michigan, Len was an enthusiastic Detroit Tigers fan, so it's no surprise that the biggest influence on his broadcasting career was legendary announcer Ernie Harwell. Listening to one Hall of Famer turned out to be very good training for occupying the booth that housed two others in Brickhouse and Caray.

"Most people understand that, without being corny, I'm trying to be the best Len Kasper I can be," he explained. "You will get the occasional 'I'd like you to be more like Harry or be more like Jack or more like Chip,' but I understand that. People get comfortable with their announcers here. Over the course of time, people get comfortable with your style. They know that you're a human being and that you have your quirks and your personality. Lord knows I have my own, but if you're genuine, you prepare well, you give them the game, and have a little fun along the way, that's what Cubs fans appreciate about good broadcasting. Those are big, big shoes to fill, and it's such an honor to sit in that chair every day."

His new broadcast partner was quickly impressed with Kasper's makeup. "Len came in here with the perfect attitude for that job," said Brenly. "There was some contro-versy the way the last crew ended, but Lenny came in with a clean slate, and he figured, 'If I work hard enough and if I do my job well enough, people will forget and forgive and move on.'" Brenly is also a fan of Kasper's work ethic. "Fans see him down here on the field every day, and the players see him in the clubhouse every day. He's got a personal relationship with every player and coach on the team and the staff, and that goes a long way toward them opening up and giving you those little tidbits that make our telecasts what they are. Guys tell him things that they wouldn't tell a play-by-play announcer normally because they feel comfortable with Len."

It's one thing to have your dream job, it's another to realize it and make the most of each day, which is what Kasper is all about and why he is so popular with the Cubs faithful. Rather than shy away from an often-demanding public, Kasper relishes the chance to mix with his viewers. "I really enjoy walking around the park before and after the game in particular and just saying hi to people," he said. "It's just so fun to be with the fans walking in and out. In a lot of the ballparks, you get on an elevator, go down a tunnel, get on the team bus, and you don't really run into a lot of fans. But here, you go up and down the ramps every day with the people that pay money to watch Cubs baseball, and that's one of the thrills for me in this job."

CUBS BASEBALL ON WGN

"It's all about baseball, and while we do have sponsored elements and things that aren't directly related to the baseball game, the number one thing is to present Cubs baseball. Number two, there is the fun aspect of being at Wrigley Field. We have such a wonderful crew, and our camera people know all the angles and the quirks, and they know the great fan shots. Our director, Skip Ellison, is very good at finding those stories that are somewhat related to the game. You have Waveland Avenue, Sheffield, Clark, Addison, things going on around the ballpark that we also try to show on occasion. I just think that we bring the entire Wrigley Field experience—it's baseball, and it's also what surrounds it before and after the ballgame. It's very unique. There's nothing quite like this, and I'm proud to be a part of it."

WORKING AT WRIGLEY FIELD

"Everybody is so friendly here. There is a reason they call it the Friendly Confines, and once the game starts, it is a big frat party. People passionately want the Cubs to win. When I walk into this place and when I see people who have never been here before, I notice that for them, no matter what the record of the Cubs is, no matter what the weather is like, it doesn't matter who the Cubs are playing, that's their Game 7 of the World Series. If the Cubs win that day, people walk out of the ballpark feeling good about themselves, and it doesn't happen in a lot of places."

CELEBRITY SINGERS

"That was an adjustment for me. You get a little intimidated when Vince Vaughn or Tim Robbins or Julia Louis-Dreyfus walks into the booth, but they are so in awe of the view, of the fact that you're looking down on 40,000 people. And when you have a night game, the spotlight turns on, and you're it. If you screw up, it's going to be on every highlight show, it's going to be on the news that night, as Jeff Gordon found out. You're going to be asked about it later. If you nail it, it almost comes off as boring. And you *have* to get the words right. Sometimes people get into that situation and don't fully comprehend how big it is for these fans to sing that song. It also doesn't necessarily matter how big the celebrity is, when Gary Pressy starts the organ and gives you that first note, these fans are going to be basically hanging on your every breath the whole time. It's such a special moment. You don't have to ask them about everything that's going on with them. They would rather talk about the experience at Wrigley Field, and a lot of times it's their first experience and they want to come back."

FROM NIGHT TO DAY

"A lot of times, the interesting thing here is when you have extra innings or you have late nights after rain delays, you come back and play the next day and everybody says, 'Gosh, it's a quick turnaround. I'm only going to get four or five hours of sleep.' A lot of times, those end up being the most memorable periods. We had a game in Houston when Rich Hill had to pitch in an 18-inning game, and he was going to start the next day. Well, the Cubs called up Ryan O'Malley, a left-hander, who pitched the game of his life in his major league debut. We had a shot of him hugging his father after the game. Bob and I were totally emotional, we had tears in our eyes, and we were worn out because it was a long night the night before. Those almost end up bringing out your emotions more and making for a more enduring broadcast."

SHARING THE PASSION

"I was told when I got this job, 'Don't try to explain it, just embrace it.' And I think that's a very good lesson for all of us who follow this team. There are people on the outside who say, 'This team hasn't won a World Series in almost 100 years. They haven't been to the World Series in 60 years. Why do they have such a passionate following?' Well, it's handed down from generation to generation. There's a family bond I think that exists when you watch a team, in a lot of ways, disappoint you year after year. I can't wait for that day when the Cubs finally get to the World Series again and win it for all these great fans, because they've been waiting for way too long." —Len Kasper

BOB BRENLY

Bob Brenly loves the game of baseball as much as anybody you will ever meet. From his childhood membership in the Tito Francona fan club to managing the Arizona Diamondbacks to a Game 7 win in the World Series, it's always been about baseball for Brenly. He is a resident expert on the workings of the baseball gods and the definition of a baseball junkie. Spend any time with Bob and you will hear,

Bob Brenly enjoys what he calls "the greatest view in the sports," his view of Wrigley Field from the broadcast booth.

"The best thing about baseball is every day at the ballpark you're liable to see something you've never seen before."

His dedication to the game was tested in college, where he was an All-American at Ohio University, but went undrafted after a good senior season. "That was a tough day as they went round and round, and I didn't hear from anybody," said Brenly. "The next day I called Major League Baseball, and the nice receptionist looked at the list for me and said, 'Son, you are free to negotiate with any team,' which was a nice way of saying nobody wanted me. Fortunately for me, the Giants were looking for somebody with a pulse to play left field in rookie ball, and that was me."

Brenly was hardly an overnight success, laboring in the minors for six seasons until several injuries on the Giants team gave him a chance with the big club in 1981. He made the most of the opportunity, carving out a nine-year playing career that included an All-Star appearance in 1984. Brenly retired after the 1989 season and applied for an open color announcer slot on WGN Radio to work with play-by-play man Thom Brennaman. That winter, Brenly and Ron Santo were sent to Florida for what amounted to a competition to see who would get the color analyst spot, using Senior League games as a venue to do some practice games.

Longtime WGN Sports staffer Jack Rosenberg was on the trip to evaluate Santo and Brenly, but instead of anointing one or the another, Rosenberg convinced the WGN Radio hierarchy to hire them both. Not only was Brenly watching the Cubs each day, but he was watching and working with Harry Caray. "I was and still am in awe," he said. "Harry was just unbelievable on and off the air, and it was a privilege to be around him."

Two seasons later, Brenly left WGN-AM to become a coach with the Giants, then got into television work before being tabbed as manager of the Arizona Diamondbacks in 2001. In one of the most memorable World Series in recent years, Brenly's Diamondbacks came from behind in Game 7 to beat the Yankees and earn their rookie manager a World Series ring. Three seasons later, the team was shedding veteran salaries and chose to send Brenly on his way as well.

With time on his hands, Bob put in a phone call to John McDonough at the Cubs. "After the firing in Arizona, I had no idea what I was going to do," he recalled. "I was sitting at home and watching a Cubs game on WGN and thought, 'You know, I should give John McDonough a call.' So I called John and said, 'If you need somebody to park cars or to sweep the stands or sell popcorn, I can do a little broadcasting, I can do some things on the field, so if any openings come up there, please keep me in mind.'"

After Steve Stone's resignation in October 2004, Brenly was the easy choice to come to the TV booth as the color analyst and the chance to enjoy, as he termed it, "the greatest view in sports." His midsummer phone call had paid off. "I had no preconceived notion that I was going to end up in the booth doing TV games," Brenly said. "I was just looking for a job in baseball, and this was a place that I always loved, and I loved the people I worked with here. It couldn't have worked out any better."

His style is easy, straightforward, and always informative. Having been in the dugout, Brenly knows that the game is much quicker on the field and that as a broadcaster he doesn't always have all the information needed to pass judgment on certain situations. More than anything, he cherishes being at the ballpark each day. "What's it like?" he said. "It sure doesn't feel like work, I know that. I can't imagine anybody else who is as excited to get to their workplace as Len and I are. We can't wait to get to the ballpark and see what happens next. We've been treated so well by everybody in the Cubs family, from the front office to the guys working in the clubhouse, the players, the ushers, everybody just treats us like family and every day is an event. I'm not a big fan of baseball as an event sport. When you try to pump it up too much, it never lives up to the billing. But a baseball game at Wrigley is an event. It doesn't matter who's pitching, it doesn't matter who's playing; every day you come to Wrigley Field to watch a ballgame, it's an event. You're seeing something that people all over the country wish they could attend, and we get to do it every day. There's nothing better."

Len Kasper calls Brenly "no maintenance," and the two quickly hit it off. "As broadcasters, we all have things that we require when we walk into the booth, and I certainly have mine," Kasper said. "I like to make sure my headset is just perfect and I can hear everything the way I like to hear it. I have my computer and my monitor, my scorebook, and everything in the right place. Bob shows up, 'Got the lineups?' 'Absolutely.' Writes them in, here's what we're going to talk about in the open, great, do the game, have a ton of fun, he gives us an unbelievable analysis every day, and that's it. That is so rare in this business. We all have egos, but Bob walks into the booth and says, 'What do you want me to do today?' That is so, so important. We have enough common interests, music and movies and things not related to baseball, but we're different in a lot of ways, as well, and I think that works well. If we were too similar, the broadcast might feel like it's too inside and people are in on the joke, so to speak. He's old school on certain baseball topics, and I guess I would put myself in the new-school category, and I think it makes for some interesting conversations."

THE MAGIC OF WRIGLEY

"It does change over the course of the season. The ivy is dormant when the season starts, and that's the fun of the baseball season blooming. Hopefully, the team comes together at the same time the ivy turns green, and hopefully, you take off from there. I can't imagine a better place in the world to go to work every day. You show up and you see the same smiling faces and you know that something is going to happen on that field that you've never seen before and on almost a daily basis. I don't think there's another place in the universe like Wrigley Field." —*Bob Brenly*

PLAYING AT WRIGLEY

"I couldn't wait to get to the ballpark. I had a modicum of success here at Wrigley, but it always felt like I did better than I did because the fans were so knowledgeable. That ground ball to second base that moved the runner to third—30,000 people knew you did something good because they appreciate good baseball. I played my best in front of fans who appreciate the little things. Certainly those fans at Wrigley, although they don't always get to see those little things executed on a daily basis, know when it happens, and they show their appreciation. I always thought it brought out the best in me. I loved playing at Wrigley."

SINGLE-DAY AMNESIA

"We talk about the fans here starting with a clean slate. It's a little lifetime every day. It starts with the national anthem, and even before that, the drama unfolds; and if it happens to be a loss, everybody mourns that loss until the national anthem the next day. If it happens to be a victory, then it's a celebration until the anthem the next day. I don't want to put down Boston or New York, two great baseball cities, but I don't think there's another place like Wrigley and the fans at Wrigley for the way they take the game to heart. They die a little bit with the losses and they experience the utmost joy after the victories. I don't see that at other ballparks."

BEING ON WGN

"I could think back to watching WGN way, way back in the day. It's scary if you let yourself think about it too much, how many people are tuned in, watching that ballgame. I try to just make it Len on one side, me on the other, nobody watching us, try to ease into the telecast, and let the action carry us. If you stop and think of how many people are watching that ballgame all over the world, it can be a little intimidating.

"Every day the Cubs were on and every day you knew the Cubs were going to be playing a day game at Wrigley Field. When I was a player, when I was a manager, your daily preparation kind of revolved around what the Cubs were doing that day. Many times the Cubs were out of the race at that point, the team they were playing was out of the race, but you still watched. You still watched; maybe Harry was going to say something outrageous, maybe the fans were going to do something outrageous. Like I said earlier, it was always an event, so as a visiting player, whether you were in San Francisco or New York or Atlanta, you had to watch. It was an event."

THE GREATEST VIEW IN SPORTS

"I still feel that way. There are some great ballparks in the major leagues and I'm sure football stadiums and basketball arenas, but on a daily basis to sit up in the booth where we sit and [have] the view that we have…. First of all, the field, it's pristine. There's not a blade of grass out of place. Everything is where it should be, and then you look out over the outfield bleachers and you can see the neighborhood out there. You can see the lake with the sailboats. I catch myself up there some days just staring. I should be filling out lineup cards or doing something productive for the game, but it's just such a great view. It's like having that awesome apartment with a view of the city and you just want to sit in your window and look out, and that's the way I feel sometimes up in the booth." ●

One more to go—Ernie Banks is welcomed home after hitting his 499th home run.

The Moments

>>

ERNIE BANKS'S 500TH HOME RUN

Only 5,264 hardy souls made their way to Wrigley Field on May 12, 1970, but they saw one of the great moments in Cubs history as Ernie Banks became the first member of the franchise to hit 500 home runs.

Banks had finished the 1969 season with 497 homers, so the countdown to 500 was the topic of conversation throughout the winter. He was also transitioning to a part-time role with the Cubs and struggled with limited at-bats. When the season started, the pressure intensified as he went almost three weeks before his first home run of the season. Number 498 came on April 25, a high fly ball that floated into the left-field bleachers against Houston off *Ball Four* author Jim Bouton. Fourteen days later, Ernie hit number 499 against the Reds and Don Gullett, a towering blast that landed on Waveland Avenue.

"It was exciting working up to that," Banks said. "I didn't think about it that much, but there was a lot of talk about it. People were pulling for me to do it. My daughter was getting a little irritated that it was taking so long. She said, 'Dad, hit the home run so we can get the media off of our backs.' I told her, 'All right, Jen, I'll get it over with.' That day, against the Braves, May 12, 1970, in the [second] inning I hit the home run." Number 500 came off Atlanta's Pat Jarvis and was a signature Banks home run—a low line drive that sailed into the left-field bleachers and bounced back onto the field.

Mr. Cub's teammates shared in his joy and his relief. "Ernie was pretty happy running around the bases, knowing he got to that milestone," recalled Ferguson Jenkins. "Back then, there were only a few hitters who had 500 home runs. It was a milestone for Ernie and for the Cubs. Everybody was pretty happy. The dugout was jumping around, patting everybody on the back, and happy for Ernie."

"I realized the impact of it and what it meant to people," Banks said. "Jack Brickhouse was there, and he was so enthusiastic about it. I still play that tape and hear him saying, 'Oh, it's outta here. Wheeee, attaboy!' It kind of lifts up my spirits and all that. It's one thing I do when I get down, I play that Jack Brickhouse tape of my 500th home run. I was overjoyed by it. I went around the city and lots of places, and everyone was happy for me. I learned from that. Sports and the Cubs are just one thing that make people very happy, not just for a moment. People still come up and tell me, 'I was at that game.'"

>>

"When I get down, I play that Jack Brickhouse tape of my 500th home run. I was overjoyed by it."

—Ernie Banks

>>

The highlight quickly became one of the treasures of the WGN Sports vault, and sports editor Jack Rosenberg was delighted for Banks. "Ernie's first full year (1954) was the same as mine, so I always felt like we came up together," he said. "That was a big moment, one of the mostly highly anticipated home runs you will ever see."

At the time, Ernie was only the 10th member of the 500-home-run club. The solo shot also set a milestone as Banks reached 1,600 RBIs for his career. In a strange twist, ex-Cub Frank Secory was one of the umpires for the game. Secory was also working the game in 1953 when Banks hit his first home run. Reaching the milestone provided a brief glimpse of sunlight following the dark days at the end of 1969 and gave fans the satisfaction of seeing the Cubs' greatest player join one of baseball's most exclusive clubs.

GREG MADDUX'S 3,000TH STRIKEOUT

Baseball players and fans talk about respect more than Aretha Franklin, but occasionally they get it right. Greg Maddux, the four-time Cy Young Award winner and Cubs prodigal son, received that respect of the highest level on a rainy night in July 2005, when more than 30,000 Cubs fans braved the elements and a long rain delay in order to see him get his 3,000th strikeout.

They had waited a long time to honor one of their favorites. At age 22, Maddux was the Cubs' youngest All-Star in 1988, led the team to a division title in 1989, and was clearly a star on the rise, with an understanding of the game that was not lost on his teammates. "He was a great teacher," noted his catcher Joe Girardi. "I was a young player and he was a young player–he's actually younger than I am–but he had been up. He was a great teacher and was always willing to offer advice, talk about how to get hitters out. When I think of Greg Maddux, I think of a guy who studied the game as hard as any player I've ever been around, never missed anything, was always on the bench, paid attention to detail, and that's what made him so great."

When it came time for a long-term contract after his Cy Young Award–winning 1992 season, the Cubs allowed their ace to be lured away by the Atlanta Braves. Twelve years, three more Cy Youngs, one World Series ring, and 194 victories later, Maddux re-signed with the Cubs to bolster what promised to be a sturdy rotation as well as to provide guidance for the team's young guns in Carlos Zambrano, Kerry Wood, and Mark Prior.

Jim Hendry relayed a typical Maddux story during spring training in 2005. "Greg was standing on the side with some of our young pitchers. Whoever was on the mound was really bringing it and got some ooohs and ahhhs after a few good fastballs. Greg said to them, 'If you're standing on the side of the road and a truck races by, can you tell me if it's going 85 or 95 miles per hour? It's not about speed.'"

The previous year, Maddux had become the 22nd pitcher to win 300 games, but that victory happened in San Francisco, not at Wrigley Field, so when Maddux went into his start on July 26, 2005, two strikeouts shy of the 3,000 mark, Cubs fans readied themselves to share the moment with their hero. "The interesting thing about that night was we had a rain delay," said play-by-play announcer Len Kasper. "It would have been an easy night for the regular fans who come out or the season-ticket holders to not hang around for the entire night, but they did."

Like so many other facets of Cubs fandom, it was no piece of cake. The start of the game was delayed two hours and 43 minutes by rain, but in tribute to Maddux, a full house stayed through the downpour to make sure they were on hand for his milestone. (Maybe the greatest tribute is that beer sales had stopped well before the first pitch, but the crowd stayed anyway.) In typical Maddux fashion, he wasted no time, putting away Jason Ellison to lead off the game. Two innings later, with two outs, Maddux painted the corner on Omar Vizquel for number 3,000, and the crowd erupted. After walking straight to the dugout, Maddux smiled sheepishly and finally allowed himself to be pushed out for a curtain call as the standing ovation continued.

From his perch in the booth, Bob Brenly soaked in the moment. "That's something that you may never see again," said Brenly, who contributed two punchouts during his playing career to the Maddux total. "Certainly it's possible that we'll never see it again at Wrigley Field. For everything that Greg Maddux did for this team, for everything that Greg Maddux did for the game of baseball, those fans wanted to be sure that when that moment came, they were here. There could have been lightning striking the towers, there could have been snow falling, they were going to stay until he got that strikeout and show their appreciation, and that's the kind of fans they are."

Manning first base that night, Derrek Lee marveled at his teammate's achievement. "Greg Maddux is a guy who commands respect wherever he goes, and I think the fans respect him tremendously," said Lee. "They wanted to be here to see him get that 3,000th strikeout, and they gave him a standing ovation. It was a great moment." In the dugout, Kerry Wood understood the cheers were especially heartfelt. "It's just the respect for him," Wood said. "The fans wanted to show their respect for him, and they sat through the rain. The umpires didn't want to call that game. They said we're gonna get it in. It was a special night, it really was."

There was a fitting Cubs symmetry in Maddux's accomplishment of becoming the second man in major league history to strike out 3,000 batters while yielding fewer than 1,000 walks. The first man, Ferguson Jenkins, also wore No. 31 during his years with the Cubs. "I've got to quit before I hit 1,000 walks," joked Maddux.

"It was a very nice moment," he admitted. "You know, I've never really considered myself a strikeout pitcher. I've always thought strikeouts were overrated, to be honest with you. You've got to get 27 outs. You don't have to get 12 strikeouts and give up five runs to do it, you know what I mean? Strikeouts to me have always been overrated. To pitch long enough to get that many strikeouts is special, and I'm just kind of glad I've hung around for as long as I have."

Numbers don't drive Greg Maddux. Wins and championships do, but he does allow himself a smile when asked about that night and the response from the Cubs fans. "They are special people. It's just an honor and a privilege to play here. It always has been."

CUBS FANS

"You really can't compare anyone to them. You know, I've heard a lot of good things about Boston and New York, but playing here every day and seeing it firsthand and seeing it after the games, how the city is, it's like no matter what restaurant you go to or what cab you jump into, everyone is always on the Cubs bandwagon, and they are always excited and anxious to find out what is going on with them. Everyone appreciates people that try to do it the right way, and hopefully I've done that."

WRIGLEY FIELD

"To me it's the best place in baseball, really. I mean, day games, the sun is shining, the wind is blowing, great atmosphere, great fans. There is always the excitement. The old field. There's bumps here and there in it. It's the way they played it like a hundred years ago. It's definitely a special place, and I cherish every day I come to this ballpark."

PLAYING ON WGN

"My parents back in Vegas got a chance to watch when I was first starting up, and I guess it was pretty cool. You don't really think about it at the time, but looking back on it, to have the opportunity to play on TV and have your friends and family watch 500 miles away, it's pretty special."

LEARNING FROM RICK SUTCLIFFE

"He taught me a lot of stuff that helped me three or four years down the road. I wasn't smart enough to understand what he was trying to tell me my first year. After I had pitched four or five hundred innings, I started to understand what he was talking about. It wasn't something I was able to do my first or second year, but down the road it helped me a lot. A bunch of little things here and there. One of the small things that comes to mind is he told me don't get a hitter out the way you should get him out unless you have to get him out. And I'm like, 'Okay, what does that mean?' At the time I was really trying to get to the fifth inning, I was pitching so bad. That was the last thing on my mind. As I started to go deeper in the games, I started to understand what he was talking about. I think that it was something that helped me out a lot down the road, not so much tomorrow, but three or four years down the road it helped me a lot."

WINNING IN 1989

"It was the first time I ever experienced winning. We made the trade in the off-season to get Mitch Williams, and I remember [thinking], 'We have our closer now,' and he walked the bases loaded [on Opening Day], and he struck out the side. We kind of went from there. It ended in Montreal. I remember we clinched in Montreal that year, and we were seeing pictures of Wrigley, of the downtown Chicago area, and the Wrigleyville area, and it was jam-packed with people. It was a hero's welcome. You come back from the airport, and everyone is waiting at the airport to greet us. Unfortunately, we didn't do well against the Giants, but overall, it was a great experience and probably one of the most fun years I've had."

THE 300TH WIN IN 2004

"It was very exciting. At the time, we were in a pennant race. We were chasing the Cardinals, I think, at that time and trying to get in the wild-card. You know, I just didn't want it to be a distraction from what the team wanted to do. As much as I wanted to win 300 games, I wanted to go past that because I wanted another taste of the postseason here in Chicago. Obviously, it was a very special day for me personally, and the support I received along the way from the city of Chicago, it was phenomenal." —*Greg Maddux*

THE SANDBERG/ SUTTER GAME

One of the fashionable themes in popular culture today is the notion of a "tipping point," an occurrence of some sort that changes everything. For the Cubs, June 23, 1984, was the tipping point for more than just the season. The team, the fans, and the neighborhood were never the same after Ryne Sandberg stunned Bruce Sutter and the Cardinals with two game-tying home runs as the Cubs entertained a national audience on NBC with a 12–11 win. So while WGN didn't broadcast this game, give me a little leeway on this one. It's the most important game of the modern era. Plus, I interviewed a stunned and wide-eyed Sandberg in the locker room after the game, and it was my birthday. Like I said, it was a big day.

The irony of the "Sandberg Game" was that it didn't start off as a national telecast, but due to a rainout of the other scheduled network game, the Cubs were seen coast to coast. "It was the backup game," said Sandberg, and he should know. He's talked about this one more than a few times. "There were two *Games of the Week* and it was the backup game, so it was Bob Costas and Tony Kubek doing the game. Back then, that was a really big deal. We used to call those the 'Games of the World' because it was the only game on TV and it was a Saturday afternoon and everybody would be watching, including all the players in the league. We were on TV there and it was against the Cardinals, and it was a great atmosphere which we always had when we played St. Louis."

For a good part of the game, what the nation saw was the same old Cubs, who couldn't get things right and were down 7–1 in the second inning. But they pecked away, helped by three singles and four RBIs from Sandberg, and opened the ninth inning trailing the Cardinals 9–8. With Sutter on to close for the Cardinals, Sandberg led off the inning for the Cubs. After taking a ball and a strike, he turned on an inside pitch and launched a home run to the last row of the left-field bleachers, sending the packed house into delirium and the game into extra innings.

In the bottom of the tenth, the Cubs were down 11–9, and Sutter was working in his third inning. After two quick outs, Bob Dernier coaxed a walk on a close 3–2 pitch, bringing Sandberg to the plate again. Willie McGee, who had hit for the cycle, had already been announced as the NBC player of the game as Sandberg stepped in for another crack at Sutter. Same count, same swing, same result, and a legend was born as Ryno's second Roy Hobbs imitation tied the game again.

With the foundation rattling at Wrigley, no one was more shocked than Sandberg himself. "Hitting the two home runs was just somewhat of a shock because Bruce Sutter was such a ground ball–type pitcher, and he was a lights-out closer," he said. "When he came in, he was lights-out. I mean the game was almost over. At best, he would

give up a couple of ground balls that might hurt him. To swing underneath his sinking ball, his split-finger, and hit the bottom of the ball and to have it go out twice, I was amazed at myself. That's how it was."

For leadoff man Dernier, the other half of the "Daily Double," Sandberg's performance was almost par for the course. "In that game, I remember being on base all day. I think Ryno and I were on base nine times between us. He hit those two homers and drove in all those runs and was just incredible. Anything Ryne Sandberg did never surprised me though. He was just built to win."

Lost in the legend is the fact that Sandberg's second home run didn't win the game but tied it for a second time. In the eleventh, the hero's mantle fell on unlikely 25th man Dave Owen, whose bases-loaded single sent the crowd into further hysterics while giving the Cubs a 12–11 win. With the end of the game came a new type of pressure, which hit Sandberg like a Mack truck.

"After the game, about five minutes after the game, I was asked to do the Cardinals postgame show with Jack Buck over in the Cardinals dugout," said Sandberg. "So I come out of the dugout and I start to go across the field, and everybody is still there! Everybody is cheering still five minutes after the game is over. So I go over there and I do that interview and I'm on for maybe 10–12 minutes with him, and so now I come out of their dugout, go across again, and people are still cheering. Now I make it inside and I couldn't see my locker there were so many media around there. That was my first taste of that, and it all happened that day. For the rest of the season, we had that attention. The games that we won, the big games, we had to deal with all that attention and keep that under check a little bit."

Faced with a horde of reporters at his locker, Sandberg was unable to put his accomplishment into words. "He was overcome," said the *Chicago Tribune's* Fred Mitchell, who was used to Sandberg's reticence during postgame interviews. "Over the years, you see athletes who, quote unquote, are in the zone for that particular game, whether you are talking about Walter Payton or Michael Jordan or

whoever. It just seemed that Ryno was in the zone for that game, and it was pretty much inexplicable for him to say what happened, how he did it. He just reacted and just had one of those great days."

The '84 Cubs had arrived, and everyone knew it. "It was almost like we knew we were competitive, we knew we belonged with everybody," said Jody Davis. "That game when we were dead, then came back and beat the Cardinals and to do it against, at that time, the premier reliever in the game in Bruce Sutter, it kind of made us feel that we could play with anybody, we could beat anybody, we were never out of it. And I think the fans felt the same way we did."

Larry Bowa won a World Series with the Phillies in 1980 and felt the win signaled things had changed. "That sort of put Ryno on the map and put the Cubs on the map," he said. "People obviously at that time didn't think we were for real. It was all 'wait for August or September and the Cubs will fold.' It didn't happen. Ryno went on to have a tremendous season. That sort of put everybody on the map at the same time."

> "*It just seemed that Ryno was in the zone for that game, and it was pretty much inexplicable for him to say what happened, how he did it. He just reacted and just had one of those great days.*"
>
> —Fred Mitchell on Ryne Sandberg

Sandberg's heroics were the first validation for manager Jim Frey's spring training message to Ryno that he could be the best player in the National League. "In anything you do and especially in sports, there seems to be something that clicks at a point where it turns people on," Frey

Rightfielder Sammy Sosa watches his 62nd home run sail over the wall. (Photo courtesy of AP/Wide World Images)

said. "There seems to be a team coming together, a team excitement, spirit. That game, I think, was the thing that turned our season around. We were a pretty good team, and when we won that game, especially against the Cardinals, I mean that's a big series for the Cubs. When we won that game against the Cardinals on national television, it seemed to give everybody in the organization a lift. I think it gave our players a sense of confidence that maybe we can carry this through."

SAMMY SOSA'S 62ND HOME RUN

The pop and the hop, the kiss to the camera, and the running salute to the right-field bleacher fans were the unmistakable signatures of Samuel Peralta Sosa, whose power and magnetism made his at-bats must-see TV for the better part of a decade with the Cubs.

Slammin' Sammy's feats included nine consecutive 100 RBI seasons and being the first Cub to post a 30-homer/30-steal season, but those are merely sidenotes to his prodigious totals during one of the most prolific power runs in baseball history. In 1998, he started a string of six straight 40-plus home-run seasons that included seasons of 66, 63, 50, and 64 round-trippers.

The most indelible moments in Sosa's career came in 1998 when he competed with Mark McGwire of the Cardinals in a yearlong race to set the single season home-run record. "The great home run chase" captivated baseball fans across the country and added an extra element to a surprising Cubs team that was making an unlikely playoff run. Coming off a season in which he hit only .251, Sosa turned himself into the best all-around hitter in the game that season, lifting his average to .308 and driving in 158 runs.

But the headlines were about the home-run mark. McGwire's 58 homers in 1997 had served notice that he was the man to break Roger Maris's 37-year-old mark of 61 in a season, but after belting 20 home runs in the month of June, Sosa happily made it a two-man race.

The two sluggers traded the home-run lead throughout the summer, but on September 8 in St. Louis, McGwire won the race to 62, breaking Maris's single-season record against the Cubs with a home run off Steve Trachsel. Three days later, well aware that the spotlight had shifted entirely to McGwire, Sosa thrust himself back into the chase with an epic weekend performance in one of the most exciting series ever seen at Wrigley Field.

The Cubs lost the series opener on Friday, falling to the Brewers 13–11, as Sosa hit his 59th home run off Bill Pulsipher. On Saturday, the Cubs trailed 10–2 before a rally including Sosa's 60th home run (this one off Valerio de los Santos) led to a 15–12 Cubs win. That wild game ended on Orlando Merced's walk-off homer, but all that was merely a prelude to the excitement of the next day.

With Sosa poised to tie Maris, no one on the North Side cared one bit that McGwire had gotten there first. By game time on Sunday, there was not an inch of available real estate on Waveland Avenue as hundreds of souvenir hunters joined the regular ballhawks hoping to grab a piece of history. Sosa didn't disappoint, tying Maris with his 61st home run in the fifth inning off Bronswell Patrick (there's a trivia-question name for you) as the Cubs built an 8–3 lead. Being the roller-coaster Cubs of '98, Trachsel and Terry Mulholland gave back the lead, and the home team went to the last at-bat down 10–8.

In a season in which he truly was Superman, it strained reality to think that Sosa could come through again in the ninth inning, but he was up to the task. Facing Eric Plunk with a 2–1 count, Sosa launched a no-doubter, bounced out of the batter's box, and watched as his 62nd home run soared over the back fence in left field and landed in between two houses across Waveland. WGN's Chip Caray had the call on Sosa's historic shot: "Swung on, there she goes! Number 62! Move over Big Mac, you've got company!" Left on the sideline five days earlier, Sosa had thrust himself back into the spotlight and a tie for the home-run lead.

With the theme from *The Natural* playing on the public-address system, the ovation continued for six minutes while Sosa obliged the crowd with three curtain calls, soaking in his part of history. Dominican flags waved throughout the ballpark, and Sosa's eyes filled with tears as he struggled to maintain his composure. "I had a beautiful, great moment there," he said. "I was very happy to be part of that moment. It was my time."

Cubs president Andy MacPhail was happy that Sosa was able to embrace his season in the sun. "I know people don't appreciate Sammy as much as they will in the years to come," he said. "At the time, whereas McGwire was scuffling a little bit with the attention attitudinally, Sammy was enjoying every minute of it, and I think the fans enjoyed that."

Minutes later, Gary Gaetti drove in Jason Maxwell to send the game into extra innings. With two out in the tenth, Mark Grace ended Slammin' Sammy's weekend in fitting style with a walk-off home run of his own, a shot that still brings an instant smile to his face. "I remember that series," Grace said. "It was just wild, it was nuts. I ended up hitting that walk-off home run in the last game of that series, and we ended up winning some big games. That was just as loud as I've ever heard this place, and it was awesome."

The Cubs went on to advance to the postseason with a wild-card playoff win over the Giants before being swept by Atlanta. McGwire hit five homers the last weekend of the season to finish with 70 to Sosa's 66, but Sammy was awarded the National League's Most Valuable Player award for leading the Cubs to the postseason.

"Being a part of the McGwire/Sammy show was amazing because the nation was following it," said Kerry Wood, who had seen it all in his wild rookie season. "Obviously, we got a ton of exposure; we're on TV all the time, and then those two guys were doing what they were doing. I don't know if we'll ever be able to duplicate the energy we had in '98 when he did that," said Wood. "He hit 20 home runs in June. To be able to witness that and be a part of that is obviously something I'll never forget."

"We did the best we could in the field, and everybody was happy," said Sosa. "After that, we can't control what

happened. We did what we were supposed to do: play baseball the way it was supposed to be played. I'm very happy, and I'm very proud."

COMING FROM THE DOMINICAN REPUBLIC

"I'm very proud to come here. When you are born in the United States, everything seems so easy for a person here to be well-educated. When you come from a country that you don't know nothing about it and come to a country to play this beautiful game and you have a successful career, that's something you have to look at."

CUBS FANS

"My relationship with the fans was great. They knew I played hard every day. They know I didn't cheat myself and went out and did the best that I could. They appreciated that. When you do give to a place where they know about baseball, they appreciate that."

WRIGLEY FIELD

"I like it. I played many, many years in Wrigley Field. That was one of the great moments in my life. You know, I made a lot of people happy there on the North Side, and it's always going to be my house."

THE HOME-RUN KISS TO THE CAMERA

"That was for my mom. I always did that to show her respect."

THE CORKED-BAT INCIDENT

"Everybody knows what happened. I explained it to everybody and took the responsibility for that. That was a mistake on my part. I never needed it. That is one mistake I have to carry with me all my life, and I will always regret it."

THE HALL OF FAME

"For anybody who played this game, the numbers don't lie. I want to be in the Hall of Fame. Definitely, that's my dream, and hopefully, when I'm retired for real, I hope

I have the opportunity to go into the Hall of Fame. That would be perfect for me."

MILT PAPPAS: NEARLY PERFECT

A "disappointing no-hitter" sounds like the baseball oxymoron of all time, but Milt Pappas's 1972 gem over the San Diego Padres has come to be known as exactly that. On September 2 of that year, after the Cubs opened up an 8–0 lead, all eyes turned to Pappas, who went to the ninth inning with a perfect game on the line.

"A pitcher is aware of what's going on, and by the time you get to the seventh or eighth inning, the bench knows what is going on," said Pappas. "That day, when I came in after the eighth inning and I still had the perfect game, I walked down the bench and no one said a word. That was ridiculous, and I wanted my guys to get going, so I said, 'Hey guys, I'm throwing a no-hitter,' and that got them loose and were laughing. Then I got tight because where I was sitting in the dugout, the cops and ushers were gathering and making a racket, so I had to ask them to be quiet."

The ninth inning opened with a routine fly to center field off the bat of John Jeter, but Cubs center fielder Bill North slipped when his feet went out from under him, and it looked like the perfect game might fall with him. From out of nowhere, Billy Williams raced in, hat flying off, and reached out to grab the ball for the first out. "When I saw Billy North slip down, my heart sank down to my toes, and I thought, 'There goes everything,'" said Pappas. "Thankfully, Billy was hustling."

Williams never took anything for granted as a player, especially with history on the line. "As I was drifting over I could see him, and all of a sudden I had to come in and make a shoestring catch to catch the ball," he said. Moments later, Fred Kendall (Jason's father) ripped a drive to left that was barely foul, then grounded to Don Kessinger at short for the second out.

The Padres sent up Larry Stahl to pinch-hit with the perfect game on the line, and Pappas quickly got ahead 1–2. After having everything go his way throughout the game, fortune (and the home-plate umpire) deserted him at the last minute.

"I'm one pitch from the greatest thing a pitcher can do," he said. "Next pitch was a slider on the outside corner, ball two. Next pitch, another slider on the corner, ball three. All these pitches were right there, and I'm saying, 'C'mon, Froemming, they're all right there.' Now comes the 3-2 pitch, again on the outside corner, ball four. I went crazy. I called Bruce Froemming every name you can think of. I knew he didn't have the guts to throw me out because I still had the no-hitter. The next guy, Garry Jestadt popped up to Carmen Fanzone, and I got the no-hitter, which was great. But those balls should have been called strikes."

Randy Hundley was behind the plate for his second no-hitter of the year (Burt Hooton had thrown one in April). "That was a little disappointing in that we didn't get the perfect game," said Hundley. "There were a couple of pitches that were questionable, but I think if Bruce Froemming had called those pitches, nobody would have ever said a word about it. We ended up walking one hitter and the next hitter pops up and we get the no-hitter. It would have been wonderful to have had a perfect game. We probably wouldn't be talking about it if we had a perfect game at this time."

The Cubs catcher still marvels at Pappas's pinpoint control that day. "One of the things about Milt was he hardly ever shook me off," Hundley said. "I would go down with the sign, and he would come with the pitch right away. The same thing happened this day. He only had a fastball and slider to work with. It was frustrating at times to get hitters out with just two pitches, but I'm telling you, I could sit there and close my eyes, and he could hit that mitt. It was just unbelievable how he did and what great control he had that day."

In the *Chicago Tribune* the next day, Pappas talked about understanding the close pitches, but the years have hardened his stance. "When you look at the last pitch to Dale Mitchell in Don Larsen's perfect game, it's not even close, but there was a perfect game on the line. The thing that got me was that smirk on Froemming's face after the pitch. The next day, he actually asked me to sign a baseball, and I said, 'I would be more than happy to, Bruce, and you know where you can stick it.'"

Ferguson Jenkins never threw a no-hitter in his career, but was excited to see another teammate join that exclusive club. "I was on the bench charting the game," he said. "Milt to this day said Bruce Froemming should have called it a strike, but, hey, the umpire is going to call his game. He pitched a no-hitter, but not a perfect game. Not bad."

Rick Monday was with the Cubs at the time, but he wants no part of the controversy. "I was at a banquet one night with Bruce, and he was asked by someone in the audience, 'You know, you were the umpire behind home plate when Pappas had the no-hitter going. There were two outs in the top of the ninth, and you called ball four. Did you know you had a chance to become only the 13th umpire to ever call a perfect game in major league history?' Bruce looked at the guy and said, 'Was it really that important?' and the guy said 'Oh yeah.' And Bruce said, 'Name the other 12 home-plate umpires during the perfect games.' And that is Bruce's take. Don't get in between them. If you are invited to the same dinner party, you might want to stay a little bit farther away from them. Was the pitch outside? Two guys had real good looks at it, and they both differ in their opinions."

"That was the only time I ever pitched a no-hitter all my years of Babe Ruth, high school, minor leagues,

anything," said Pappas. His gem ended a run of four Cubs no-hitters in four seasons (Holtzman 1969, Holtzman 1971, Hooton 1972) and is the last no-no thrown by a Cubs pitcher. Pappas is the only man in major league history to lose a perfect game with one out to go and complete a no-hitter by retiring the next batter. He is also the only pitcher to lose a perfect game by walking the 27th batter.

CUBS FANS

"There is nothing like them. I played in Baltimore, Cincinnati, and Atlanta and have been to stadiums all over the country, and bar none, the Chicago Cubs fans are the greatest fans in the world. They are phenomenal fans who stick by their players. It's a little more difficult today than when I played because now guys can jump from team to team because of free agency. We were locked into one team, and a general manager told you at contract time, 'We own you,' so the only way you could move was if you died, were traded or released. We stayed with the same team for a long time."

WRIGLEY FIELD

"There's no doubt about it. There's only one Wrigley Field. It's amazing when I bring friends who have never been here before, and maybe after the game I can take them down on the field. They go nuts! It's hard for me to relate to because I played here. They want to touch the ivy, and I say, 'How would you like to throw it and watch it go over the ivy, like I did?' I still come to games, but it looks a lot easier sitting there than it is to play the game on the field."

PITCHING TODAY

"Paul Richards with the Orioles preached that pitching was 75–80 percent of the game, and I firmly believe it. You need your staff to stay healthy and things can fall into place, and it seems like the Cubs have not been able to keep their group healthy a lot of years. When I listen to games and I hear that a guy is up to 100 pitches, who cares? The pitch count is so ridiculous at times, especially when a guy has good stuff. We pitched every fourth day and didn't have the set-up man, the quasi-closer, the closer, all that stuff. The game has become hard, and there is too much thinking going on. Also, the talent is diluted today, much more so than it was when I played when there were only 16 teams."

SUPERSTITION DURING A NO-HITTER

"I don't believe anything about a jinx during a game. I'd rather be lucky than good any day. If it's going to happen, it's going to happen. If it's meant to be, it will happen." *—Milt Pappas*

ANDRE DAWSON'S HOMER TO END '87

sa·laam \suh-'läm\ *n* **1 :** a very low bow or obeisance, esp. with the palm of the right hand placed on the forehead **2 :** a salute to Andre Dawson, offered after each Wrigley Field home run by extending both arms and bowing from the waist.

One of the greatest individual seasons in Cubs history opened with Andre Dawson on the outside looking in. As the Cubs opened camp in Mesa, Arizona, in 1987, Dawson was a free agent without a contract, looking for work. To show he meant business, Dawson made the team a bold promise, offering to work one season for a fill-in-the-blank contract.

Cubs ace Rick Sutcliffe made sure everyone knew how badly he wanted to see Dawson's bat in the lineup. "I remember that year, him standing outside the gate in spring training, and I came out publicly and said I'd give $100,000 of my money to sign him," said Sutcliffe. "Well, I got a pretty nasty letter from Dallas Green saying, 'You just pitch, and I'll be the president of the club.' There was a lot going on as we know. I knew one thing, I knew that in '86 we weren't any good, and the only chance we had to get better was to get that man in the lineup and out into right field. When he signed on, all of a sudden we had a chance to win. He was the MVP, I led the league in wins (18), and

without him, I might not have won 10 games that year."

A sixth-place finish wasn't the magical year Sutcliffe was hoping for, but Dawson was nothing less than incredible. Green and the Cubs received a handsome return on their $500,000 investment as Dawson finished with a staggering 49 home runs and 137 RBIs. After finishing second twice in the MVP voting, Dawson won it in 1987, the first-ever winner from a last-place team.

Dawson was an immediate favorite with the Wrigley faithful, especially the natives in the right-field bleachers who applauded each of his home runs with what Harry Caray quickly dubbed "salaams." With the Cubs going nowhere, fans had little to cheer for except the new right fielder, whose booming bat and rifle arm virtually guaranteed a can't-miss highlight every game. On the last home game of the season, Dawson gave Cubs fans one final thrill for the ages.

With two out in the bottom of the eighth, Dawson came to the plate for his last at-bat of the season at Wrigley Field. In the booth, Caray echoed every Cubs fan's thoughts when he wished aloud, "Wouldn't it be great if he could do it one more time?" As the crowd stood as one and demanded a giant exclamation point on his MVP season, Dawson delivered with a rocket into the left-field bleachers off Bill Dawley for his 47th round-tripper of the year.

"That's what you call pressure," laughed Dawson. "You know the fans want it, and I had done it so often for them during the course of that year. You can't swing for a home run because you're going to overswing, you might just miss it, and if you get a good pitch to hit you might foul it off. My thinking was that I was going to work the count and get a pitch that I could drive. It happened to be against a pitcher who woke me up because he pretty much threw a pitch behind me earlier in the year, and at that point, he couldn't get me out anymore. I worked the count to 3–1, he threw me a 3–1 change-up, and it just happened to be in the zone that I was looking in. I was able to get the bat head on it and hit it out of the ballpark."

Ryne Sandberg watched in admiration as Dawson pulled it off. "It was his last at-bat and the fans were on

Andre Dawson offers a tip of the cap to his fans after homering
in his last home at-bat of the 1987 season.

their feet, and of course, they were wanting a home run. So for the guy to go up there and hit a ball like he did, he just crushed it to left field—way out. It was amazing. He was amazing that summer."

For a consummate pro like the Cubs' second baseman, Dawson's arrival added a kindred spirit to the clubhouse. "He was a great teammate," said Sandberg. "He was a guy who came to the ballpark every day and did a lot to prepare for every game. I just watched that and I knew, having Andre on the team, what kind of effort he would give every day, and it was always top-notch. He was a big part of the '89 team as one of the leaders, a quiet leader. That first season he had in '87 when he signed a contract, a blank check that contract, and he went out and hit 49 home runs that year. It seemed like he hit one every other day. Forty-nine, three years ago, that would have been the middle of the pack, but in 1987 that was a ton of home runs. It was unbelievable. He's a guy that had a Hall of Fame career in my book."

Ten years on cement covered by the barest of Astro Turf in Olympic Stadium ravaged Dawson's knees. "It was part of my makeup, part of my upbringing, and I was told that I would probably last all of four years because of my history of knee problems," said Dawson. "I won't say it motivated me, but it made me aware of just how fast things can end. I took the attitude that my work ethic had to be impeccable. If I was going to go down, I was going to go down leaving everything on the playing field. My attitude every day was to give it all I had and not worry about what the outcome was."

Dawson's daily routine was not lost on his teammates. "You really looked up to him because you saw what he went through on a daily basis just to play," marveled Joe Girardi, who was a rookie catcher in 1989. "To me, that's the love of the game. Andre Dawson had a love of the game. I was fortunate enough when I managed in Florida, he came to the ballpark every day and worked with our guys. I just think he's a great example of what a ballplayer should be, and he should be a Hall of Famer."

WRIGLEY FIELD

"Wrigley Field has always overwhelmed me. The city of Chicago and coming here when I was embraced in 1987, my first year, I couldn't have imagined what it was going to be like, but the fans were just magnificent. Every time I get an opportunity to come back, it's just the same. It's the same feeling, the same excitement, and I guess that's the magic of Wrigley Field. It's like a second home, and I always look forward to getting back to Wrigley Field. Regardless of what my agenda calls for during the season with the Florida Marlins, this is one trip that they know I'm coming on, and they pencil it in. You get to rehash moments here, see old friends, and for the most part rehash great relationships."

FAN SALUTE FROM RIGHT FIELD

"Well, it got to be old habit, and at the end I said, one of these days I'm going to stop and salaam back just to show my gratitude for what they have instilled in me over the years. It was a wonderful feeling. It made you feel accepted as a ballplayer, knowing that you went out and did something that was pleasing to the crowd. You don't want to be a crowd-pleaser, but you want to make sure that when they go home, you leave them with the impression of, 'Okay, well, I came out today and I saw something exciting.'" —*Andre Dawson*

1987

"It was the best year of my career, despite the way it all started. I lost my grandmother that year. I was a free agent without a team. I was being hassled about a contract after 10 years of service. It wasn't really looking up, but I guess I prayed a lot, which is what she always told me to do. I didn't set any goals that year. I dedicated the year to her. I said I'm just going to go out and have fun and what happens, happens. I came to Chicago with the blank contract, and that was a huge burden lifted because I knew that, well, now there's somewhere I'm going to play. I wasn't concerned about numbers or anything like that because if

I was healthy all that was going to even out. It just turned out to be a dream-type year. Every time something would happen from a positive standpoint, I would look up to the heavens and think of my grandmother. Just the fact that things turned out the way they did, the MVP and all that, it made it just that much more rewarding. At the end of the season, I said I knew that I could honestly let her go now because I knew all along that she was with me."

FAVORITE MOMENTS

"My favorite moment had to be when we clinched it in Montreal to win the division in 1989. Playing here at Wrigley, there were so many. There was a three-home-run day when we beat the Phillies. I was exhausted after the game. It was almost 100 degrees, and it was very tough running on and off the field for nine innings soaking wet. I could barely swing the bat up at the plate, but I found the energy to deliver three home runs, which was a first for me. We won that ballgame but only scored five runs."

WRIGLEY REBIRTH

"I always marveled at the fact that there were so many Cubs fans everywhere you went. To me it was a rejuvenation, it extended my playing career. I just wish I had the chance to play here a little longer."

WILLIE SMITH'S OPENING-DAY HOME RUN

After Opening Day in 1969, there was no doubt that it was going to be the Cubs' year. They had posted back-to-back winning seasons in 1967 and 1968 and were poised for a breakthrough as they took the field against Philadelphia on April 8 to open the season. What followed that day set the stage for a Wrigley Field summer of love like no other.

The love-in started for Ernie Banks when he received a standing ovation during the pregame introductions. Banks then celebrated his 16th Cubs Opening Day with a home run in the first followed by his second standing O of the day. The crowd rose again for Banks as he came to the plate in the third, then stayed on its feet after Banks launched another homer. By the day's end, the *Chicago Tribune*'s George Langford counted nine standing ovations for Mr. Cub to go with his two home runs.

"I don't think Leo [Durocher] or Mr. Wrigley or anybody on the ballclub realized what was going to happen that particular year. It just started when Willie Smith hit that home run on Opening Day, and I think things just took off from there."

—Billy Williams

On the strength of Banks's heroics, the Cubs held a 5–2 lead going into the ninth inning. However, rookie Don Money's second home run of the game (and second of his career) wiped that out and chased starting pitcher Ferguson Jenkins as the first game of the year went into extra innings.

The Phillies broke through in the top of the eleventh as Money, who had five RBIs on the day, drove in a run against Cubs reliever Phil Regan, and it appeared that the Cubs might have let one slip away. In the bottom half of the inning, Randy Hundley picked up a one-out single off another Phillies rookie, reliever Barry Lersch, to keep hope alive at Wrigley.

Enter Willie Smith. The Cubs' backup outfielder and left-handed pinch-hitter went to the plate so jacked up that he got a stitch in his side after a vicious warm-up swing. Smith winced a bit, then laced a 1–0 pitch from Lersch into the right-field bleachers to set off the first of many postgame celebrations at Wrigley Field that season. As Willie was joyously rounding the bases, a familiar voice was hitting a new octave overhead, where Jack Brickhouse was nearly falling out of the booth. His call was one of his finest, sheer exultation on the Cubs' dramatic win: "Well hit, deep to right. Back…back…back, it's all over!!!! Willie Smith just homered!! The Cubs win the game!!"

Hundley was relieved the ball carried out. "I can still see that ball going over my head at first base," he said. "It was kind of like a knuckleball. It didn't have a lot of spin on it, and I didn't know if it was going to carry enough to get out, so immediately I'm hauling fanny to try and score from first base if the ball was off the wall. Luckily, he got the ball out of the ballpark, and what a thrill!"

A mob of 24 teammates and several fans met Smith at the plate. He managed to fight his way in to step on the plate, and for his efforts, one of the Cubs accidentally spiked Willie's right big toe.

Billy Williams would win the game on Opening Day 1971 with a tenth-inning home run of his own, but he still maintains that 1969 was his favorite opener. "I don't think Leo [Durocher] or Mr. Wrigley or anybody on the ballclub realized what was going to happen that particular year. It just started when Willie Smith hit that home run on Opening Day, and I think things just took off from there. I can still see him now; he was running around the bases proud as a peacock. All of a sudden we won that game, and from then on, it was a beautiful summer."

For Glenn Beckert, Smith's blast couldn't have come at a better time. "I was in the dugout trying to keep warm, and I wanted to give Willie a big kiss for doing it because I was freezing. That was a big ballgame. To get a win on Opening Day, you could just see the momentum starting."

The home run jump-started the Cubs in a big way. "Being down and hitting that home run in the tenth inning was unbelievable," said Ron Santo. "It just inspired us, and then we went on to win. I think we were 11–1 to start the season. I think we all knew this was our year."

Smith hit only nine homers in 1969, but none was bigger than his first swing of the year. After his death in 2006, in his honor the home run was played as part of the opening ceremonies at that year's Cubs Convention. The roar was as loud as ever.

GLENN BECKERT

Glenn Beckert was a grinder long before the term was commonly used in baseball. The scrappy Cubs second baseman manned his position with the team from 1965 until 1973 and was paired with shortstop Don Kessinger throughout his years in Chicago. "Nine years was a long time, but now you don't have players staying together that long," said Beckert. "They will have a good year, and then salary-wise they will move on to another team or whatever. Back then, we knew that for five or six years that's how we were going to open the season."

His familiarity with his double-play partner improved both his and Kessinger's play in the field. "Kess had a lot more ability than I did fielding-wise," said Beckert. "I could look at where he was playing so I knew what range he had, and he could look at me to know what I could get to. Staying together that many years was sure beneficial to us. I don't think you see that too much anymore."

"Turning double plays is like a godsend," said Ferguson Jenkins in appreciation of Beckert and Kessinger. "Ground balls in the infield, they were gonna turn that double play quick, in seconds, and that gets you out of the inning. The double play can make or break a pitcher. To have a strong infield and to know that they're strong up the middle, that's a reassurance for a pitcher. Beckert and Kessinger were that strong."

Beckert's tenacity was not lost on manager Leo Durocher, and he quickly became one of Durocher's favorites for his solid glove, heads-up play, and ability to handle the bat in the number two hole. He made the National League All-Star team four years in a row from 1969 to 1972 and won a Gold Glove in 1968. In 1971, Beckert had a breakout season at the plate, hitting .342 to finish behind Joe Torre in the National League batting race.

Cubs second baseman Glenn Beckert's hard-nosed play made him a favorite of manager Leo Durocher. (Photo courtesy of Getty Images)

Beckert roomed with Ron Santo on the road through-out his years with the Cubs and, somehow, they remained close friends. "Nine years as my roommate. That's got to be some kind of record!" laughed Santo. "He is the best one-liner guy I ever met in my life. He could never sit still."

In 1965, Glenn offered up some advice to his room-mate that would haunt him to this day. Sandy Koufax was on the mound for Los Angeles at Dodger Stadium, and after making the second out in the first inning, Beckert told Santo not to worry. "I've been known to say a lot of things at the wrong time. He struck me out in the first inning and I hated that. Before, I had hit a line drive down the left-field line that missed being in by maybe an inch. I thought, 'Jeez, I had that one.' So Santo says, 'Rooms, what's he got?' I said, 'We've got him tonight. He's not throwing anything.' Well, a perfect game is a lot to throw! Santo tells that story all the time, but I can't get out of it. It's the truth." Koufax outdueled the Cubs' Bob Hendley that night and threw a perfect game against the Cubs, the last time the team has been no-hit.

Beckert remains an avid fan of the Cubs from his home in Florida. "I just know before too long we're going to be in the World Series. I can't wait until we start setting this place on fire and win it all."

1969

"We all went down together. I don't know if we were worn out and that Leo might have used a few extra players. We played our hearts out; we did our best. Even though we lost, we created a lot of interest in Chicago about the Chicago Cubs. I played on the same team with three members of the Hall of Fame, and that's something. I don't know a lot of teams that has happened to. There's a fourth that should be in, and that's my roommate, Ron Santo. He definitely should be in."

FANS STILL LOVE THE 1969 TEAM

"It's probably because back in those days teams were together. There was no free agency. Plus, we had turned it around to win. We were contenders. We didn't win at that time. We brought them contenders and played real good baseball. I wish we had it the way it is now, where you fin-ish second you can still get a wild-card."

CUBS FANS

"For some reason, it's one of those relationships. Each year it expands with Cubs fans because we're the last team that hasn't won since 1908, and I think everybody has dreamed that. I just dream of the time I come here to Chicago and Wrigley Field and see a World Series."

PLAYING WITH KESSINGER AT SHORT

"I give a lot of credit to Don Kessinger. We knew each other's style, where we would play, how we would move on it, where to throw the ball on a double play. That knowl-edge certainly helped. When I was traded to San Diego, I knew we were in bad shape when the shortstop didn't speak English and I didn't speak Spanish!"

HITTING SECOND

"Billy Williams was one of the best hitters I've ever seen. I was fortunate enough in my playing career to bat in front of him. By him hitting behind me along with Santo and Ernie Banks, they were not going to worry too much about me because I'm not a home-run hitter. I knew I was going to get a good fastball, usually down the middle. I picked up on that, and things worked out good for me." —*Glenn Beckert*

WRIGLEY FIELD

"I don't think much has changed except the salaries. I played nine years there and it was a great thrill. Walking onto Wrigley Field still brings the goose bumps out in me. The majority of the ballparks are new now. If you say to some-one, 'Have you ever been to Wrigley Field?' they always say, 'I've been there once, and I'll never forget how beautiful it is and I want to go back.' That's Wrigley Field."

SECOND BASEMEN

"The best second baseman I ever saw was Bill Mazeroski of the Pittsburgh Pirates, as far as fielding and durability are concerned. For the Cubs, no question, it was Ryne Sandberg. He was number one, and hopefully I finish number two!"

THE '84 WALK

If ever a moment perfectly illustrated the love affair between the Cubs and their fans, the postgame atmosphere on September 30, 1984, would be that snapshot. The final home game of the magical '84 season provided an exclamation point that will be remembered as one of the happiest afternoons in Wrigley Field history.

The day was not memorable because the Cubs rallied in the ninth inning to score two runs off Bruce Sutter for the win (been there, done that, right, Ryno?). The lasting image will always be the impromptu lovefest that followed on the field. It was a moment shared between baseball's most victory-starved fans and the surprising cast of players who gave it to them.

>>

"The phone rang, and Dallas Green said, 'They're not leaving. They're not going home. They're staying.'"

—Manager Jim Frey

>>

The finale was supposed to be a meaningless playoff tune-up and a chance for the reserves to get a few at-bats, but with the Cubs of '84, every day brought a new surprise. Down 1–0 in the bottom of the ninth, Henry Cotto and Dan Rohn singled off Sutter to open the inning. Thad Bosley singled in the tying run. A Gary Woods walk loaded the bases, and Keith Moreland followed with a bouncer to third. Terry Pendleton threw home for the force, but Glenn Brummer's wild throw to first allowed Bosley to scurry

home with the Cubs' 96th win and sent the 33,100 on hand into a frenzy.

It was a fitting end to a memorable season, but the ticketholders weren't about to let it go so easily. "We were in the clubhouse walking around, and I went into my office," said manager Jim Frey. "The phone rang, and Dallas Green said, 'They're not leaving. They're not going home. They're staying. Why don't you go outside and wave to them? Get a couple players, and wave to them.' In Baltimore when I was a coach, one time we went out after the game and stood by the dugout and waved, so I said, 'We can do that.' I thought the whole team should, out of respect to the fans, go out, and not just a few players. So I went in the clubhouse and I said, 'Get everybody outside.' There were two or three of them that didn't want to go, but I made them go. The whole team got out there, then I said, 'Let's go thank them.' So I started to walk, and we went around to right field and left field. It turned out it was a lot of fun. Even to this day, I have fans come up to me who say, 'I was at that game when you took the players around the field.' The fans enjoyed it. I thought it was great, the way it turned out."

The victory lap surprised the players every bit as much as the fans. "It was totally improvised," said Bob Dernier. "The game was over, and we were in the tunnel, and the fans just kept cheering. That was in the first year of the new clubhouse. As we were on the way up the tunnel, the crowd got louder like there was something going on. Then somebody hollered, 'Hey, you've got to come on back.' So off we went. That was really unique. I don't think I've ever seen anything like that on TV or in person. It was really a neat day."

Ryne Sandberg was already in the clubhouse and had to scramble to put his pants back on. "I didn't know what that was all about," he said. "We played the game, we went inside, guys were half dressed, in the shower, or in the training room, and all of a sudden, Jim Frey comes in and says, 'They're not leaving. We have to go out.' I was looking around thinking, 'Who's not leaving?' We go out there in long underwear and shirts and shower shoes, and we look

Cubs manager Jim Frey leads his team on an unforgettable victory lap after the last game of the 1984 regular season.

out and nobody had left the stadium. They were cheering, so we circled around out there, and it was awesome."

"That was a totally spontaneous, unscripted situation where Jim Frey and the players showed their appreciation to the loyal Cubs fans in 1984," said *Chicago Tribune* writer Fred Mitchell, who had covered the team the entire year. "They came out on the field and sort of serenaded the fans, I guess you might say, by going around the field and acknowledging the bleacher fans and all the people who had stuck by them for so many years."

The significance of the day was not lost on the Cubs' veteran shortstop. "It was a special moment," said Larry Bowa. "There's not a lot of times you get to mingle with the fans. Spring training you do, but during the season, it's tough. That special moment stands out because it was our way of saying thank you, and they really appreciated that. They were going crazy. Everybody was walking around, and there were standing ovations. Nobody wanted to go home, they wanted to enjoy the moment. Those are moments that as a baseball player, when you're in it a long time—I've been in major league uniform since 1970—those are moments that always stick with you, and when you're going through bad times, you sit down and reflect a little bit and say, 'You know what? There were some good times.' Those are the moments you look back on."

For Rick Sutcliffe, it was another sign that he had landed in the right place. "That's part of that family," he said. "It didn't matter if you were Ryne Sandberg or Dan Rohn. I mean, they just wanted to touch your hand, and they wanted to thank you for ending the 39 years of suffering that every Cubs fan had gone through."

JIM FREY

After two losing seasons while "building a new tradition," Cubs general manager Dallas Green was forced to fire Lee Elia as Cubs manager in 1983. For his next dip into the managerial pool, Green turned to Jim Frey, a former Orioles coach who had taken the Kansas City Royals to the World Series in his first season as their dugout boss in 1980. *Chicago Tribune* beat writer Fred Mitchell saw the team take a cue from the no-nonsense manager, who had logged 14 years as a minor league player without making it to the bigs. "Jim Frey was a very candid baseball guy," said Mitchell. "He was a baseball lifer. He has a tremendous relationship with us in the media and really didn't hold anything back in talking with the players, and I think they appreciated that honesty."

Frey's tenure got off to a rocky start under the Arizona sun in Mesa. Dick Ruthven and Mel Hall had a well-publicized fight, and the Cubs stumbled through 11 straight losses while posting the worst spring training record in baseball. With only days until the beginning of the regular season, things began to look up when Green added the outfield help Frey had been asking for. "Mel Hall was playing in center field, Leon Durham was in left field, and [Bill] Buckner was on first," said Frey. "What I said to [Don] Zimmer one day was, 'Every time a ball goes into the outfield, it seems like it's a triple. I'm tired of this. We've got to get a center fielder who can run and catch the ball.' So I said that to Dallas, and he ended up getting [Bob] Dernier and [Gary] Matthews. All of a sudden, we had a pretty good team, and I liked our team. Our pitching wasn't straightened out yet, but anyway, we came out of the box and went to the West Coast and started playing pretty good."

The Cubs went 12–8 in April, but Green and Frey continued to work on the makeup of the club with another deal in May. "I loved Billy Buckner as a player when he was young, but by the time I got to Chicago, he couldn't run, he didn't have any range, and he really didn't have much power," Frey explained. "I thought we were going to be a lot better with Durham on first base and Matthews in left. So Dallas traded Buckner and we got [Dennis] Eckersley. He was an experienced, strong pitcher, and again our defense was improved, and we became a pretty good team."

Green had one move left, dealing for Rick Sutcliffe before the June trading deadline, and Frey now had the team he envisioned in spring training. "One night, he had a little cookout at his house for me and the coaches in March, and I said, 'If we could get a center fielder who could run and catch the ball, and we get a couple starting pitchers, we can compete.' Well, he went and got 'em. We got hot, and we got hotter, and we got hotter, and all of a sudden, as in the great movie where the guy said he could be a contender, we were a contender."

With a warm summer breeze blowing out to left most days, Frey could afford to follow the advice of his Baltimore mentor Earl Weaver and wait for the big blast. "I can remember managing against some people who came in there, and they were bunting for one run or two runs early," he said. "I used to love it because I knew our big guys were going to get it up in the air, and the wind was blowing out. We were going to score runs, and we did. A bunch of our guys had real good years in '84. I remember there were times when we'd be in a bunt situation, and you know somebody on the bench or a coach would nudge me, and I'd say, 'Nah, let 'em go, and bang, they'd hit one out.' I lived in an apartment you could see over the center-field fence. The first thing I did in the morning when I woke up was run to the window and look out to see which way the wind was blowing. When the wind was blowing out, I put those big fat guys in there, and they just lofted the ball. That was wonderful."

The Cardinals struggled throughout the season, so the key for Frey and the Cubs was handling the Mets head to head. "For me, the most exciting thing that happened to me as a manager was we went to New York in the second half, in late July," said Frey. "We played the Mets four up there and four at home not long after. [Dwight] Gooden beat us 2–1 on Friday night, and we took the next three at Shea. Then we took the four in a row in Chicago. When we took those four in a row at Wrigley, I thought, 'You know what, maybe we can do this.'"

Do it they did. The Cubs had a winning record in every month of the season, then took the lead in the NL East on August 1 and never relinquished it, finishing six and a half games ahead of the Mets. For his role in leading the Cubs turnaround, Frey was named National League Manager of the Year. Like the rest of his well-decorated squad that season, Frey would have gladly traded the individual honor for one more October victory against the Padres.

Despite the disappointing playoff loss in San Diego, Frey felt even better about the team's prospects the next year. "In 1985, I thought we had a better team," he said. "People forget that we were in first place, and I thought that we had a better team than we had shown. I thought even then we were going to win in '85. Then we lost all of our starting pitchers; Dernier went down for a while, Davis went down for a while, and all of a sudden, we started losing and couldn't win a game. We ended up fourth. That was unfortunate because I thought we were better in 1985 than we were in '84. We had a better bench in '85, too."

> *"There were a lot more games where I was nervous sitting upstairs than I was in the dugout. In the dugout I was doing what I thought I should do. When you're up there, it's like you are helpless. "*
>
> —Jim Frey, on being general manager

The Cubs struggled again in 1986 and Frey was fired as manager, but he stayed in Chicago. After a stint in the WGN Radio booth, he replaced Green as general manager of the Cubs in 1988 and immediately set about finding new blood and removing some familiar faces from his 1984 team. With his longtime friend Don Zimmer managing the club, a young Cubs team surprised baseball by winning the National League East in 1989. For Frey, not being on the field took some getting used to. "I can tell you this honestly. There were a lot more games where I was nervous sitting upstairs than I was in the dugout. In the dugout I was doing what I thought I should do. When you're up there, it's like you are helpless. It's like watching one of your little grandchildren play T-ball. You get nervous, you know? You don't get nervous when you're playing. When you're watching somebody else, you get nervous. I had a lot of anxiety watching those teams. It wasn't that I didn't have confidence, it's like you have a helpless feeling. When things are going well, you feel bad because you are helpless."

Frey served as general manager until the end of the 1991 season but decided it was time to chase some other pursuits during the summer. "I wanted to see my family and play some golf, and that's what I've done," he said. "I was in baseball for 43 years, with several organizations, and the nine years in Chicago were without a question the highlight of my career, the way the Tribune treated me and the way the fans treated me. There's no question that was a big period in our life, and we had a lot of fun there and we had some success. We didn't quite get where we wanted to go, but we gave it a scare a couple of times. Chicago is very important to us."

CUBS FANS

"Have they been good to me? They've been terrific. I can remember when we would go on the road, especially in places like Houston and St. Louis, sometimes we would say there are more blue jackets than red jackets or whatever the other home-team color was." **—Jim Frey**

FAVORITE GAMES

"My favorite game would be the one where [Ryne] Sandberg hit the home runs off [Bruce] Sutter. The most important games would be the one in Pittsburgh where we clinched it, and then in '89, we clinched it in Montreal. Those would be the most important games from an organizational standpoint. There were a lot of great games. Things happen that the fans or the writers don't realize. Things happen with players and things that you try to do don't work out. Sometimes they

do, but you always remember. I remember going to bed sometimes, seeing something happen on television, and I would remember a game I managed. There were a lot of exciting games, a lot of exciting times."

THE 1984 CUBS

"Turning it on in the summer of '84 was the result of having about six guys who could loft the ball up in the air. We didn't have a speed team. We had Dernier and Sandberg. Bowa could run some, and Durham could run some. The rest of them were big guys like Cey, Davis, Moreland, and Matthews. What I meant by that was, the makeup of our team was we had a power team. If we could control the other team by throwing strikes and keeping the ball down, we were going to score. A bunch of our guys had real good years in '84. Six of them had 80 RBIs or more. We were just a slam-bang team in '84, with pretty good pitching. We had pretty good starting pitching."

1989 NL EAST WINNERS

"Zimmer had a different team. We had Jerome Walton and Dwight Smith. By this time, we had gotten rid of some of the older guys on the club. We had a younger, faster, not as much power—a different type of team. That suited Zimmer's style. He just did everything. He bunted, squeezed, hit and run, steal, stuff that I didn't have to do. I just said hit one out of here. No take, just go for it. Zimmer played more of a speed game that year. That was exciting, too."

HARRY CARAY

"In terms of WGN, I don't think you can talk about WGN and the development or the growth of WGN without talking about the importance of Harry Caray. When I was there, he was new in Chicago. He had been with the White Sox. Everybody knew Harry Caray was kind of like a clown, but I want to tell you, he was an important guy. I had a lot of respect for him because he helped with this development and this excitement and love of watching the Cubs on WGN, and I don't think you could talk about the Chicago

Cubs and the growth of WGN and the excitement without at least mentioning Harry Caray. He was a true character, but he was an important guy."

THE LEGACY OF '84

"When we started filling it up, that was quite a change. The media sometimes presents this thing as if it's been going on forever, but that's not quite accurate. When I got to Chicago, I wasn't aware of what this all was. I was an American League guy. I don't think the hysteria had quite caught on yet, at least I wasn't aware of it. I can remember in '84, when we finally got in a position late in the season, getting into September and the ballpark was full every day. My pitching coach, Billy Connors, had pitched there, and he said to me, 'After Labor Day when the kids went back to school, this place was pretty empty. Every day now, they're filling it up—37,000.' That was really exciting, and that's when I first realized the extent of the coverage which WGN was starting to build this thing. It was a very exciting time for us. The last 15 or 20 years has been great. I think on WGN, with their expanded coverage, we became like the Braves, and we became the national team. Everybody in America, no matter where I go, even to this day, I can't believe it, I honestly cannot believe it, Nashville or Miami or whatever, and someone will say, 'You were with the Cubs, Jim Frey.' There are Cubs fans all over the world! It's great, and I enjoy it."

8/8/88: THE FIRST NIGHT GAME

Easily the most recognizable date in Cubs history, even though it has nothing to do with action on the field, is 8/8/88. The first night game at Wrigley was the culmination of years of action off the field that included a threat from Commissioner Peter Ueberroth to move future postseason games out of Wrigley if the city did not relent and allow the installation of lights. When the magic date arrived, it was the Oscars, Super Bowl, and Christmas all rolled into one.

"The first night game was a spectacle. It was a happening thing," marveled Ryne Sandberg. "I did the pregame interviews, and even in the pregame, there was a buzz that was going on like a playoff game." The WGN announcers (except Harry Caray) were clad in tuxedoes to mark the occasion, not the most comfortable attire for the hot, humid evening. "I've had cooler nights," laughed Steve Stone.

For John McDonough, it was the chance to create an evening that could match the hype. "The first night game at Wrigley Field was the single biggest event I have ever attended, that I ever felt. I've been to six or seven Super Bowls, and I've been to the World Series, but there's really only one first night game. All of the details about getting Harry Grossman to hit that button and getting Jack Brickhouse involved in the ceremonies and the 40,000 caps that people received, hearing the Phil Collins music when people came in, 'Tonight, Tonight, Tonight.' It had the feeling almost of walking into a heavyweight fight, that you're going to see something tonight that you've never seen before. For me, it was the most memorable night in my years with the Chicago Cubs."

>>>

"The first night game was a spectacle. It was a happening thing."

—Ryne Sandberg

>>>

Ninety-one-year-old Cubs fan Harry Grossman was chosen to turn on the lights, and with Jack Brickhouse at his side, he asked the crowd to say these words: "Let there be lights!" At 6:06 PM, Grossman pushed down the ceremonial red button, and seconds later, the newly installed fixtures came to life.

Rick Sutcliffe had the honor of starting for the Cubs, and the Phillies batting order posed the least of his problems. "That was by far the biggest event I was ever involved in," said Sutcliffe. "Everybody from Bill Murray to Mark Harmon to Brooks & Dunn to Alabama, all my buddies, everybody wanted tickets to that game. I had 10 Opening Days, and there was always going to be another Opening Day, but we didn't think there was going to be another Opening Night."

Once he got to the mound, Sutcliffe wished he had borrowed a pair of sunglasses from his celebrity pals in order to survive the barrage of flashbulbs that accompanied the first pitch. "As I'm warming up in the bullpen, I'm thinking, 'Fine, everybody's got their tickets, I'm in,'" he laughed. "I go out on the mound, and I'll never forget the Hall of Fame said, 'Hey, whatever you do, don't let them put the first ball in play.' So I was told to just miss the outside corner. They wanted to take the ball to the Hall of Fame. So I try to do that, but as I turn to go to home, I thought the stadium exploded. I went, 'What in the world was that?' Nobody had ever taken pictures of me like that. Everybody in the ballpark took a picture. I was kind of blinded, I was blurred, and I went, 'C'mon, you've pitched in big games before. What's the problem with this one?' I mean, the next thing you know, I'm trying to settle down and figure out what just happened. It was special. I'm sure it was a great night for the people at Kodak. I'm sure they sold a lot of film that night."

Two pitches later, Sut found himself on the short end of a 1–0 deficit after Phil Bradley launched his offering onto Waveland Avenue. In the bottom half of the inning, the spotlight turned to Sandberg, who got a lot more than he bargained for in his first trip to the plate under the Wrigley lights. "My first at-bat I'll never forget because, you know, I was excited; it was a big moment, and the first guy got on base. Then on the PA, 'Now to bat, Ryne Sandberg.' There was a huge roar all of a sudden, and I was thinking, 'Wow, this is kind of cool.' I looked up and Morganna the Kissing Bandit was running toward me from right field. She's the lady who went around and kissed Pete Rose when he got his big hit, Nolan Ryan with no-hitters, and George Brett when he was trying to hit .400. So now she chose the first

night game, and I was on her list at that time. I looked up and here she was, running at me. As it happened, the crowd was going nuts, and she was running so slowly that, by the time she got to first base, security took her off and everybody booed. And there I am trying to get my first at-bat under my belt under the lights. I actually hit the second pitch for the first [Cubs] home run under the lights, so that was a big thrill."

This being the Cubs, Mother Nature was not about to let 74 years of uninterrupted baseball under the sunshine go without a fight. In the fourth inning, as lightning flashed all around the park, the skies opened with a cataclysmic fury that exceeded even the wildest dreams of the anti-lights faction, while chasing spectators under the stands. "I thought the ballpark was going to blow down," said Cubs general manager Jim Frey. "I thought we could lose the lights, everything. Within two hours, I went from a high to feeling as bad as I could possibly feel. When we lost that night, it was a terrible storm. It turned out to be a terrible evening. I didn't like that at all."

As the rain delay progressed, the spotlight moved back onto the field when four Cubs decided to entertain the fans with some good old-fashioned belly slides on the tarp. Greg Maddux blamed his veteran catcher for starting things. "Jody Davis started talking about, 'Let's go slide on the tarp,'" Maddux said. "I was young–I bit. I went out there and I remember sliding on the tarp. It was Jody, Al Nipper, Les Lancaster, and you know that was what I remember about the first night game." Frey voiced concern about the players' safety at the time, but deep down he wasn't too worried. "If I was a young player, I'd have done the same thing," he laughed.

The downpour continued throughout the night, and the game was finally called. The next night, the Cubs beat the New York Mets 6–4 in the first official night game, but 8/8/88 will forever be "Lights Night" in Cubs lore. ●

On August 8, 1988, the Cubs played their first night game, ushering in a new era of play for the franchise and the fans.

A new era begins at Wrigley Field, August 8, 1988, with the first pitch at the first night game.

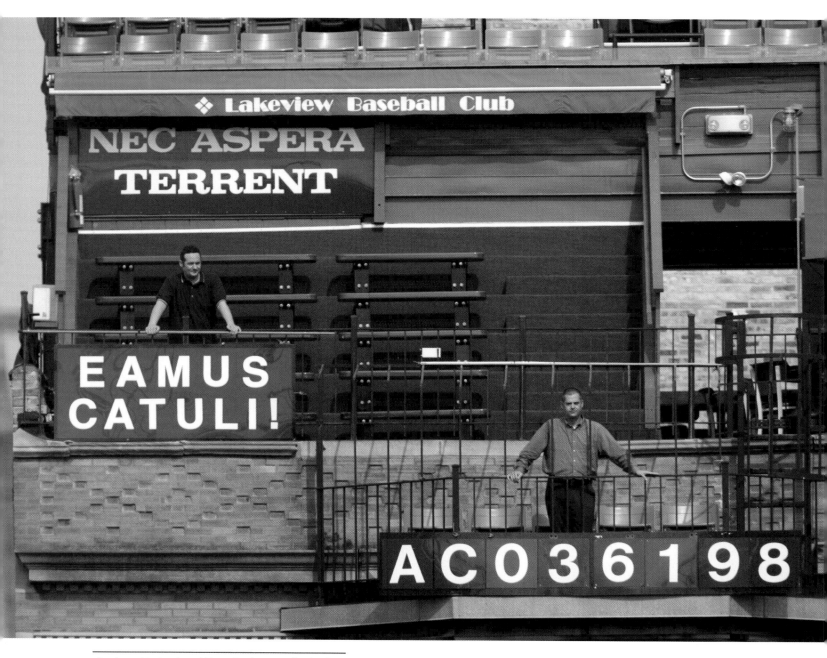

Brothers Michael and Tony Racky proudly display
the signature signs of the Lakeview Baseball Club.

The Faithful

THE LAKEVIEW BASEBALL CLUB

One of the biggest changes to the Wrigley neighborhood began in the late '80s, with the commercialization of the roof-tops across the street from the park. The fans with folding chairs and coolers were replaced by open-air extravaganzas on Waveland and Sheffield. One of the first big renovations occurred in 1988 at 3633 North Sheffield, with the construction of the Lakeview Baseball Club.

"We come from a long line of Cubs fans," said Tony Racky, who now runs the club with his brother, Mike. "My great-grandmother was a season-ticket holder. My grandfather met Babe Ruth the day he called the shot. It's kind of in our blood. As small kids, we watched games from these other buildings. One day we looked over and said, 'Dad, why don't you get one of those for yourself?' The rest is history."

Their father, Bob Racky, purchased the property in 1987 and set about remodeling the entire building. The club officially opened for the Cubs' first night game on August 8, 1988, after a thorough and not-quite-finished overhaul. "The building was in rough shape," remembered Tony. "There was a lot of work to get things in shape and safe."

It was a labor of love for a family of Cubs fans. The Racky family connection to the Cubs goes back over a century and really is in their blood. Two great-grandfathers played for the team: William Traffley in 1878 and Lawrence Hoffman in 1901.

The most recognizable features of the club are the blue signs that face Wrigley, one with the words "Eamus Catuli" (which roughly translates to "Go Cubs") and the other "AC046299" (this changes yearly). "That's my dad," laughed Mike. "He's a little bit of a Latin scholar, and that's how he came up with 'Eamus Catuli.' I guess his original idea with the sign was to have it as a contest and see who could figure it out. Everybody thinks [AC] means 'after championship,' which it doesn't. It means 'anno catuli,' which is 'year of the cub.' The numbers go: first two—years since we won a division; next two—years since we've won a pennant; and last two—years since we've won a World Series. Let's hope that they're all zeroes real soon!"

"We come from a long line of Cubs fans."

—Tony Racky of the Lakeview Baseball Club

"The numbers are a really good marker, and everybody knows the numbers," said Tony. "It's been fun, everybody asking what they mean. Everybody has their own theory of what they think they mean, and it's been good for the building."

The club can hold 200 people and is full of amenities, including bleacher seating for 100, an upper deck that features stadium-style seating, an air-conditioned third-floor club room with a view of the park, and full catering services. At the end of the day, though, it's still about the Cubs. "We started off with aluminum chairs and Weber grills, and now are up to high-tech plasma TVs and an antique English bar. I would have never guessed that," said Tony. "It's the Cubs—win or lose, rain or shine—everybody wants to see the Cubs, and that's what we're here for."

The power of Wrigley Field is such that the club sometimes holds events even when the Cubs aren't playing. "A lot of people would come just to see this place empty," said Mike Racky. "It's not like any other place. I could look at it empty, too, and I've been here almost every day of my life."

This Eric Karros home run lifted the Cubs
to a key 2003 victory over the Yankees.

The brothers aren't ready to do anything else except enjoy the family business. "I really never get sick of it," Mike said. "I thought I would. People who work in a pizza parlor never eat pizza because they get sick of it, but I could watch the Cubs every day, day in and day out, and never get sick of it. I loved the Cubs long before we had this place, and I'll love them my whole life."

ERIC KARROS

Eric Karros is a Cub. Sure, he played 12 seasons with the Dodgers and only 114 games in one year with Chicago, but he's a Cub. Karros was acquired before the 2003 season with Mark Grudzielanek in exchange for Todd Hundley, a deal that at the time was seen as swapping high salaries and underperforming players. While Hundley did little in L.A., Grudzielanek hit .314 as the Cubs starting second baseman, and Karros was in the middle of the most exciting moments of the season, while marveling at the passion and loyalty of the fans he played before each day.

At the time of the trade, Karros wasn't exactly jumping for joy and had no idea he was about to experience an unbelievably memorable year. "Going to Chicago, I had been there for two or three days at a time and that was fun, but I was leaving L.A. and a familiar area where I live all year round," said Karros. "My initial thought was, 'Look, I'm going to find a place to live, and I don't care what it cost me because if I'm going to be miserable in Chicago, it's going to have nothing to do with my living conditions.' I ended up finding a place that was a few blocks away from Wrigley Field, ironically on Grace (where a Cubs first baseman should live) right by Southport, and it was an unbelievable place. My initial thought process was, I know Dusty and that's good, and I have no idea what I'm getting into in Chicago. I know they just had a struggling season. I don't care what it costs, I'm getting a place that's just nice, and I'll go from there."

It didn't take long for Karros to change his tune about life as a Cub. The North Siders were off to a good start,

and as he walked to work each day, it became clear he was involved in something special. "The best experience that I've ever had in professional baseball is playing for the Cubs," said Karros. "Playing in Los Angeles, I thought was the ultimate. Going to Chicago, though, and having the opportunity to walk to and from the park—that's how baseball used to be for the guys living in Brooklyn playing for the Dodgers, like turning back the clock."

On June 7, Karros hit what was probably the signature home run of the Cubs season and cemented a place for himself in the hearts of diehard Cubs fans everywhere. The Yankees were the opponents at Wrigley for the first time since 1938, and after winning the opener on Friday, the New Yorkers sent Roger Clemens to the mound in search of his 300th victory, while the Cubs countered with Kerry Wood. Karros didn't start the game but came on in the fourth after Hee Sop Choi injured his head in a collision with Wood on a pop-up. Clemens left the game with two runners on in the seventh nursing a 1–0 lead. Juan Acevedo came on in relief, and Karros greeted him with a three-run homer to left to give the Cubs their first-ever win over the Yankees. "That was one of my greatest experiences as a baseball player," recalled Karros. "I had my dad in the stands. I hit the home run, and that was one of the best nights to be Eric Karros in Chicago. I went out to dinner at Joe's, which is my favorite restaurant in the country. It was probably my most gratifying moment as a baseball player."

With the Cubs in the pennant chase, Karros decided to chronicle his days in the dugout and began taking his video camcorder everywhere he went at the ballpark. "In September, I was thinking that this might be it for me as a player, especially because we win it, it's my last season," Karros said. "It just started off as, well, this could be my last month of pro baseball, so I started to document it. We were still a couple of games out, and as the month began to unfold, in the games I wasn't playing, I would take shots of stuff in the dugout. I even got a letter from Bob Watson [from Major League Baseball], telling me I couldn't have the camera in the dugout. I shot a ton of behind-the-scenes

Thank you to the Chicago Cubs fans and the entire
Cubs organization for your support. You have all
provided my family and me with an unbeatable
experience and memories to last a lifetime.

Warmest Regards,

stuff. Then the closer it got, it became, 'Hey, we may have an opportunity to be in the postseason.' There were people who were talking to me that depending on how far the Cubs go, it could be a great program or a video. I'm glad I did it, and I wish I would have done even more. I put all the stuff on DVD. I don't know what I'm going to do with it. The tapes are in a safe-deposit box. I don't know if I'll ever do anything with it because there's a lot of great stuff on there. There's a lot of stuff, well, let's just say there's a lot of other stuff, too."

On September 27, the Cubs hit their final stride during a Saturday doubleheader against Pittsburgh at Wrigley Field. While the Cubs were taking the first game behind Mark Prior, the Milwaukee Brewers had defeated the Astros, so when Karros and the Cubs hit the field for game two, they knew a win would sew up the division. Two hours and 26 minutes later, they did just that, ending the game by turning a double play where the game ball ended up in Karros's glove. "I have the ball, and I've got 30-some odd signatures on it. It's in my office," said Karros. "I don't have a lot of stuff up, but I've got that ball, and I had every player on that team sign it." The celebration on the field also gave Karros another chance to record some magnificent memories. "When we clinched against Pittsburgh, I ran with the camera all the way around Wrigley Field," said Karros. "When we were in Atlanta and we clinched there, I've got all kinds of footage of the fans, too."

Karros hit two big home runs to help the Cubs past the Braves in that first-round playoff series and was in the lineup as the team took a 3–1 series lead over Florida before losing three straight. He took the loss personally, especially because of the heartbreak for the fans he had come to love. "I still can't believe we lost," he said. "This is the reason why I did the thank-you. I had a great time in Chicago. It was easily the best time of my life, baseball-wise. My family loved it when they were out. I stayed for a couple of days after we lost, kind of cleaning up stuff. Wherever I went publicly, I had people across the spectrum saying to me, 'You know I just want to thank you for a great season. You brought our family together.' Never once did I have a problem, not even some teenaged kid saying we choked or some guy sitting in a bar saying, 'You screwed us.' Not once did that happen. When you lose, you feel bad, sure. But I genuinely felt so bad for the fans because I thought we let them down and pulled the rug out from under them. I understand the history. It's one thing to talk about it, but it's another thing to actually have those feelings. Just talking about it now, it still hurts me."

The thank-you Karros was talking about came in the form of a full-page ad in the Sunday *Chicago Tribune* shortly after the end of the season. Chicagoans opened their *Tribune* sports page and found a message from Karros, thanking them for an unforgettable year. "Obviously, it helped that the *Tribune* owned the Cubs," said Karros. "I called some people there and said, 'Look, I want to take out a full-page ad.' At that time, let's face it, I was making some ridiculous money. I was saying, 'I don't care what it cost, I want to say thanks because baseball-wise, this was the greatest year of my life.' They were gracious enough to let me know that as a *Tribune* employee, I got a special rate! I don't know how many employees take out a full-page ad, but I know there aren't many *Tribune* employees that get to play first base for the Cubs. I got to pick the picture, and the *Tribune* helped me out with the design and the caption. To have that put in the Sunday paper was really outstanding. I'm really proud of that."

Karros was a great ambassador for the team both on and off the field that year, and his efforts did not go unnoticed. "What Eric Karros did that year is he cemented his legacy and he found a place in the hearts of Cubs fans for the rest of his life," said the Cubs' John McDonough. "When we talk about a Valentine to our fans, that's exactly what that ad was. He really was the guy that understood it. As the season, that magical season, was unfolding, he wanted to make sure that he had the video camera all the time because he wanted to capture it. He had that one great line that we all wish we said about other major leaguer players, 'Everybody should be a Chicago Cub for one year.'"

Exactly. That's why Eric Karros is a Cub.

"There's no place left to win a championship on any professional sports level other than for the Chicago Cubs. There will be nothing greater. Winning with the Yankees, been there, done that. Chicago is the last great place to win a world championship." **—Eric Karros**

VIDEO MEMORIES

"I've got stuff that's not necessarily incriminating, but it's fun stuff that you wouldn't expect. I've got shots when Sammy [Sosa] got thrown out of a game, and he is just going off in the clubhouse. I've got Mark Prior doing some stuff that you wouldn't expect him to be doing, and Kerry Wood, too. After the game, there would always be one song playing, and I can't stand 50 Cent, but that was going all the time. I caught a lot of fun stuff."

AFTER THE 2003 LOSS

"To a person I didn't run into anybody who said anything other than, 'Hey, I want to thank you for this summer. Thank you for the memories.' That will forever stick with me. I played on some teams in L.A. where we went to the playoffs or were in it until the last week. There you would inevitably run across someone who would give you a hard time. Not here. That's my memory of Chicago."

CHICAGO LOVE

"I think at that stage of my career, that fact that we won, the way that the city embraced us as a team, I should have retired after that year. In 2004 I had asked for my release from Oakland, and I called Jim Hendry. I said I'd like to come back here. I don't even care if I play. I'll sit on the bench. I thought I could help the club. I thought that dealing with Sammy and all that stuff I was kind of a buffer there. I wanted to go back to Chicago, even if it just meant sitting because there's only one place left in all of sports to win a championship, and that's playing for the Chicago Cubs. I truly believe that."

THE BUDWEISER HOUSE

The Budweiser House sits on the corner of Kenmore and Waveland, looking directly at its younger neighbor across the street to the south. For Pat Kelly and his family, the house is more than a source of income. It has been a home, a living landmark, and a spot for family and friends to come and celebrate their love for the Cubs.

The advertising on the roof has been around long enough that it is allowed through a grandfather clause with the city, which is why its painted roof and a billboard on a Sheffield roof are the only advertisements across the street from the ballpark. For many years, the roof had a sign for Ricketts Restaurant on Clark Street, then with the television era, the spire on the southwest corner of the roof sported WGN TV-9 and Radio 720 logos. In recent years, after a one-year flirtation with Sapporo beer, the roof has been emblazoned with a bright red Budweiser logo (not a bad deal for WGN since Budweiser is one of our biggest and most loyal sponsors).

If you are looking to rent the building for a shindig, forget about it. The Kelly family doesn't rent their "skybox." Instead, it is used by family and friends: BYOB and come prepared to soak in the roars from across the street. If you want to be a regular, don't call it a rooftop. "For a long time, with the friends I grew up with, it was called the attic," Kelly said. "They'd say, 'You going up to the attic today?' and I'd say, 'Yeah, come on up to the attic.' I'd buzz you in and boom—we're watching the game. It's a party, a gathering of family and friends. That's how it's been. I consider ourselves the first skybox. Before Wrigley had skyboxes in their area, we were here."

The view is partially obstructed by the new bleacher construction, but still offers a great look into the lush outfield of Wrigley Field. Speaking of bleacher construction, don't expect any across the street on the four wooden rows in Kelly's beloved attic. "It's still the same old bleachers," Kelly said. "The bleachers were here when my grandfather

Pat Kelly sits on the wooden bleachers in the attic of the Budweiser House.

bought the place back in 1940. I couldn't even tell you how old they are. The bleachers in the ballpark have come and gone, and these are still here!"

>>

"The things people [in the bleachers] do when they have a couple of beers is amazing."

—Pat Kelly

>>

A day in the attic also offers some great people-watching, courtesy of the bleacher denizens. "I've seen many things," Kelly said. "People in the bleachers as they face the field sometimes don't realize that we're behind them. The things people do when they have a couple of beers is amazing. When balls come out of the park, we can see the people scrambling for the balls in the street. I've got an inside and outside view of the park, and it's great."

Even mundane tasks such as yard work take on a new dimension when tackled across from a major league ballpark. Kelly never felt the need to wear a hardhat while being outside, but cutting the grass could sometimes take an interesting turn. "I would tend to take care of property on off days when people weren't around, but the team would be having a workout. I can remember so many times I could hear the crack of the bat, then a ball would come flying over. I'm out there cutting the lawn, and balls are flying out and nobody is around. I'm stuffing them in my pockets and got balls coming out of everywhere. I probably picked up 15 balls with nobody shoving for them on some of those days."

Kelly and his family are uncertain on the future of the building but know nothing can put a price on the memories shared with their celebrated neighbor. "The adrenaline that people bring to the ballpark is amazing, and I can see it from over here," said Kelly.

"I guess it builds up a lot of adrenaline in me. It's been pretty exciting. You know, when you live in a place for 30 years, across the street from Wrigley Field, you sort of take things for granted until you get to be a little bit older, then all of a sudden you realize you've really lived a helluva life living across from the ballpark."

BOB DERNIER

Successful seasons for the Cubs in recent years have always had one thing in common: a great leadoff man, such as Jerome Walton in 1989 and Kenny Lofton in 2003. The modern gold standard for Cubs leadoff men was set by Bob Dernier in 1984.

With just a few days left in spring training that year, general manager Dallas Green wasn't happy with the makeup of the Cubs, who had the worst exhibition record in baseball at that point. Green tapped into his extensive knowledge of the Philadelphia organization and engineered a trade for Dernier and fellow outfielder Gary Matthews.

Dernier's arrival filled a void for the Cubs and made life easier for manager Jim Frey. "We wanted a center fielder who could fit in the leadoff spot in terms of getting on base and base-running ability, stolen bases, and Bobby Dernier fit that bill."

For Dernier it was a chance to be a starter and instill a different attitude in his new team. "[The Phillies] had just played in the World Series the year before, so we expected to win and we did," he said. "We didn't go all the way, but certainly that team presented itself as a day-in, day-out competitive team."

Dernier meshed immediately with Ryne Sandberg at the top of the order, forming a one-two punch Harry Caray quickly dubbed the "Daily Double." Ryno was quick to credit Dernier's success with helping launch his MVP season. "When he came over, it was great because he was a guy who could run. He was a leadoff hitter. I knew him, and he fit right in. He really made me become a better hitter, having him on base so much. We created some havoc out there for the infielders and the defense."

Dernier stole 45 bases and scored 94 runs as the catalyst for the Cubs offense that season. For his brilliance in center field, he was awarded a National League Gold Glove.

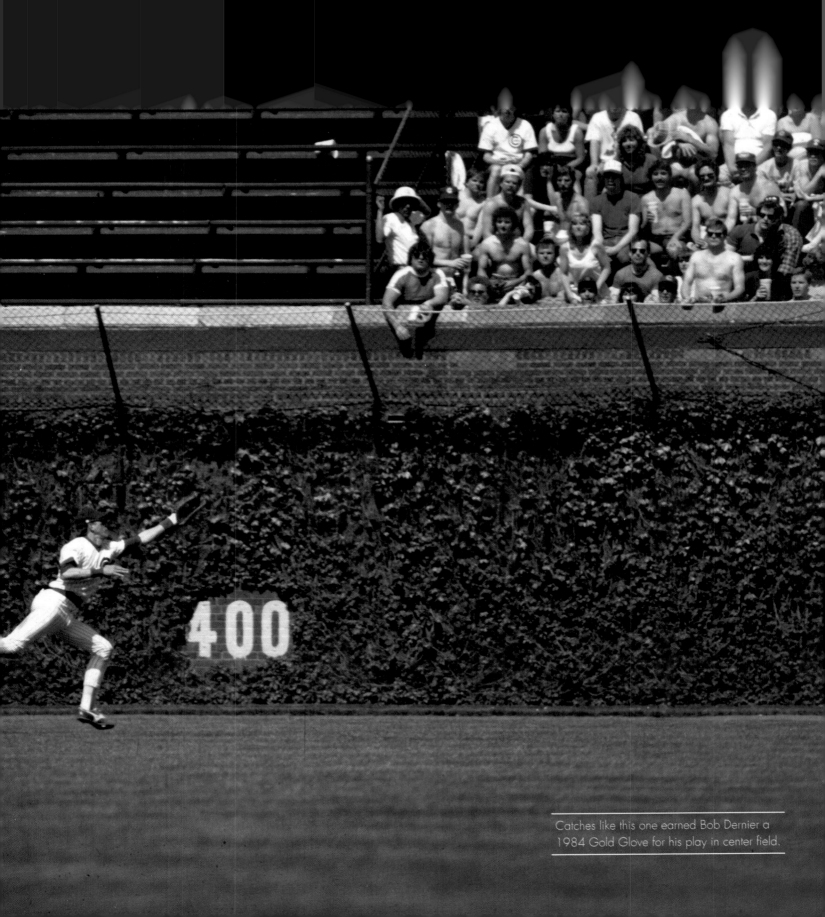

Catches like this one earned Bob Dernier a
1984 Gold Glove for his play in center field.

Hampered by a foot injury, Dernier never approached his 1984 numbers and signed as a free agent with the Phillies after the 1987 season. His popularity with Cubs fans continues as a regular at Randy Hundley's fantasy camp and the Cubs Convention. In 2007, he rejoined the organization as a base-running/outfielder coordinator, determined to help the Cubs get to the World Series they just missed in 1984.

BEING TRADED TO THE CUBS

"I felt like I had a greater opportunity to play every day in Chicago, so I really looked forward to it, although I had great friends there and ended up finishing my career in Philadelphia. I wanted to play there—everybody wants to play for their first team—but that wasn't going to happen. I knew the opportunity was awaiting in Chicago with Dallas here, Ryno was already here, and so was Keith Moreland. I really felt like I was where I belonged. For Gary, I'm not sure he knew at the time. I do know this. When we got on the plane, he said to me, 'Look here, we're not playing all that losing stuff. We're going over there to win.'"

CELEBRATING THE CLINCHER

"After we won that game and clinched, we went about our different ways of celebrating. I remember Ryno and I walking down the hall at around 5:00 in the morning, and we had a date to be on *Good Morning America* at about 6:15. He looked at me, and I looked at him, and I said, 'We're not going to make it, are we?' and he said, 'Nope.' I'm sure we made them mad, but we weren't capable at that point, and it just wouldn't have been right. But Ryno made the call! We certainly celebrated and enjoyed that moment. That was the culmination of a lot of great moments up to that point."

THE LEGACY OF 1984

"The relationship we had with the fans who were able to watch us play at that time is a big part of it. Our generation of players appreciated it. We followed the Hundleys and Beckerts and Jenkinses of the world, and we learned from them how to go about things. We put our spin on it. I think

we really appreciated that relationship, and I think most of us still show that, and the people treat us great because of it."

CHANGING THE CULTURE

"As a visiting player, I remember the stands weren't nearly as full as they became in 1984, but we had to earn that. We were winning a little bit and looked like we were fun to watch. People started talking and then they would come, and before you knew it, here we go. From that point on, Wrigley Field numbers have continued to improve, but it is still all about winning or at least being competitive. I think that is what the Cubs fan demands. They don't demand a world championship every year, we all know that, but they keep showing up. If you give them a good effort, are competitive enough, and have a good chance to win, they will keep coming." —*Bob Dernier*

HARRY CARAY

"Harry and I always had a great relationship. I just thought the world of him. The reason why is something he told me one night on the road. He said, 'Bobby, you will never get booed at home because even when you stink, it looks like you're trying.' That was a great compliment from Harry the fan, that he appreciated my style of play and could suffer along with me when I'm 0-for-15 or popping the ball up too much. Instead of getting booed, the fans would really pull for me. Even when I had a tough time, I hustled, ran the bases hard, and played defense. I think those are the kinds of things Cubs fans really appreciate."

PLAYING IN WRIGLEY FIELD

"The truth for me was thinking that Gale Sayers used to run around out here. Babe Ruth used to stand in that dirt right across the plate. That's what got me stoked. I used to look around and think, 'Wow, there's a lot of things that have happened in this ballpark.' I was always a big fan of the past. Baseball has always been a game of decades anyway. Did you play in the '40s, '50s, '60s? I used to always reflect on how many decades they had played baseball there. I was from Kansas City, so I was a big Gale Sayers guy. Those were the things that got me when I walked up out of the dugout and onto the field."

COMING BACK TO WRIGLEY

"I've been there to sing, to help out in the broadcast booth, hoist Ryno's flag, and throw out a first pitch, but every time I come back, it's like being in my old gym. It's a place that I know, and I know where the rust on the hoops is. I know the walls out there, what they are before the ivy starts to appear. I know the little nooks on the steel door out in left-center that can cut your elbow wide open if you don't look where you are running. It's like an old gym you were so used to playing in when you were growing up. I hope it never goes away."

GARY MATTHEWS

After losing 11 straight spring training games in 1984, it was apparent to Cubs general manager Dallas Green that his team needed a spark. By swinging a deal with his old club to bring over Gary Matthews from Philadelphia along with Bob Dernier, Green added a raging bonfire. Matthews's take-charge personality galvanized the Cubs, and the Sarge (a nickname given to Matthews by Pete Rose) became the unquestioned leader of the team, a point he quickly made to his fellow outfielder. "I remember Dernier telling me how excited he was when he got the word that he was being traded to the Cubs," said Cubs beat writer Fred Mitchell of the *Tribune*. "He called Sarge and said, 'Hey, guess what, you're coming with me to the Cubs,' and Sarge said, 'No, you're coming with *me* to the Cubs!'"

After first hearing the news, Matthews wasn't sure he liked the deal. "To tell you the truth, I didn't like the trade at all in the beginning because I was in the World Series in '83 with the Philadelphia Phillies and thinking that we had a chance to go back."

Green was looking for leadership, and it was apparent to his new teammates that Matthews was the new sheriff in town. "When Sarge walked in that clubhouse after that trade, it was almost like throwing the switch of confidence for everybody," remembered Jody Davis. "Sarge wasn't going to take any crap from anybody. 'This is the way we do it,' and that Phillies team was so good and it was, for me, just like night and day. 'We can do this,' and we had somebody to lead us, and that was huge."

For Ryne Sandberg, Matthews's arrival changed the way the Cubs approached everything. "He came over and he was 'the Sarge,' and he had that nickname for a reason," Sandberg said. "I mean, he was 'the Sarge.' He wanted things done a certain way. He wanted guys taking batting practice seriously, working on their stroke, and it got to the point where we all watched each other in batting practice, just to see where a guy was. If a guy wasn't taking a good batting practice, we weren't afraid to say something to the player. It became somewhat competitive during batting practice in a fun way, and Sarge brought that."

Matthews walked the walk in a big way. He led the league in bases on balls and on-base percentage, and also posted a National League–best 19 game-winning RBIs.

"The Sarge" was never better than on the sunny Friday afternoon of August 24. As patrons entered the left-field bleachers, they were handed a white painter's cap with a sergeant's stripes visible on the underside of the bill, courtesy of their beloved left fielder, a grand gesture that had the fans in left roaring with approval as Matthews took the field. Sarge was never one to miss a moment. He trotted out to his position, head down as the cheers rained down, then suddenly stood straight up and snapped off a salute to the bleacher fans, sending things up for grabs. Matthews said, "We had a good time. I was wondering and talking with John McDonough, who was actually in charge of all the entertainment in the ballpark. I was going to just give out free beer for the left-field bleachers from the first to the seventh innings, but John said, 'Oh no, no, no. We can't do that.' We came up with the painter's hats that had a Sarge

In his role as "the Sarge," Gary Matthews was the unquestioned leader of the 1984 Cubs.

stripe. To see the fans stand up, the love affair that I had with the bleachers guys who were out there was just something that motivated you on a daily basis."

Matthews was seemingly in the middle of every Cubs rally down the stretch, and after his two home runs in Game 1 against the Padres, it appeared he was headed for a return visit to the Series. Three straight losses in San Diego ended that dream. "It was bittersweet, obviously, not finishing what we set out to do," said Matthews. "Going to San Diego, losing three in a row, was something that you will never forget. That particular series, my son, Gary Jr., was there, and that's when he had determined right then and there after we had lost that he was going to be a major league player."

After that season, "the Sarge" traded his stripes for a role as a goodwill ambassador. Both the Cubs and WGN-TV received crates of mail from all over North America during the Cubs run in 1984, but the greatest volume that year came from the country of Belize in Central America. After the season, Matthews was dispatched to Belize to donate used equipment and hold a clinic. "We had a great time. There was a parade there, and I spoke to the whole country," he said. "Actually at that time, in speaking with the ambassador there, the only larger crowd they had for a parade was when the pope was there. I told the ambassador, 'I don't mind taking a second seat to the pope!' We had just a great, great time."

Matthews was traded to Seattle in mid-1987 and retired following that season. He rejoined the Cubs for a four-season stint beginning in 2003 as a coach on Dusty Baker's staff, coming oh-so-close once again to being part of a World Series team on the North Side. Despite being let go after the 2006 season, the Sarge still has strong feelings for the Cubs. "I am sincerely pulling for them, wanting them to have good years," he said. "I think it would be selfish on all of our parts from Dusty Baker on down to say or to think or to not want to wish them well because there was nothing that we did wrong. We can hold our heads up proud."

NO NONSENSE

"Being able to be in an organization with Mays and McCovey, you learned right away that it doesn't always take a hit to win the ballgame. There's other things that you can do from catching a ball to throwing out a runner, from breaking up a double play. When your teammates see that you are giving and that you sacrifice, it's very easy for them to do that. Hitting third for the most part all year and considered by most as the best hitter on the team, you display it not so much by stats, but by actions and by giving your heart to what you should be doing, which is winning first and hits and stats second." —*Gary Matthews*

PRIDE IN '84

"Nineteen eighty-four, that team, we like to feel that we're responsible for all the people and the fans being in the stands today. To back it up, you could look at the stats prior to '84. You could actually come up and buy a ticket and just about sit anywhere. After '84, it was pretty difficult to get tickets, and it remains that way today. That team, a lot like the Philadelphia team, these guys stick together and we played unselfish ball, evidenced by how many guys drove in 80 or more runs, I think we had six guys who did that in '84."

SITUATIONAL HITTING

"The game we played in batting practice was get 'em over and get 'em in. A lot of times, guys were thinking, 'Well, I've got to get 'em over with a ground ball.' No. You can get them over with a deep fly ball. What I like to do is get them over but stay in your strengths within yourself in being able to do that. Keith Moreland was probably our best hitter in being able to get the guy over to second just because he could inside-out a fastball that was inside and hit the ball over the right side in giving up himself. If a guy didn't get them in behind you, trust me, he heard about that and not in any really nice, nice ways as well."

Fireman John Sampson has seen it all from his post across the street from Wrigley Field.

WRIGLEY FIELD

"It's a great ballpark in a historic district. It's one of our few ballparks, like Boston, that's in a regular neighborhood. It has a homey feeling. You know yourself, when things start going good here, they rock this joint, and it's good to see. You look at all the different venues here from the way that it's set, from the Bleacher Bums to all the different seats, it's really quite a venue. To be able to have played here, you really feel blessed. There couldn't have been a better spot for me to finish my career for sure."

THE FIREHOUSE

Across Waveland Avenue from the left-field entrance to Wrigley Field sits Chicago's most famous firehouse, Engine Company 78. For firefighter John Sampson, his assignment there lets him indulge in his two passions: fighting fires and rooting for the Cubs.

Sampson was always fascinated with both. Like so many Chicago kids of his generation, his TV was turned to channel 9 each afternoon. "It was through my mom, watching WGN black and white, back in the '60s, when I can first remember watching television," said Sampson. "It was watching Ernie Banks, Don Kessinger, Ron Santo, Glenn Beckert, all those guys. My favorite number is 11 because I wanted to be a shortstop like Don Kessinger. Everything I do is 11."

Sampson is the longest-serving firefighter at Engine Company 78 and has no plans to relinquish his crown. "I was sent here as a rookie 27 years ago, and why would you leave? Back then this neighborhood was kind of rough, and we were fighting a lot of fires in Uptown. It was just so busy, and I like being a fireman. Now it's kind of like my retirement home because the whole neighborhood has changed. It's pretty much slow now, which is good for the neighborhood. We pretty much boast that we are the safest battalion in the city."

When asked to name his favorite season, Sampson wastes no time and is an unabashed admirer of the 1984

Cubs. "People ask me all the time, 'What do you think about this year compared to another?' and I say, 'To me, in '84, it was pretty much how bad are you going to get beat by the Cubs?' It wasn't whether they were going to win or lose. They were going to win. It's how bad were you going to get beat? Now every year, it's kind of like something is going to happen, they may win, they may lose, the pitching kind of falters, but you just don't get that feeling like, how bad are you going to get beat? Nineteen eighty-four, that was it."

>>>

"I'm all Cubs. I can't stand the Sox. During the Sox World Series, I was watching reruns of Little House on the Prairie.*"*

—John Sampson

>>>

The firehouse received national attention late that year when it became the self-proclaimed "Official Firehouse of the 1984 World Series." Sampson and company hung the designation on the front of the firehouse for all to see. "My officer at the time was John Kelly, who owned Kelly's Pub," he said. "He's a big baseball fan, and in a really scruffy voice he said, 'We need a sign for the top of the house.' That was the year of the Olympics, and everything was the official fire hydrant of the '84 Olympics, official dog bone, all of that. I said, 'Why don't we make this the official firehouse?' and he liked that. So we got two big pieces of plywood, and I wrote on there, 'Official Firehouse of the 1984 World Series,' and we put it up. A few of the players would drive in, and we could see them looking at it. They actually put it in *Sports Illustrated* and did a watercolor of it."

Ten years later, the media converged on the firehouse again, this time as the site of manager Tom Trebelhorn's ill-fated town meeting. With the Cubs mired in a season-opening slump that would see them drop their first 16 home games of 1994, manager Trebelhorn used the bench in front of the firehouse as his pulpit to meet with an angry mob of fans. "We had Trebelhorn over for dinner several times," recalled Sampson. "He was great. This place was almost a relief for him to just sit with the fellas. That day, all the cameras and all the people were around. He was fielding questions on why the Cubs were bad, but no real answers came out of it."

The firehouse has long been a haven for Cubs players. "One of nicest guys here was Shawon Dunston," said Sampson, running down the list of players who have frequented the firehouse during his tenure. "Turk Wendell would sit here all day long and pull up his pickup truck, put his flap down, and sign autographs until everyone left. He would bring over venison stew for us. Billy Williams usually stops by when he's at the park. Ryan Dempster's father and brother are firefighters, so he has been here to hang out. There's a neighborhood feel here, especially when there is no Cubs game and there is an off day, you always see some of the players over here. It's a lot of fun."

Firemen in Company 78 are not required to be Cubs fans, and a fair share of the group roots for the White Sox. They have learned to expect no quarter from Sampson, who is as diehard as they come. "I'm all Cubs. I can't stand the Sox," he smiles. "During the Sox World Series, I was watching reruns of *Little House on the Prairie*."

In addition to turning on the hydrant outside to cool off the masses, the other big duty on game days is saying "cheese." "We see a lot of people," said Sampson. "People just want to know about the firehouse, how many runs you have a day, let alone a month, a year. It's gotta be one of the most photographed firehouses in the country. Little kids, dogs coming through, it's like a big family neighborhood, which is nice."

Only at Company 78 could you have a foul ball end up in the kitchen, but that's what happened to Sampson. "Ron Cey hit a foul ball out of the park, and it must have hit something, but it just came dribbling into our kitchen. I picked it up and shoved it in a locker, and there it sat. About 15 years later, a little kid came in all dejected. He

was a fireman's son and had come this close to getting a foul ball at the park. I grabbed that ball out of the locker and gave it to him. I can still remember how he just stared at it. It totally made his day."

From the roof of the firehouse, you can see the entire field, except home plate, so it is a popular place to visit, especially for White Sox and Cardinals games. Regardless of the opponent, the firehouse has no shortage of visitors. "Most game days the place is jam-packed full of firemen," Sampson said. "It's usually firemen from out of town. We get them from France, Australia, Japan, Sun City, Arizona. L.A. comes in a lot, New York comes in a lot. So we've got a little bond now with the New York firemen and the Boston firemen. They always come in, and you always see the same guys. When we go out to different ballparks, we look them up, and they treat us the same way."

According to Sampson, it wasn't interleague play that sparked the visits from other cities. "That was more because of 9/11," he said. "The camaraderie between firemen because of that is really magnified now. After 9/11, it's a cohesive fire department now across the country and across the world." And what better place to celebrate that cohesion than Wrigley Field? It will always do just fine for Sampson. "It's like home," he said.

"I've been here 27 years, and I spend probably more time here than I do at home. Once I retire it might be tough because I would have to come back here just to wean myself off of being by Wrigley Field."

CUBS HISTORIAN ED HARTIG

Did you know Wrigley Field once hosted a ski-jumping event? That 8/8/88 was not the Cubs' first night game at Wrigley Field? The Harlem Globetrotters played in the Friendly Confines? The Cisco Kid hosted a rodeo there? Ed Hartig knows it all, and through his role as a baseball historian, he brings to life some of the forgotten footnotes of the Cubs' past.

Cubs historian Ed Hartig in the outfield.

Hartig's passion for Cubs baseball melded early with his love for numbers. "I was lucky that my mom didn't throw out my baseball cards," he said. "I had boxes and boxes of baseball cards and the books. You would turn the card over and, 'He's hitting .290 in April....' Okay, here we go. This guy is going to win the MVP. Oh, wait a second, he hit .211 in May.' Baseball is a game of numbers. I'm a statistician by education and training. My full-time job is in statistics. I worked in sports information in college. I used to clip things out of newspapers. It's just fun. It's a way to keep interested in the team and in the ballpark."

His association with the Cubs came about because of his love of the team's history. "I actually signed up to be a Wrigley Field tour guide about 14 or 15 years ago. I was giving tours and someone heard one of my tours and he worked for *Vineline*." That someone had gone to high school with Hartig and convinced him to write a monthly history piece for the Cubs magazine. A subsequent introduction to Chuck Wasserstrom of the Cubs media relations department led to the chance to proofread the history section of the team's media guide and a new title for Ed. "The following year when the media guide came out, he had to give me a credit, so he could have put 'baseball geek' or 'research historian.' Luckily for me, he put 'research historian.' I'm a baseball geek, but call me research historian."

Play-by-play announcer Len Kasper has been the beneficiary of Hartig's quest for timely and interesting trivia. "Ed Hartig was a guy who, when I took the job, I asked a few people, 'I want to learn more Cubs history, and if I have questions about certain things that have happened, who should I speak with?'" said Kasper. "Ed's name came up at every turn. So a couple of months after I got to Chicago, we got together for lunch and I had a list of about 12 or 15 questions that I was curious about or had read about, and Ed filled me in on all those things and essentially said, 'I have this big database of information.' I've asked him many times, 'Why don't you write a book?' He said, 'I'm not a writer. What I'm good at is compiling information and giving that to somebody else.' So if we can find a writer, somebody who wants to write the entire

history of the Chicago Cubs, we have his right-hand man.

"Ed has supplied us with a lot of great information. Some of it is so off-the-wall and so specific that I wonder if he's making it up. But knowing Ed the way I do, he's not making it up. It's somewhere in a book. There was one we loved about the Cubs record when a country wins the World Cup. Who would think of something like that? Ed Hartig, of course."

That game note was the one that floored Bob Brenly as well. "We were playing a Sunday game in 2006, and moments after Italy beat France to win the World Cup in soccer, Ed lets Len know that the Cubs are 4–0 on dates when the Italians win the Cup. How great is that?" When asked about that one, Ed is quick to add, "The Cubs were also 1–0 on days that France won the Cup. I was ready either way."

As much as Brenly loves the information, he has no clue as to how Ed gathers it. "How do you know this stuff?" he said. "How do you find this stuff? Apparently, he's got every media guide and every baseball resource book and every computer program imaginable covering Cubs minutiae, and he is as on top of it as anybody I've ever seen."

BECOMING A CUBS FAN

"Believe it or not, I grew up on the South Side. I was from a family of White Sox fans—six kids, five White Sox fans and myself. I would always win the arguments. I used to get beat on pretty good. I became a Cubs fan because of WGN and day baseball, there is no doubt about that. My older brothers and sisters were at school. I was home. My mom would fix me lunch, I'd sit and watch the ballgame. I got to know Jack Brickhouse, Jim West, and you got to trust the Cubs. And you believed Jack Brickhouse that this was going to be the year." *—Ed Hartig*

NUMBERS AND BASEBALL

"Most statisticians love numbers, and baseball has more numbers than any other sport. I'm also a soccer fan, but if last night's score was two goals to one, well, you're done, your stats are finished. What happened in the sixth inning, what happened in the seventh inning, how does this reliever do against left-handed batters? Stuff like that is why baseball lends itself to many slices of the data that it's just a natural for a statistician to love baseball."

RESEARCH TODAY

"Especially in the last 15 years, things have changed, especially with the Internet. You can go online and get the complete run of the *Chicago Tribune* back to the 1880s, sitting at your home. Now, before you would have to file through pages and pages of the daily reports. You go to the Hall of Fame, and they've got every player's day-by-day account, but it's just on accounting paper, just files and files, and you would have to go through that. But obviously over the last 10 or 15 years with the Internet, there's a group called the Society for American Baseball Research [SABR] that has done a tremendous job of making the data available for anyone, and with all the major newspapers you can go online. The access to data is just so much easier today. I don't deal with too much stuff in the current, so I'm not going to tell you who's leading the Cubs in batting this year, but 20 years ago, where the data is a little more scarce, that's where I do most of my work with the Cubs."

CALLS FROM ALL OVER

"I do get some interesting requests. I've gotten some requests obviously from the baseball magazines, the baseball publications. But I've gotten calls from public libraries to come give a presentation. I've gotten calls from a cigar magazine that was doing an article on baseball and smoking. I've talked with people from Australia who have come out here. It's fun, it's interesting, it's not paying the bills, but it keeps you busy. It's a great hobby, it's a great way to meet people, and we're talking about baseball of all things."

GETTING IDEAS TO RESEARCH

"You only hear part of the things. Some things Len and Bob look through and say, 'Nah.' Obviously, I do have a little

benefit there. I love sports. I love the history. I'm watching the game anyway. I've got the computer turned on. For the most part, I just listen to cues from the announcers. If something happens, I wonder when the last time that happened. Boom! There it is, you pull it up. I've also got a lot of stuff already done, on a spreadsheet and so forth, so that if something comes up, it's just a couple of mouse clicks away and I've got the numbers. You only hear the good ones, not the clinkers, and there's been plenty. You can ask anyone in media relations. There have been ones that they looked at and said, 'Uh-uh, that's not gonna happen.'"

WATCHING THE CUBS ON TV

"I'm a product of the '70s, so you're going back to the days of José Cardenal and Jack Brickhouse. There was always a special bond between those two. There was a game back in '72 or '73 or so when there was a rain delay, and somehow José Cardenal got hold of a microphone. Well, Jack was upstairs talking to José, and here was Cardenal in the dugout trying to interview players. I remember Rick Monday saw Cardenal coming over and realized this was going to be a train wreck, so he went scampering off. Now José cornered Randy Hundley in the dugout. You've got José with his thick Latin accent trying to interview Randy Hundley with his thick Southern drawl. José was asking him questions, and Hundley had no idea what he was saying. Hundley was answering, and I had no idea what *he* was saying. The interview went back and forth until finally Hundley said, 'José, I have no idea what you're talking about,' and he walked away."

WRIGLEY FIELD TRIVIA

"This place just oozes history. Wrigley was one of first multiuse facilities. Besides being home for the Cubs and the Bears, they played soccer here even in the '30s. They have had rodeos, circuses, and the Harlem Globetrotters play here. They once set up a ski jump behind home plate. They actually played a night game here in the '40s. When was the first night game at Wrigley—8/8/88? Actually, it wasn't. In June

John McDonough was always on the lookout for ways to enhance the Wrigley Field experience.

of 1943, they played a night game here, the Cubs against the Cardinals. They played it on one of the longest daylight days of the year, started at 6:00, and the game was over by 8:10, and it was still light out. By major league definitions, that was a night game, but no one remembers that."

FAVORITE PLAYER

"Billy Williams had a certain elegance, a certain grace whenever he stepped to the plate. I could watch Billy Williams hit any day. I've met him a couple times through the ballclub, and as great a player as he was, he's an even greater gentleman. He was my first Cub hero."

BEING A CUBS FAN

"I hate the idea of being called 'the lovable losers.' I'm not a Cubs fan to watch them lose. I want to see them win. I want to see ring ceremonies. I want to see them raise a banner."

JOHN McDONOUGH

Beanie Babies, conventions, singers, and attendance records tend to be the subjects that come front and center when discussing the remarkable career of John McDonough with the Cubs organization. Focusing only on those achievements undersells the man whose true love is baseball and who has never wavered in his search for excellence during his tenure with the Cubs marketing department and rise to the team's presidency. (In November 2007, McDonough left the Cubs and was named president of the Chicago Blackhawks.) He always wanted the best for the best fans in sports, a sentiment he echoed in his first words as the team's president—"It's time to win."

He joined the Cubs in 1983 after working with the Chicago Sting and has been an integral part of building and marketing the mystique that surrounds the team and Wrigley Field. After all these years, McDonough still marvels at the resiliency and optimism of the Cubs faithful. "It's all about today," he said, when asked to define what makes Cubs fans unique. "It's something that you really can't explain. They live

for today. They're very forgiving, they do have amnesia, they have short-term and long-term amnesia. When you have an event that is a great comeback victory, that really registers. That is a snapshot for the rest of their lives."

McDonough is reluctant to take too much credit for the creation of the monster known as the Cubs Convention. The fan gathering was the first of its kind, and although it has spawned many imitators, nothing can compare to the return of 15,000 Cubs fans to the Chicago Hilton each frigid January, all seeking a dose of North Side baseball to get them through the winter. "You can never imagine what happened," said McDonough, discounting the notion that he developed a special Cubs Kool-Aid and made it available to the masses. "I think in many ways we really labeled that originally as Harry Caray's first cocktail party. I asked Harry if he would be the honorary chairman. As soon as he had ownership of it, he talked incessantly in 1986 about this event that was going to happen. Once Harry gave it the papal blessing and he stamped it, it started this rush and wave of interest we see right now. But never did we think that it would get to the level that it is right now. It's a wonderful success. It bridges the end of one season, and for Cubs fans, it's too long for them to wait for February, and it's far too long, it's unthinkable, for them to wait until Opening Day. They want that Cub fix in the middle of winter, and that's what we've been able to provide for them."

In 1998, after examining ideas on how best to honor the memory of Harry Caray, McDonough introduced the concept of guest conductors to sing "Take Me Out to the Ballgame," a ritual that has now become an integral part of the Wrigley Field game-day experience. "I think the beauty of the seventh-inning stretch is that it's imperfect," he said. "In many instances, it's really bad performances, but it's consistent with the imperfection of baseball. All of this I think was given to us by Harry Caray.

"I think it's got an extended life. What that is I don't really know. If done properly, I think this could go on forever. I think invariably what you will get when people come to this beautiful ballpark, they want to know who you're playing, they want to know who's pitching, and they want to know who's singing. Just to get into that group is really—for something on the business side—a very high compliment, and we really recognize that a big part of this, a major part of this is WGN television and the presence that they have given us, because a lot of these celebrities, they love singing to the multitude, but they want to sing on WGN-TV."

McDonough has been the target of unfair criticism over the years, with critics claiming that, by promoting hope, bricks, and ivy, he is responsible for a game-day atmosphere with an emphasis on fun over winning. Nothing could be further from the truth. The reason he was so successful, the reason he identifies so closely with the Cubs fans is that he is one of them. He should not be faulted for doing his job brilliantly over the years and doing everything he can to improve the Cubs product on and off the field. At the end of the day, no matter what happened, John burned as much as anyone can with the desire to see a championship flag raised at Wrigley. "The best marketing tool of all time is winning," he always says. "Nothing else is even close."

THE CUBS PHENOMENON

"Don't try to understand it, just let it wash over you. There's a unique mystique, there's a phenomenon, there's kind of an urban culture that none of us can understand. We haven't won in 99 years. We play during the day when people should either be at work or at school. We have limited parking. All of the games are on television and radio, yet you can't get in. It's a Valentine of 41,000 people every day that embrace that brand, that embrace those players, and it's really nothing short of a baseball romance." —*John McDonough*

HARRY CARAY

"Those of us who knew him very well, we realized that we all wanted to be him. Harry violated every law of nature. People are concerned about cholesterol or eating late or drinking late or make sure you get eight hours of sleep. None of

those ever crossed his mind! He wanted to squeeze as much as he could out of life, and that was the lesson that he gave us when he would say, 'Live it up, the meter is running.' I'll constantly find myself during a game thinking of a Harry-ism. Just recently, in some of the games when we were outplaying the White Sox, I remember what he used to say; he used to say, 'Cross your fingers, cross everything.' He's a huge reason this franchise is as strong and as powerful as it is right now. Here is a guy who sold tickets to a stadium. People wanted to experience coming to Wrigley Field, they wanted to see a game, but they wanted to see an 80-something-year-old guy sing 'Take Me Out to the Ballgame.'"

WRIGLEY FIELD

"I love the majestic beauty of it. When the team is on the road and you might have had a rough day, a lot of places people will have to go into a cafeteria, people will go into a lounge, and they'll go outside. I get to sit and walk into the most beautiful ballpark in America. I remember many years ago on WGN television before we had the seventh-inning stretch, Harry Caray invited Bill Cosby to come on the broadcast, and Harry had asked Bill a question. I'm not sure if Harry thought it was Bing Crosby or Norm Crosby or Bill Cosby or whatever, but I remember Bill Cosby stopping and saying, 'Harry, before you go any further, I've traveled all over the world and this is the most beautiful sight I've ever seen—Wrigley Field.' That was one of the high compliments I've ever heard paid about this ballpark."

THE FIRST NIGHT GAME

"For me, it was the most memorable night in my 24 years with the Chicago Cubs. I also remember when we heard—this is far before the sophistication of [meteorologist] Tom Skilling's technical advancements—but I remember them saying we were about to get a lot of rain here at Wrigley Field, and Rick Sutcliffe was slowly pacing around the mound wiping his brow, tying his shoes, and we were all screaming from the upper deck or from here, 'Just throw the ball! Let's get going! We want to get one in!' Ultimately, we didn't, and it's made for some great trivia as to which was the first night game, but it was a memorable, if not the most memorable, event ever here at Wrigley."

WILD-CARD NIGHT

"People sometimes forget that Michael Jordan threw the first pitch that night, so what better way to lead that game off? You remember the late Rod Beck getting the last out, you remember Mark Grace catching the ball. You remember, as part of all this, Sammy Sosa having one of the greatest years that any player has had in the history of the game. That night of the wild-card game was one of the most enjoyable experiences you could ever have. The silhouette on the balloon of Harry Caray over the outfield wall gave it kind of an eerie feel, a surreal feel like, 'Is all of this really happening to us?' And it happened on our home ground.

In 1984 and in 1989, we clinched on the road. We clinched in '84 in Pittsburgh. We clinched in '89 in Montreal. We had never clinched here. People didn't know what this was about. So they saw that for the first time, and the setting couldn't have been better."

ANDRE DAWSON

"I would say my favorite game here at Wrigley Field unfortunately didn't come when we clinched something if you're talking about one game. It was the last home game of the season in 1987, when Andre Dawson hit his last home run of the season. I'm not ashamed to say this. Andre Dawson is my favorite Cub of all time. Class. Dignified. Very similar to Ryne Sandberg, the type of player. The way he treated our fans, the respect for the game he had. When he hit that 47th home run on that Sunday afternoon, I believe I thought that was a very magical moment here."

Mike Ditka, former Chicago Bears player and coach, performs a lively rendition of "Take Me Out to the Ballgame." (Photo courtesy of AP/World Wide Images.)

The Stretch

MIKE DITKA

When the Cubs instituted the idea of celebrity singers to honor Harry Caray in 1998, the experiment was a pleasant addition to the Wrigley Field experience that flew largely under the radar for the first few months. That is until Mike Ditka inadvertently brought national attention to the new concept when he arrived late for his July 5 date with the microphone. What followed made blooper-reel history.

The sellout crowd of 38,742 didn't have much to cheer about that afternoon as the Cubs fell behind 5–0. After José Guillen was called out on strikes to end the Pittsburgh seventh, the fans turned to the booth, prepared to belt out "Take Me Out to the Ballgame" with their Super Bowl coach. The only problem was that Ditka wasn't there, having gotten stuck in traffic on his way to Wrigley Field. He burst into the administrative office doors on the ground floor and headed upstairs just as Guillen was exiting the batter's box. While organist Gary Pressy held the opening chord on the PA system, Ditka raced up the ramps, no small feat for a guy with two artificial hips and a heart attack under his belt.

Meanwhile, Chip Caray and Steve Stone were waiting in the booth without much guidance on what to do with an AWOL singer. "Steve and I were here, and we knew Ditka was coming," said Caray. "He was late because he had been playing golf. We're waiting and waiting and waiting, and I'm pretty sure the Cubs were losing. [They were down 5–0.] Steve grabs the microphone and said, 'Well, I've got good news and bad news. The bad news is that Ditka is not here. The good news is that he's on the way, so in the meantime, we're going to start singing.' Now in comes Ditka, former NFL player, nice guy, and he's out of gas. You've got to walk up the ramps, and he's got bad knees, a bad back, and he's been on the golf course all day. He takes a deep breath, comes in the booth, and belts it out. He was so excited."

After keeping the crowd waiting, Ditka left them breathless as well when he launched into his own breakneck version of the song. Da Coach's performance lasted only 22 seconds, a record that hopefully will never be broken. While play resumed in the bottom of the seventh, the crowd did its own, much slower, rendition of "Take Me Out" as Ditka laughed from the booth while doing an interview with Chip and Stoney.

> *"You've gotta believe! C'mon, wake up! Let's go!"*
>
> —Mike Ditka

When the Cubs' John McDonough conceived of the idea of using guest conductors for the stretch, he didn't imagine that one of them would turn it into a hopped-up version of "Pop Goes the Weasel." "Mike Ditka really put this on the map," said McDonough. "He went into the hurry-up offense, and he sang as fast as he could. That put an imprint on this that we hope is going to last a long time. We all thought that Steve and Chip were going to have to sing. That was okay, too. But we knew he was on the way, and we knew that he had bad hips, and we knew that he had to run up ramps and all of the elements were against us. But when he finally showed and really gave our fans the 'let's win one for the Gipper,' I think we did score four or five in the bottom of that inning, it was as if this thing was really put on the map, once and for all." The Cubs scored a total of seven runs in the two innings after Ditka's vocal dash and went on to win 7–5.

Bonnie Hunt never misses Opening Day at Wrigley Field or a chance to lead the crowd during the seventh-inning stretch.

In his seven appearances as a guest conductor, Ditka's most inspiring moment on WGN came on September 3, 2003, as the Cubs were battling the Cardinals in a five-game series over four days. With the Cubs trailing 7–3 in the seventh, he grabbed the mike and screamed at the crowd, "You've gotta believe! C'mon, wake up! Let's go!" Buoyed by his exhortations, the Cubs rallied for three runs in the seventh en route to an 8–7 win and went on to take four out of five games in the series that began the September run to the division title.

Ditka has always been a big baseball fan and cops to being a much better baseball player in his younger days. He often tells the story of chasing brother Ashton home during a Little League game because of an error—a young Iron Mike who already hated to lose. Despite growing up near Pittsburgh, he wasn't a Pirates fan. "I was a Cardinals fan because of Stan Musial," said Ditka. "I'm a diehard Cubs fan now, though." Thanks, Coach. That's good enough for us.

BONNIE HUNT

What's not to love about Bonnie Hunt? Sure, she's beautiful, hilarious, successful, and loyal to her Chicago roots. Yes, she's a big name in Hollywood after starring in *Jumanji, Jerry Maguire, Cheaper by the Dozen, Cars,* and other projects. True, she's a talented writer and director who is also a talk-show regular. But what puts her at the top of the heap is that Bonnie is a bona fide, hard-core, blue-as-they-come, diehard Cubs fan.

"I come from a large family with seven kids in our family," said Hunt. "WGN and the Cubs on television is the soundtrack of my life. It's the background of my childhood. My parents were huge Cubs fans, and we grew up a couple blocks down Addison from Wrigley Field. When I was a little girl, my friend's father drove a pie truck, and he would drop us off at the bleachers the night before Opening Day every year about 1:00 in the morning, even though we were just young kids, 12 or 13 years old. We would sit in the back of the truck with all the pies and his deliveries, and he would go past Wrigley and drop us off. We would stay overnight to get our best, favorite seats in the bleachers."

The ride down Addison started a tradition that Bonnie and her friends honor to this day. "I've never missed an Opening Day since the '70s," she said. "I meet up with my old gang from the old neighborhood. We all meet there on Opening Day. For us, it's kind of our New Year's Eve. It really is. It's kind of that turning point for us every year where the Cubs start another great season of hope. The guys who come are always the same and don't want to let me buy a drink. They say, 'Hey, your money's no good here, Ms. Hollywood.'"

Rounding up that many seats on Opening Day is no easy task, even for a star like Hunt. But Bonnie works it out in a time-honored Chicago tradition—she's "got a guy," this one in the person of her brother Tom, whose electrical company works with the Cubs. "That is such a great day for all of us, and there's usually more than a dozen people there," said Tom Hunt. "The Cubs are such a big deal for our family, and it's great my sister can come back so we can all keep that tradition alive for over 30 years."

No doubt about it, Bonnie and family are serious about the Cubs. "My sisters and I at one point, we wouldn't answer to our real names," she said. "We were Randy Hundley, Ernie Banks, and Billy Williams. It's just been a part of our lives. I was born in 1961 and the Cubs, gosh, especially in the late '60s, forget about it. That was really the turning point for me, hearing Ernie Banks with 'the Cubs will shine in '69.' It's probably the first poem I ever recited."

Banks has some stiff competition from Bonnie's mother, Alice, when it comes to the yearly poem predicting imminent success for the Chicago National League ballclub. "Every year she hand paints a brand new Cubs sign for the big picture window in our house in the old neighborhood," said Hunt. "Everybody comes by to see the sign. In 2007 it was 'Cubs in Heaven in 2007,' and Mom always comes up with some rhyme like Ernie Banks did."

Jimmy Buffett's love of the Cubs made him an easy choice to headline the first concert at Wrigley Field.

For Hunt, the elation of the Cubs' pennant run in 1969 still outweighs the heartbreak that followed, mostly because it marked her true initiation into the realm of the Cubs faithful. "I think '69 was it for me," she said. "I was old enough to get it. Sixty-nine was that turning point where I was at the age that I really got into it and knew that I was a part of something big that my parents loved, that my older brothers and sisters loved, and it was a part of the character of the city. Sixty-nine was a tough year. But there have been a lot of tough years. We're Cubs fans. We can go through anything. It's a part of me. Always.

"I love that ballpark," she gushes when talking about the need to see the Cubs on her trips back to Chicago. "I love everything about it. I love the people, how we all feel when we're together. It's a community that we're all nostalgic for, especially during these times, and Wrigley Field is always home. It's always romantic and exciting and hopeful. I love it."

Despite four decades of unfulfilled adoration, Bonnie takes the approach that her unconditional Cubs love translates into peace in other parts of her life. "Being a Cubs fan is like a form of therapy," said Hunt. "No matter what you do professionally or personally, you have your ups and downs, and you know that you are going to start all over again. It's a whole new season. You wake up, you brush yourself off, and you hope. Certainly with my dad, Wrigley Field was kind of like our backyard. He would put all seven kids in the back of the station wagon, and we'd go down to the park and sit through the game. Those were the good old days."

WRIGLEY FIELD

"I think for me, Wrigley Field is one of the most romantic places in the world. You know I've been to Rome, I've been to Paris, I've been to Spain and Scotland. I've done a lot of traveling because of my career, and I've been really fortunate. But nothing beats the romance of being at Wrigley Field to me, and I mean that sincerely.

1969

"The Cubs of '69, we're talking about a group of classic athletes. I mean they were good guys and great role models. They had that team spirit, it was almost like they were your high school team with all that camaraderie and the mutual respect among the players. There was so much respect among those guys between each other and the way they loved the fans. They would get everybody riled up and on their side." —*Bonnie Hunt*

WGN

"WGN was in the background of my life, always having that game on, whether it was Jack Brickhouse or Harry Caray, and it's just a big part of my childhood. Living here in Los Angeles now most of the time, I have WGN on every game in my kitchen. I have a little TV in there, and I have those games on all the time. I love listening to Ron Santo on the radio, too."

LIFE AS A CUBS FAN

"When you are a Cubs fan, you just apply it to your own life. Things aren't going exactly as you expect, then you say there's always next year, there's always tomorrow. There's something so beautiful about that."

JIMMY BUFFETT

When the Cubs began exploring the notion of a concert at Wrigley Field, it didn't take long to see that having Jimmy Buffett bring his unique summer celebration to Clark and Addison would be a perfect fit, especially because Buffett was a longtime Cubs fan with a special affinity for the Friendly Confines.

"I was always a ball fan," said Buffett. "I grew up in Mobile, Alabama, which was a pretty good town for players, and we had a little minor league team, so I was always into ball." Mobile was a hotbed of baseball talent, producing such stars as Hank Aaron and Jimmy's favorite Cub, Billy Williams.

After getting to Chicago, Buffett hooked up with his friend, folk music legend Steve Goodman, who introduced him to the Wrigley Field bleachers. It was love at first sight. "Steve Goodman hooked me," said Buffett. "When I first came to Chicago, I worked at a club here called Quiet Knight. It was up on Belmont. Goodman worked down at the Earl of Old Town. In those days, there were no lights, so I'm of the pre-night-game period. Being a shameless entertainer working nights, Goodman brought me to the game, and we would sit out in the bleachers. I remembered it, and I wrote about it when we did the shows here and later for the DVD. I remember seeing Willie Mays play here when he was with the Mets in the latter part of his career. We'd come to the games and sit in the bleachers. It was great to be able to come to a ballgame in the afternoon. That's how I got into the Cubs, through Goodman and coming here to watch day games."

Buffett moved on to bigger national stages, but his baseball heart stayed in Chicago. Fortunately, the Cubs were available on the WGN Superstation, but it took a bit of work. "Now it seems like it's such an effortless thing to see a Cubs game," he said. "I remember back then, I was living in Colorado at the time in the summers and Florida in the winters, but I had one of the very first satellite dishes, one of these monstrous things—you know, it was the eight-meter dish or something. I remember we had a crescent wrench, and we'd have to go out and physically turn it. We had a Sharpie marked where we could get certain channels, and WGN was one of them so we could pick up the Cubs games. So I go back to ancient satellite technology, which I thought was an amazing thing. I think if you look back on it, that's really kind of a remarkable thing for baseball and the Cubs because the Cubs became not just a Chicago team, in my humble opinion, they became an American team."

Buffett has been a consistent presence at Wrigley Field, singing the national anthem and "Take Me Out to the Ballgame" during postseason appearances, while quietly enjoying regular-season games with his crew at the park whenever their schedules allow.

The Labor Day 2005 shows at Wrigley were a no-brainer 10 years in the making. The chance to play a show at the home of the Cubs was a challenge Buffett couldn't resist. "It was the impossibility of it, everybody saying you can't do it," he said, when asked why the lure was so great. "You know that the Cubs would never let you come in and play a rock show. I took it as a challenge, but I also knew that they were great people. It was probably a 10-year process of coming in and out as we did on our normal kind of run through Chicago, which always included coming out to Wrigley. If the Cubs were in town, we'd come to a game. Not just me, my whole group. In the process of seeing people who worked for the Cubs who then came to our show, it came up. You know, somebody like John McDonough or Jay Blunk said, 'One day we ought to do this.' And I said, 'Do you really think that's possible?' And they said, 'No, but we ought to just try anyway.' I am of the 'all they can say is no' mentality, so I said let's go and see. It was that 10-year period of coming back and forth. I think there were a couple combination factors that came into play, some of them economics, some of them interesting, and some were people in baseball who were fans of mine. I loved that connection. The parrothead-to-Cub-fans connection was really a big part of this thing once it got to the decision-making level."

Playing Wrigley Field turned out to be anything but another tour stop. Hurricane Katrina had ravaged his beloved Gulf Coast only days before. When Buffett stepped out onto his center-field stage looking back at the crowd, he made sure to take it all in. "Let's just say the Cubs' season wasn't going too great at that point," he said. "There was the emotional thing because of Katrina. New Orleans was flooding at the other end of the line, and I was deeply involved because of my family and everything else there. Then I thought, 'What would Steve Goodman say about this?' So there was a huge pile of emotions going on. As a performer, what got me through is that there's something that gets you to your appointed rounds where you can appreciate the emotion of the moment. And you've got a job to do. What made me realize that was how good this place sounded. It was never built for anything like what we did. It was not only the sound and the natural acoustics of Wrigley

Field from center field, but because it was the opposite way from where everybody sat. It was magical. Then there were the sightlines of how wonderful it set up as a rock-and-roll thing with the stage. The natural comfort of being on that stage in Wrigley Field, with all those emotions going on, the place made me feel at ease. I walked out there to start the show. And I'll never forget that moment."

After several hours of enthralling a crowd wearing grass skirts on a grass infield, Buffett closed out his first Wrigley Field concert with a special tribute. For his last song of the night, a lone spotlight illuminated the far corner of the right-field bleachers, revealing Buffett and guitar player Mac McAnally. In a tribute to the recent devastation of Hurricane Katrina along the Gulf Coast and the memory of his good friend Steve Goodman, Buffett offered up a moving rendition of Goodman's "City of New Orleans" to end the show. With a nod to the Wrigley Field venue, the moment was a grand slam for the ages.

The concert adventure only deepened Buffett's love for the Cubs, and he sees even better days ahead and hopes that the team will enjoy the success he's found. "I guess I've always loved the underdog," he said. "I think in some ways it compares to my journey along this road because career-wise in those early days I was a club singer who very few people knew. Fortunately in Chicago, I found a following here which I have been loyal to and they have been loyal to me for a long, long time. So, in a way, I can kind of understand that connection with what a great fan base this town is. I got to appreciate a little bit of it, so I kind of feel that, as things have gone along for me, hopefully they will go along for the Cubs."

WRIGLEY FAVORITES

"I have to say the bleachers—up in the corner of the bleachers where I came that first time was my favorite part. I paid homage to that when we came to do the show. That's got to be my favorite part of the park. The other rush is just to get on the field and walk around. That's cool. My favorite part on the field is in front of the ivy in front of the 400-foot sign." —*Jimmy Buffett*

THE CONCERT AT WRIGLEY

"You think about it now and it was a no-brainer. The amazing thing to me when I got up there, first of all, I don't think they've ever had anybody in there to play before we played. We were second at Fenway, which we had done the year previous, and a lot of the Cubs guys came over and saw how well it did. I think also if I can brag about my crew and all, my guys do a wonderfully efficient job, and they're unsung heroes. There's a work ethic that I think connects the people that run this organization to the people that run my organization. There's not a lot of flamboyance out there. They're just hard workers, and we do our job and we do it well. I think that was appreciated before they turned over the keys of this place to us gypsies! It was a 10-year getting-to-know-each-other thing, and it seemed like such a natural at the end. There are a lot of people that have the satisfaction of knowing they were there when it wasn't such a natural idea, and they made it happen."

BEING PART OF WRIGLEY FIELD HISTORY

"I never think of it like that, but if it is, I'm glad to be a part of it. It seemed like a natural. After doing this a long time and going all over the world and all over this country, I think you have to know the history of where you're playing. As a performer, I don't want to walk onto the stage and not know if I'm in Detroit or Chicago or Minneapolis. I want to know what's going on. I have history in this city from a musical career and a love for this great city in middle America that I have appreciated and known for almost 40 years of my life. This is a cathedral, that's the way I look at it. It's not a ballpark. So I respect the history and I respect the place, and I want to use it that way when I play here."

WHEN THE CUBS WIN

"I'd like to be here when it happens. I think it's a game-winning home run into the street. Somebody just wins it in the bottom of the ninth. I've seen too many wonderful moments like that here when the Cubs win. It's one of those desperation moments when somebody knocks one out and it's over. I like that kind of drama."

JEFF GARLIN

A successful stand-up comedian has to have a tough skin, be able to accept failure, and still soldier on with a never-say-quit attitude. Sounds just like a Cubs fan, doesn't it? Jeff Garlin is both and has successfully climbed the ladder of show business success while maintaining his love for the Chicago National League ballclub. No matter where life takes him, the star of HBO's *Curb Your Enthusiasm* is not about to curb his ardor for the Cubs.

Like so many other Cubs fans, Garlin's addiction is a family affliction. "I got hooked through my father," he said. "He is a huge Cubs fan, so you sort of fall in line with that. He made me a Cubs fan. My son is a Cubs fan. The Cubs are his favorite team only because they are my favorite team. I follow the Cubs, he follows the Cubs. We watch it on WGN out in Los Angeles. My younger son is, too. It's just been handed down. I'm proud and happy to be a Cubs fan."

Garlin was hooked in 1969 and never let go. "Obviously, my first favorite player was Ernie Banks and of course, Ron Santo and Billy Williams," he said. "I could name the entire '69 lineup. I was seven years old, and it was my first season as a baseball fan. It was also my first season collecting baseball cards, so that was a big year."

The next year is also fondly remembered for his first visit to Wrigley Field. "My first Cub game was 1970. I went with my father," said Garlin. "I don't remember if the ivy was in full bloom, but my head was in full bloom. I was so excited to be here, and it seemed bigger than life. We got here early. Seeing Ron Santo walk along the wall and the fact that I was allowed to be that close to him was amazing. Amazing. We sat over by third base. I saw Ernie Banks, and I screamed out 'Ernie!' and began running to him. When I began my journey to him there were no kids around him. By the time I screamed out his name and ran to him, so

many people had gathered, I couldn't get to him. They were playing the Mets, and Jon Matlack was pitching. Yeah, it has all stuck with me."

The Cubs remained a big part of Jeff's life, and he took things a step further when he moved into Wrigleyville and a new version of *The Odd Couple.* "I lived with Conan O'Brien, Kenmore and Waveland, right next to the alley," he said. "From our back porch, we could see into the stadium. When you watched the game and you had your window open, it was better than surround sound. I was there in 1988, the year the lights came in. People said, 'Do the lights affect you?' And, yes, they woke me up. Night games from where my bedroom was, the lights shined in my window, and the helicopters when they were first putting them in woke me up. I did a lot of napping, too, so it really irritated my sleep. That was the only thing I minded. I still don't go to night games. I'm a day-game guy."

Now that Garlin is working and living on the West Coast, he looks for ways to maintain his allegiance and tries his best to see his team in person when they visit Dodger Stadium. "Thankfully, I get to see WGN out here," he said. "That's the only way I get to see the Cubs is on WGN." He finds time to make at least one visit to Wrigley Field each year and is a regular guest conductor for the seventh-inning stretch.

At the end of the day, Garlin says he isn't about to let go, no matter what heartache may lie ahead. "I would still be a Cubs fan despite all that I've been put through," he said. "It's like life. Every year is fresh with opportunity. The Yankees, every year is not fresh with opportunity, only disappointment. I think the Yankees' disappointment is greater because they have a black cloud over them unless they win the World Series. We're just thrilled to be Cubs fans. We're thrilled to be allowed in Wrigley Field. We're thrilled that we get to play games. It's all good. I love being a Cubs fan. I would never trade that for anything."

Actor and comedian Jeff Garlin, a lifelong
Cubs fan, sings at Wrigley.

CUBS LOVE

"I have loved them my whole life, even during the late '70s, the Kingman years. Those were tough. I'm a real Cubs fan. Anyone who gives up on them during the year is a real bandwagon person. Even when we're bad, I know that next year will be better, and I'm looking forward to spring training."

BASEBALL DREAMS

"Yeah, I always wanted to hear them say, 'Garlin is on the mound.' It was never a realistic dream at any point, even during Little League. I could go 4-for-4 with a home run, but there was never a day when I was going to the majors." —*Jeff Garlin*

WRIGLEY FIELD

"God, I love this place! I love to see the 'Hey, Hey' sign. I grew up listening to Jack Brickhouse. 'Hey, Hey!' It's always an honor and a privilege to come here. I will never stop saying that."

SINGING THE STRETCH

"The seventh inning for me is about pure joy. I was terrified the first year I did it. It's really strange. What's strange about it more than anything is that at that exact moment, it's like Pavlov's dog. They're trained. All the heads turn and look right at you. That's unsettling. I've never experienced anything like that in anything I've ever done, any stand-up show, any movie, TV. Nothing compares to that moment like, 'Okay, who is it? Jeff Garlin? I don't know who that is!'"

FAVORITE MOMENT

"There used to be a television/stereo store across the street. I forget the name of it, but I was in there. It was 1987. Last game of the season. Andre Dawson is at bat, and I don't remember if it was the last at-bat, it may have been the last at-bat. Harry Caray said, I remember the exact quote, 'It would be poetic justice if he could only hit one out.' Now, why would it be poetic justice? We were in last place. I didn't

understand that, but I fell for it, and Andre hit it out! He hit it out! I remember being in the store, and I was screaming. Thank God it was in Chicago and nobody thought I was nuts because they jumped in like, 'What happened?' 'Andre just hit it!' Poetic justice."

PERFORMING WITH CUBS IN THE AUDIENCE

"I was doing a show in Atlanta when the Cubs were playing down there, and I had a laugh about some of the guys on the team who were talking at my show. I told them I didn't talk while they were performing. I went to all three games of that series. Now, Rich Hill knows me, but he was standing in the on-deck circle looking right through me like he didn't know me. Did I talk to him? No! Derrek Lee said to me, 'C'mon down to the clubhouse when you're at the game to sing.' I did not! The last thing they need is the fat comedian coming down to bother them! I have respect!"

BILL MURRAY

"T.S. Eliot, the poet, once said 'April is the cruelest month.' But I don't think even that great man would have anticipated that the Cubs would lose their first four at home. I'm here today to turn this around, and I think with the help of the overrated and *not-such-a-big-deal-after-all* Montreal Expos, the Cubs will triumph today, here at the real Wrigley Building at the corner of Clark and Addison. Today it's baseball, the Cubs and the Expos."

Thus began the nine-inning odyssey of Bill Murray's day in the WGN broadcast booth on April 17, 1987. With Harry Caray sidelined due to a stroke, WGN and the Cubs had decided to turn to a star-studded roster of guest announcers for the first few weeks of the season, but it was Murray's performance that was so, well, noteworthy, that the Museum of Broadcast Communications requested a copy of the game for its archives.

Not surprisingly, Murray showed no reticence in attacking his one-day duties at the mike. After watching Steve Stone handle the *Leadoff Man* pregame show duties,

Bill Murray watches his first pitch sail over the back screen and into the crowd.

Murray was ready to jump right in and introduce the starting Expos lineup.

"Casey Candaele–he's no good. In right field is Mitch Webster–he's no good. At first is Andres, how would you folks say that? Galla-, Gallaraga. Vance Law is overrated. He's at second base. Tom Foley shouldn't even be playing. He's at shortstop. Herman Winningham. What, you're going to be afraid of a guy named Herman? We'll just throw it right down the plate, when he's up. They're no good. Shouldn't be a problem. I don't think there's any question that the names on the Cubs are a lot easier to pronounce and they seem to be a more like baseball-player names."

With that, Bill was off and running for the next three hours, offering a stream of commentary never heard before (or since) for the WGN-TV audience:

BEFORE THE NATIONAL ANTHEM

"Frankly, I love the 'O Canada' national anthem, because there is only like 10 words and I wish they'd let me sing it. It's one of the goofiest national anthems I've ever heard. It makes the national anthem of the United States sound like Beethoven's ninth. They've only got five words in the song, and they just keep saying them over and over again. I hope you Canadian folks call up and say something to whoever is in charge of your country about that theme song of yours."

THE MONTREAL TEAM

"They're playing the game in English so maybe the Expos will be confused." —*Bill Murray*

UMPIRES' GEAR DELAY

"Steve, the real problem today is there is a delay because of the umpires getting dressed. Now what is it that umpires do when they dress? How many problems can they have? It's basically the one color that they're wearing. It's not like they are holding up different sportcoats in front of the mirror and saying 'Well, Jocko, what do you think of this look?'"

BLEACHER BUMS

"The really bad ones are in right field. That's where the real criminal element is. These are people who take bad falls down the stairs and don't really know. I think that really adds to the confusion. People hear a really big roar and they think they've missed something, and it turns out that it's someone who just bounced down to the front row. I noticed that they have cut off beer here after the eighth inning, and I think that's a great rule. I'm not going on a soapbox here, Steve, but anybody who can't get drunk before the eighth inning doesn't belong here."

BILL'S MOTHER IN THE BOOTH

"Well, my mother has finally arrived at the ballpark and there is liquor on her breath. Now what's the story? What took you so long to get here? Well, the guys from the penal institution in Joliet managed to to make themselves known. Where have you been for seven-and-a-half innings? And there was some mixup with the tickets and there was a fight, and somebody started pushing, and the next thing you know the officers had the handcuffs on you. It's a sad, sad refrain. If the Cubs weren't winning, I'd be pretty upset.

"Ooooohhh, Bull Durham. Thank you, Bull. Thank you! Look at this, Mom. This is the kind of stuff you've been missing all day long. There's Bull going to his right. There's no chance. Miraculously, he pulls it out. This is the kind of excitement that's been going on here all day while you were in the drunk tank over on Halsted Street. Terrible.

"What's that fire truck doing out there? Did you have something to do with that? Did you set a fire out there again? You weren't throwing matches in the garbage were you? What are we going to do, take your word for it? We were all at the game.

"She thinks because she had nine kids and we're all working that she gets a free ride for the rest of her life, *and that's not true!* She'll be scrubbing floors later."

Murray the fan grew up watching Ernie Banks and was so enamored with his boyhood hero that he named his son Homer Banks Murray. "I used to misbehave at school so I could get home in time to catch the last couple of outs on TV. He was really all we had," he said. "Maybe you could get excited about Moose Moryn, but it was really all Ernie Banks. It's amazing that one guy on a second-division team could somehow hit 512 home runs. He was your guy. He was always upbeat and never got down about it. He just seemed so quiet in a way like a mystery, how could he play on a team that lost so much and still play so well. There was a lesson there."

He has been a loyal Cubs fan his whole life and always willing to be a part of the action–spending time with Harry in the booth during the first night game in 1988, electrifying the crowd with a stirring rendition of "Take Me Out to the Ballgame" during the 1998 wild-card game, and visting the booth whenever he was at Wrigley Field. Perhaps Murray was the missing piece to the puzzle in 2003 when he was unable to be see the Cubs postseason run due to a commitment to film *The Life Aquatic With Steve Zissou* in Italy.

Through it all, he keeps it in perspective. "I remember getting in an argument once during the '89 playoffs with somebody who said, 'you're going to get really mad if they lose,' recalled Murray. "I said, 'you just don't get it, do you? You just don't get it.' We've been losing the whole time. We know how to lose. Cub fans know how to lose. They're good losers. That's why they are such wonderful winners, because they understand how to be on the other side."

That experience on the other side has convinced Murray that success will never spoil his favorite team. In late 2007, he bristled at notions that a Cubs world championship would change the team forever. "That's like saying you wouldn't be you if were asleep," he said. "Isn't that exactly what's like? I don't accept that because the Cubs have already won the World Series (in the past) and they are the Cubs. Would the Cubs be the Cubs if they lost the World Series? That's sick thinking. You have to watch out for people like that."

You tell'em Bill. That's the confidence, hope, and understanding we expect from America's number one Cub fan.

BECOMING FRIENDS WITH MARK GRACE

"I've been in the minor league baseball for awhile. I was the part-owner of the Pittsfield Cubs, and it was an amazing team with Mark Grace, Joe Girardi, and a few other guys that made it to the big leagues from that team. Every time I would go to Pittsfield, they would get rained out. That's when I met Grace, during a rainout, and we just stood in the pouring rain for hours while they tried to get the game in. We were in the dugout, and I was just there trying to be funny. Once you've owned a slave and set him free, you always feel connected to a guy like Grace. Whenever I would go to the ballpark, I would scream 'Pittsfield' from the stands and watch his neck twitch. He realized that his former master was in the audience and he had better perform. We played together at Pebble Beach and became good friends, so I was never afraid to hit him up for tickets. For a guy who acts like there is feathers in his head, how he managed to show up every day and play Gold Glove baseball, well, just say his friends and family are just as excited as heck that he's still with us."

SUPREME COURT JUSTICE JOHN PAUL STEVENS

Many Cub fans tend to point to the heartbreak of '69 as the year they fell in love with the team, but for one of our nation's most celebrated jurists, his love affair with the Cubs goes back to the heartbreak of '29. Supreme Court Justice John Paul Stevens has the third-longest tenure in the Court's history, but long before he was interpreting and upholding the Constitution, he was head-over-heels in love with his hometown Cubs.

Justice Stevens cultivated his passion for the team by holing up next to the radio at every opportunity. "I'd listen to almost every game I could," he said. "I had done that for two or three seasons before I ever saw a game. At that time, which was back in 1927–29, quite a long time ago, the Cubs were a very fine team and they were a contender every year, whereas the Sox were contending for the cellar. So you tended to gravitate toward the contending team. I got hooked on the radio and primarily it was listening to Hal Totten, who was the WMAQ broadcaster, and Pat Flanagan, who was the WBBM announcer and who announced the game when the Cubs were away, using the ticker-tape approach."

Asked to recall his first game at Wrigley, Justice Stevens can clearly recount both the details and the disappointment. "The first game I went to was the first game of the World Series with the Athletics in 1929, when Connie Mack was managing. The Athletics had two excellent pitchers, Lefty Grove and George Earnshaw, and both were fastball pitchers. My dad got seats right behind home plate, and this was my first chance to see a ballgame. I was going to see all my heroes—Hack Wilson, Riggs Stephenson, Kiki Cuyler, Charlie Grimm—all the big hitters. Connie Mack, instead of pitching his fastball pitchers, pitched Howard Ehmke, who was a nothing-ball pitcher. He was a has-been, and I thought the Cubs would kill him. He struck out 13 Cubs, and that was the saddest day of my life. My first game, to see all my heroes, and have Howard Ehmke lay them down. I'll never forget that day." The A's won that game 3–1, before 50,740 stunned fans at Wrigley Field and went on to win the Series in five games.

Justice Stevens witnessed one of the most famous moments in baseball history three years later at Wrigley Field when he attended the 1932 World Series. He had a clear view of Babe Ruth's called shot and still keeps a scorecard of the game on display in his office at the Supreme Court. "My dad took me to the game. We had box seats behind third base, about 15 rows back. There are millions of people who claim to have been there, but I can assure you we were. I saw it, and it was really something."

At the end of World War II, his duties as a code-breaker in the United States Navy kept Justice Stevens from attending the Cubs' last World Series in 1945, but he remained near baseball after receiving his law degree. He worked with the House of Representatives committee that examined the game's anti-trust status in the early 1950s. While in private practice, Justice Stevens was witness to the inner workings of the game when he represented Charles O. Finley, the mercurial owner of the Athletics who made his home not far from Chicago in LaPorte, Indiana.

His work at the Supreme Court forces him to follow his boyhood team from a distance, but Justice Stevens found time to make a triumphant return to Wrigley Field in 2005. After taking a tour of the field and posing for pictures with players and umpires, he earned a roar from the crowd by firing a high fastball from the mound on his ceremonial first pitch.

WRIGLEY FIELD

"It does stand the test of time. Of course, they have lights now, which is new. The ivy is the same, and there are more seats across the street from left field. Basically the park is the same, it really is.

"I was away a good deal during the intervening years, but I did not follow it as closely as I grew older as I did when I was a kid, but I have always remained a fan and gone through one disappointing season after another in recent years, although I feel much more optimistic this year."

FAVORITE PLAYERS

"I had several from those early teams. I liked all the outfield. Riggs Stephenson was a great hitter. Hack Wilson, as I'm sure you know, was a great home-run champ, and Kiki Cuyler, who played in right field, stole a lot of bases. He was a great base stealer and he was a distant relative of our family, so he was a particular hero. Rogers Hornsby was a great player. The pitchers were Guy Bush, Charlie Root, and Pat Malone. I really admired the team at that time. They were a really powerful team."

BABE RUTH'S CALLED SHOT IN 1932

"There was a byplay going on between Guy Bush and Babe Ruth. I don't remember what the issue was, but they were razzing one another. Bush came out of the dugout and yelled something at Ruth. I thought Babe was responding to Bush [as he] pointed his bat at the scoreboard. I remember thinking he was saying, 'I'm going to knock you to the moon' or something like that. It seemed to be part of the interchange. I didn't interpret it as saying 'I'm going to hit a home run,' which, of course, he did. He then hit the next pitch out of the ballpark."
—*Supreme Court Justice John Paul Stevens*

Del Rice, Walt "Moose" Moryn, Don Cardwell, Ernie Banks, and Jerry Kendall
celebrate Cardwell's no-hit shutout against the Cardinals on May 15, 1960.

The Games

DON CARDWELL'S NO-HITTER

On May 15, 1960, newly acquired Cubs right-hander Don Cardwell took the mound and proceeded to mow down the St. Louis Cardinals for one of baseball's unlikeliest no-hitters. "I had been traded on Friday the 13th, but that certainly was not a bad omen two days later," said Cardwell. "Coming over to a new ballclub, you try to do your best."

Cardwell started the second game of the Sunday doubleheader, and it didn't take long to see that he was on his game. He walked Alex Grammas, the second batter of the game, on a close pitch, but after that, he used a blazing fastball to set down 26 Cardinals in a row. Years later, Cardwell recounted, "I said, 'Alex, how did you take that pitch?' He said, 'I never saw it.'"

"On that particular day, I have never seen a pitcher throw a baseball any harder," declared WGN sports editor Jack Rosenberg. "That would include Koufax and all the rest."

"He was in really good spirits and throwing the ball well," said Ernie Banks, who was at shortstop that day and had been presented with his 1959 Most Valuable Player trophy before the game. "Playing behind him, the feeling, the tension, the emotion was really going. It uplifted me, and I was just so inspired by it. I was really focused, and I hit a home run in the game. Later on, I saw Stan Musial, and he was in that game. He was telling me, 'Boy, you remember that game when Cardwell pitched the no-hitter against us? I was up there swinging at sound.' He was throwing the ball so hard and with so much stuff on it that they couldn't hit it." Musial's strikeout ended the eighth inning. In the WGN booth, Vince Lloyd read a live commercial for Oklahoma Oil, then scurried down to the field, hoping to do a live interview after the game.

The season's biggest crowd of 33,543 watched anxiously as Carl Sawatski opened the ninth inning with a screamer to right, but George Altman was able to back up to the doors along the wall to keep the no-hitter alive. George Crowe flied out to Richie Ashburn in center, leaving Cardwell with one out to get.

"The last play of the game, Joe Cunningham was a good left-handed hitter for the Cardinals, and he hit one of those semi–line drives to left field, and your head just pops instantly when you see it's going that way. And here is Moose [Moryn], and he's coming. I had never played with Moose except watching for a couple days, and he made a great catch. Then you all know what broke loose. There were all kinds of people coming onto the field, and the ushers couldn't hold them back."

In the booth, Rosenberg watched as Moryn's catch sent Jack Brickhouse into a frenzy. "I still remember it as if it were yesterday on the final out when Joe Cunningham hit a fly ball that was sinking to left field, and Jack was about ready to jump out of his chair. I can hear Jack yet, 'C'mon, Moose!' Moose Moryn scooped that ball up for the no-hitter, and what a mob scene at Wrigley Field."

As the crowd stormed onto the field to mob its new hero, Cardwell had more trouble getting to the locker room than he did with the Cardinals. "I was with Vince Lloyd, and I didn't want to hurt anybody. In those days we had metal spikes. I wanted to get away because they clustered us. Vince Lloyd was down on the field and he said, 'Don, let's get out of here before somebody gets hurt—me!'" After a chaotic postgame interview on WGN, it took Cardwell 20 minutes to make his way down the left-field line to the Cubs locker room.

The postgame scene in the locker room was a bit muted, only because Cardwell barely knew his new teammates. He would go on to an 8–14 season with the Cubs that year and played two more seasons in Chicago before heading to Pittsburgh, then New York. He passed away in January 2008. Cubs fans can be forgiven if they overlook the fact that Cardwell won eight games and a World Series ring with the 1969 Mets. For one afternoon's magic, he will be a Cub forever.

THE HEROES OF HIS NO-HITTER

"I think I had a great catcher in Del Rice. He came out early in the ballgame and asked if there was anything I wanted him to call. He was an experienced catcher, and I said, 'You call the game.' As it turned out, he called a pretty good ballgame. The savior was the play that Walt [Moose] Moryn made for the last out. People would say he wasn't agile, and I say I don't think so either, but he sure did a fine job, didn't he?"

THE AFTERMATH

"It was a great feeling. You didn't realize it until later because you really didn't have time to let it sink in. Then you say, 'There it is. It's a no-no.' It's something that you will never forget. If everybody you meet who says they were there was there, that ballpark would have to have held over 100,000 people." **—Don Cardwell**

PITCHING AT WRIGLEY FIELD

"There's a lot of heartaches pitching in this ballpark. Certain times of the year you have to pitch under the plate because certain times of the year the wind comes out of the south, and I have seen pop flies where the shortstop goes back. The next thing you know, he gives up on it, and the left fielder starts backing up to the left-field wall and then it's gone. You try to take advantage of it when the wind is coming in. You just put it in there and say, 'Here, hit it.' A lot of times it's a home run when it leaves the bat, but the wind holds it up and brings it back in for your outfielders. I had a center fielder who backed up to the wall, figured it was gone and dropped his head, and the ball hit him right on his button on top of his hat and knocked him out. I think it's a great park to pitch in, but you have to keep the ball down."

PLAYING WITH RON SANTO

"The first time he joined us was in Pittsburgh. Either the first or second ball that was hit to him, he threw 30 feet over the first baseman's head. I was sitting on the steps of the dugout and said, 'Welcome to the big leagues.' I just told him when he came in, 'Ron, don't try and do everything yourself.' I said, 'Relax like it's the minor leagues or in spring training. Just catch the ball and zip it over there. Everything will be all right.'"

THE 23–22 GAME

The notion of Wrigley Field as a hitters' paradise doesn't take into account that the wind actually blows in about 60–70 percent of the time.

What sticks in the mind of baseball fans are the days when that wind is howling out and any pop fly up into the breeze has a chance to be a souvenir in the bleachers. Days like May 17, 1979, when the Cubs and Phillies hooked up in a 23–22 donnybrook at the Windy Confines.

A game-time glance at the jet stream headed toward the bleachers served notice that the pitchers were in for a long day. "I remember going out that day and the wind was howling. It was howling!" said Larry Bowa, who was playing shortstop for the Phillies. "Any time you go to Wrigley Field, the first thing you do is look up at the flags because if it's blowing in, it's gonna be real quick, 3–2, 2–1. But if it's blowing out, you've got a chance of missing your dinner reservations downtown. I remember the flag was at attention, just blowing straight out, and I said, 'This could be a long game.'"

Not for Cubs starter Dennis Lamp, who had been injured and expected to miss his start that day. Mike Krukow was set to take the ball for the Cubs, but Lamp said he felt good enough to go, a decision that didn't exactly leave Krukow up in arms. "As soon as we came down Irving Park,

Mike Schmidt swats the final home run in the 1979 slugfest between the Cubs and Phillies.

took a right, came down Clark, and checked out the flags, and it was like howling, Jack!" laughed Krukow. "I charted pitches that day. I had to go on the disabled list because I had carpal tunnel syndrome or whatever they call it, but I had it. It was bad. Fifty hits, the chart was like four pages. I went through three pens, and I had the ink all over my uniform. It was unbelievable."

The Phillies set the tone from the get-go, scoring a touchdown in the first inning off Lamp and Donnie Moore, capped by a home run from their starter Randy Lerch, who had a 7–0 lead to work with before he stepped to the mound. "This game is four days old, and we haven't even batted yet," said Jack Brickhouse, emitting a rare gripe in the booth after watching the carnage in the first.

Lerch didn't get a chance to hit again because like his counterpart Lamp, he was showering in the first inning. Cubs hitters wasted no time getting in their hacks against him, opening the game with four straight hits culminating in a Dave Kingman home run. Two more runs followed, and at the end of one wild inning, the Phillies led by an extra point, 7–6.

Both starters had lasted only a third of an inning, and the fun was just beginning, especially for the Phils, who bashed about Moore and Willie Hernandez to go up 15–6 after three. With all the offense on both sides, anybody who wasn't hitting homers got lost in the shuffle. "The thing I remember is that everybody was hitting home runs, but I got five hits that day!" said Bowa. "It was a big game for me." Bowa and Pete Rose scored runs 20 and 21 in the top of the fifth, and the Phillies extended the lead to 21–9.

At that point, the winds of change began to blow the Cubs' way. After the Phils walked Ivan DeJesus to force in a run, momentum shifted to the Cubs dugout. "Tug McGraw threw a 3–2 curveball, whoop, ball four and we score," remembered Krukow. "I turned to Bruce Sutter and I said, 'We're going to win this game.' We all felt we were. I'll never forget that game."

Bill Buckner, who had a huge day with four hits and seven RBIs, continued McGraw's woes when he drilled a grand slam to right. Two batters later, Jerry Martin followed with a two-run shot, and the crowd was going crazy as the Cubs pulled to within five. Buckner can still remember the offense coming to life. "I had four hits, seven RBIs, and a grand slam, and I didn't even have our best game," he said. "Kingman had three home runs!" After five innings, it was Phillies 21, Cubs 16.

In the sixth, two Cubs RBI groundouts cut the lead to three before Kingman unloaded again. His third homer of the day pulled the Cubs to within 2, at 21–19, a titanic blast that carried over Waveland and landed three houses down Kenmore. The Phils added a run in the top of the seventh, but the Cubs weren't finished. In the eighth, Buckner and Martin each drove in a run with a single. Barry Foote followed with another single that plated Steve Ontiveros, and the Cubs' comeback was complete at 22–22. Bobby Murcer had a chance to put the Cubs on top, but his roller to second left two men on and sent the teams to the ninth.

At this point, Brickhouse felt the need to inform the audience the unfathomable score on the screen was indeed correct. "If you've just gotten home and you are looking at your television set and you see the superimposition of the score, you are probably saying to yourself, 'I have to call the television repairman because of the ghosting on [my] screen. I see a two and a two and a two and a two.' Ladies and gentleman, forget it. That happens to be the score." After a day of offensive fireworks, the bats on both sides took a well-deserved breather, and neither team scored in the last frame.

Both clubs were at the back of their bullpen, and the Cubs looked to have the advantage with Bruce Sutter over Philadelphia's struggling Rawly Eastwick as the game went to extra innings. Mike Schmidt had started the scoring for the Phils with a homer in the first, and in the tenth, he added a bookend as he got hold of a Sutter splitter that didn't drop and yanked it over the left-field wall to put the Phillies on top. Maybe the biggest surprise of the day was that Schmidt had only two home runs, because he hit 50 in his career at Wrigley Field.

In the Cubs tenth, Kingman had a chance to match Schmidt's 1976 Wrigley feat of four homers in a game and send the contest to the eleventh, but he struck out wildly for the second out. Steve Ontiveros followed with a weaker grounder to Schmidt to end it, making the final 23–22 Phillies and adding another ignominious notch on the Cubs' franchise belt. "I remember coming all the way back to tie it up," Buckner said. "We had the best relief pitcher in baseball available, and they had used everyone up. We thought we were going to win, but we ended up losing on that Schmidt home run. We lost, but it was quite a game. It was fun, but it was still a tough game."

Included in the final stats were 24 hits and five homers for the Phillies, who were also the beneficiaries of 12 Cubs walks. The Cubs tallied 26 hits and five homers in the seemingly endless display of offense. "I think maybe that game is still going on," said WGN sports editor Jack Rosenberg, who saw the whole thing. "I may have to check."

BILL BUCKNER

Bill Buckner may be known for other things in other cities, but on the North Side of Chicago, he is revered for his lethal bat and fierce desire while playing on some victory-challenged teams during eight seasons at Wrigley Field. After coming to the majors as a fleet-footed outfielder with the Dodgers in 1970, Buckner's game changed drastically when he severely sprained his ankle sliding into second base in 1975. He was traded to the Cubs for Rick Monday in 1977 and quickly became a fan favorite for his relentless style of play. Among his many accomplishments while with Chicago, "Billy Buck" won the National League batting title in 1980 and added a Gold Glove to go with it.

Cubs shortstop Ivan DeJesus watched Buckner lay it all on the line every day and feels the Cubs first baseman never got enough credit. "He was an outstanding player," said DeJesus. "He gave everything he had. He went through a lot of injuries in his career, but when he was here he was the batting champion. Not only as a player, he was a great person, a great teammate, and he tried to help everyone. Even though he didn't have the greatest tools, he gave it everything he had, just like Pete Rose."

He is too modest to bring it up, but Buckner will grudgingly acknowledge how hard he worked to get on the field each day. "I was a decent player, but I don't think too many people could have done it, playing under the conditions I played under," he said. "I iced my body down three times a day for 16 years. To me, it was worth it. Some people probably wouldn't think so. I loved to play, so I did whatever I had to do to get out there."

Buckner's grit was not lost on his teammates and cemented his stature as a leader. "I think Bill Buckner was a great player," said Larry Bowa. "Not a good player, a great player. The thing that bothers me most is that all you hear about Bill Buckner is the ground ball that went through his legs, which completely is a joke as far as I'm concerned. He was a great hitter; he played in a lot of pain. He loved the game of baseball. You could tell by the way he prepared himself for every game. He could hardly walk, and he would go out there with bad knees, bad ankles, bad everything. He was a tremendous player, and his numbers back it up."

When he was out there, the fans needed to be ready in the stands because foul balls off Buckner's bat were almost automatic each time he came to the plate. Buckner never struck out more than 40 times in a season and finished his career with only 453 strikeouts in more than 9,397 at-bats. "I hated to strike out, ever since I was in Little League," he admitted. "It may have hurt me at times, but I could always put the ball in play. If I had a borderline pitch a couple of inches off the plate, I tried to put that in play. If I were going to go back and change anything in my career, I might have struck out some more. Not intentionally, but I could have been a little bit more aggressive with two strikes in certain situations. Now, there's a time when you can't afford to strike out, like a runner at third with less than two outs, and you have to put the ball in play. Instead of lunging at a pitch two inches off the plate

Bill Buckner drove in seven runs, but it wasn't enough
during the Cubs 23–22 loss to Philadelphia in 1979.

to put it in play, maybe I could have been a bit more patient and hit for a bit more power. I just hated to strike out. I didn't want to deal with it. I probably had 10 hits in my career where I literally threw the bat at the ball with two strikes. I can remember a few times where I hit it on the bounce."

In 1982, Buckner tallied 201 hits, an impressive total for a player who wasn't beating out many infield hits. Despite his injuries, he was so competitive that he could find another gear if needed. "For the first couple years I was with the Cubs, I struggled from the standpoint of just getting around," said Buckner. "It started getting a little better later on. If I smelled a hit, I could pump it up a little bit. Something about base hits makes you run faster. I was able to get a few infield hits. Even though I wasn't fast, I could pick the right time to steal a base. If I had the opportunity to do it, I did it. The injuries certainly changed my game from being a fast guy to a slow guy. It made me a better run producer: hitting further down I had to drive in some runs. The first year I drove in 100 runs with the Cubs, I did it with only 15 home runs. You know you have to be pretty good with men in scoring position when we only scored 500 and some runs that year, so that was probably my best year run production–wise for the opportunity."

"Bill Buckner and I became very good friends," said pitcher Mike Krukow. "He was the heart of that club. Buckner was a guy who was an absolute champion; he was a winner. It was tough for him to play here in those years when they did the rebuild here. He had an ankle that did not move. It was frozen. There was no flexibility in his ankle. It was just locked. What he did before the game and after the game to even play was excruciating to watch. He was the heart of the Cubs. He was the darling of Chicago on some pretty bad teams. I'll tell you one thing. You can have champions on bad teams, and he certainly was one of them."

He was certainly a champion in the eyes of the Cubs fans throughout the drought seasons of the late '70s and early '80s, and his popularity continues to this day. "Those fans are Midwest, blue-collar, get your uniform dirty, play hard," said Buckner. "They like that stuff. The Midwest people as a group are probably the most solid people in the country. They're good. They love baseball. Obviously, the winning in recent years helps. They sell out every game. When I played, during the summer they would sell out, but during the school year they didn't fill it up like they do now. It's a pretty exciting place to be now. I enjoy going back. You know it will be a full house, with a lot of enthusiasm."

THE CUBS' GREAT START IN 1977

"That was probably the most exciting months I had there playing. When you're on a team that is overachieving, better than everybody expected, and having everybody get excited. That's the only team I ever played on where you got a standing ovation just for taking the field to start the game. That was a pretty exciting couple of months. It was a little bit of a letdown when Sutter got hurt. For those few months, it was exciting." —*Bill Buckner*

THE 1980 BATTING TITLE

"I came on at the end of the season. I got hot, and some of the other guys slipped down. I really didn't come into the picture until there was about a week left. All of a sudden, I jumped in front, and we had the last game of the year. I could have sat out, and there was no way I could have lost, but the only way I was going to lose was if I went 0-for-4. Joey Amalfitano was our manager, and he kind of wanted me to sit out. I decided to play because I thought if the shoe was on the other foot, I would want the leader to play. We were in Pittsburgh, and I did go 0-for-4 while Keith Hernandez of the Cards got a hit his first time up, but then he didn't get another hit. I had to sweat it out a bit. What was fun was to have your teammates and coaches pulling for you. They were pretty excited about it, which made me feel better."

CUBS FAITHFUL

"The Cubs were pretty well the national team largely because of WGN. For people all over the country, that was their daily soap opera. That was pretty cool. As we traveled around, we had a big following in every ballpark, but now it's even bigger. People come from all over to see them in spring training in Arizona. Here in Boise, probably the favorite team for people to go watch during the spring is the Cubs. It seems like anybody I know that goes down there, the first ticket they buy is to the Cub game. I played with L.A. and then later Boston, so I was in some big markets. Probably my best memories are with the Cubs, though. I think if I were going to pick a team, they would be it for me."

CHICAGO LIVING

"I lived down on Belden in what used to be an old Lutheran church. They left the steeple part of it, which was about five or six stories high, and then they built around it. It was pretty interesting. It had the big arch windows in it and stained glass. I think maybe it helped me out living there—I didn't have to go too far to pray for the wind to be blowing out! It was funny because the first thing I would do in the morning is climb up to the top floor and see how the flags were blowing down at the ballpark. If the wind was blowing out, I was in a hurry to get to the park. If it was blowing in, I fiddled around and wasn't exactly racing to the park."

WRIGLEY FIELD

"It is great. The fans here have been great to me. Probably the highlight of my career was playing seven years at Wrigley Field. I played with the Dodgers at the start of my career, and they were a great organization back in the '70s. The people in the Midwest and especially at this ballpark were so friendly that you looked forward to coming to the park. They made you want to play hard. They appreciated hard play."

FENWAY AND WRIGLEY

"They are two very different ballparks, yet they both can have a big outcome on the game. You can have big scores, or sometimes the conditions keep the score down, but both places make it fun to watch. I never hit a home run over the Green Monster because all my power was to right field."

FAVORITE PLAYER

"I grew up in the Bay Area, so I was a big Willie Mays fan as a kid. I was fortunate enough to see Stan Musial play at the end of his career, so that was great."

STRIKING OUT

"I never struck out three times in one game. I came close once when we were playing the Pirates. I had struck out the first two times up, and the next time up, I popped the ball up behind home plate. It was the only time in my life I ever hoped the catcher would get my pop-up."

SUCCESS AGAINST STEVE CARLTON

"I did get a bunch of hits in about three years. He used to get me out a lot with that nasty slider. I said, 'You know what, I'm gonna move right up on the plate and look fastball for the first pitch of the game, and after that, I'm sitting on the slider.' So I did that for about three years, and I got him and hit some home runs off him. Sometimes, it was like he was in a trance, and he didn't know who was hitting, so I don't think he knew how well I was doing over that period of time. After about three years of me wearing him out, he woke up and drilled me in the ribs, and that party was over. I wasn't sitting on that slider anymore!"

LAST HOME RUN

"I hit my only inside-the-park home run when I was at Fenway. I was 40 years old and in my last year. I hit it out to right field, where Claudell Washington was tracking it, and he ended up falling into the stands. He came out of the stands with hot dog and mustard all over him, and the ball

Burt Hooton's knuckle-curve mystified
the Phillies during his 1972 no-hitter.

came in with mustard on it. I made it around the infield in about two minutes."

BURT HOOTON'S NO-HITTER

On April 16, 1972, making only his fourth major league start, 22-year-old Burt Hooton electrified a chilly crowd of only 9,583 at Wrigley Field with a stunning no-hit win over the Philadelphia Phillies, 4–0.

It was only the second game of the season for the Cubs because of the players' strike that spring. Cubs vice president John Holland almost canceled the game that day because of the wet conditions and a bitter north wind, but there was a good advance ticket sale, so the game went on. The few fans who stuck it out were rewarded with a gem delivered by the Cubs' top draft pick out of the University of Texas.

"The things I remember were that it was cold, damp, and the wind was blowing in from the north," said Hooton. "Somebody [Denny Doyle] hit a line drive, and Don Kessinger jumped up to make a real nice catch on it. I remember Greg Luzinski hitting a ball that I thought was out of the ballpark, but of course the wind kept it in the park, and Rick Monday caught it in the ivy just in front of the basket."

Randy Hundley was behind the plate and happy to be a part of history after having missed both of Ken Holtzman's no-hitters. "It was a pretty chilly day," he said. "It was cloudy, a little bit nippy, and a little bit damp, too. It had rained some. The wind was blowing in, and Hooton had this knuckle-curveball that was unbelievable. How he threw it I have no idea. But he pushed the ball out with his knuckles, and the ball just turned over and got to the plate and boom! Just like rolling it off the table. He had pretty good command of his fastball. He didn't have much speed, but he could throw it in and out. We just dazzled them that day, and what a thrill it was."

Hundley guided Hooton in and out of several jams as he walked seven Phillies through the first eight innings.

On another day, Cubs manager Leo Durocher might have lost patience with the rookie who struggled with his control, but Durocher was home sick with a virus and acting manager Pete Reiser let Hooton continue.

Hooton was at his best in the ninth inning. Willie Montanez grounded to Glenn Beckert at second, then Deron Johnson flailed at Hooton's knuckle-curve for a strikeout to set the scene for Luzinski to get another crack. The Bull went down swinging, and Hooton was now the one who was overwhelmed. "I walked seven guys, so the best inning I actually had was the ninth inning. That was a three-up, three-down inning with two strikeouts. After it was over, I didn't know what to do."

Rick Monday played center field that day and tracked down Luzinski's seventh-inning blast but got more of a kick out of watching television when he got home. "My biggest memory of Burt Hooton's no-hitter," he said, "was not the day of the no-hitter, it was the evening of the no-hitter, and here's why: Ernie Banks was doing some sports on WGN television, and he came on that night when they went to the sports segment. Ernie said it was a big deal at Wrigley Field, and he went on, and all of a sudden you see Ernie on camera and he says, 'At Wrigley Field, everybody was rootin' and tootin' for Burt Hooton.'"

Handling the instant fame turned out to be Hooton's toughest task that day. He went 8–14 for the Cubs that season, and after two more losing years was traded to the Dodgers in 1975, where he flourished and pitched in three World Series.

HIS FAMOUS "KNUCKLE-CURVE"

"First of all, it's a curveball. Everybody thinks it's a knuckle-ball, but it was a curveball. It's just a different way of throwing it. I was 14 years old, sitting at home, watching *The Game of the Week* in 1964. Hoyt Wilhelm was pitching, and he was a knuckleballer who had been around forever. I even got to pitch against him at one point when I finally caught up to him. Dizzy Dean and Pee Wee Reese were going on and on about his knuckleball. I was always one to experiment, and I had a

Pony League practice that afternoon. After the game was over, I shot off to practice and started playing catch and decided I was going to learn how to throw a knuckleball. The problem was nobody showed me how to throw it. I just figured if it was a knuckleball you had to put your knuckles down on the ball. Later, I found out it was a fingertip ball. Anyway, I folded my knuckles down on the seam of the ball, and I had heard them say you have to push it out. I was always really loose-wristed, and when I would flip my wrist and push it out, it would always have a forward rotation on it. I never could throw a regular knuckleball. I even had guys like Charlie Hough try to show me how to throw a regular knuckleball. With my knuckle-curve, the harder I threw it, the better it got, but at that time I didn't know what I had, so I figured I would start throwing it in games and see what happened. I kept throwing it and nobody could hit it, so it became my curveball."

AFTER THE NO-HITTER

"What I remember was that when the no-hitter was over with, here I was a kid from South Texas who hadn't even been in pro ball for a year, and now I'm at Wrigley Field pitching a no-hitter in my fourth major league start. All of a sudden, the city went crazy for a while, and there was a media onslaught, and I was thinking that I don't know how to handle this. What do I do? I wasn't expecting all that. I was used to pitching games and going home and getting ready for the next game. That probably sticks in my mind more than anything."

PITCHING AT WRIGLEY FIELD

"If you're pitching in Wrigley Field, the first thing you do as you're coming to the ballpark is see which way the flags are blowing. If it's blowing out, it's the worst ballpark to pitch in. If it's blowing in, it's the best ballpark to pitch in. I've seen balls popped up to shortstop that you think are going to be easy go out to left field. I've seen other balls, like Luzinski's blast, that, I don't care how hard you hit it, you can't get it out of there." **—Burt Hooton**

THE CUBS FAITHFUL

"I got my career started here, but back when I played, I still remember the stadium with 1,500 fans in it in September when we were out of it. Now to look at it, and to see it full every game they play, no matter what the standings are, no matter what the weather's like, no matter what the situation is, to me it gives you a good idea of how faithful these fans are."

KERRY WOOD'S 20 STRIKEOUTS

Sixteen years after Burt Hooton's no-hitter, another big Texan and top Cubs draft pick burst onto the stage at Wrigley Field in only his fifth big-league start. On May 6, 1998, 20-year-old Kerry Wood turned in one of the most dominant single-game pitching performances in the history of the game when he struck out 20 Houston Astros and allowed just one base hit in a complete-game 2–0 win at Wrigley Field. Wood gave up a single to Ricky Gutierrez in the third inning and hit Craig Biggio with a pitch in the sixth. His 20 strikeouts tied the major league record for a nine-inning game, set twice by Roger Clemens (April 29, 1986, and September 18, 1996). Wood opened the game with five straight strikeouts and later had stretches of five and seven in a row. His stuff was electric, his composure amazing, and his performance simply dazzling.

On the mound, the rookie was totally locked in. "Honestly, it felt like I was playing catch out there," Wood said. "The game just slowed down. I took in everything. I was able to look around and enjoy the fans that were doin' it up. Not too many times when you're out on the hill does the game slow down that much where you can really take it all in. For whatever reason, that day it seemed like everything was kind of in slow motion."

In the broadcast booth, it was quickly apparent to Steve Stone that this day was going to be different. "Watching how the Houston Astros approached him that day, for one day in the life of Kerry Wood, he probably understood how it

Kerry Wood's 20 strikeouts came in only his fifth major league start.

felt to be godly, as far as a pitcher is concerned, because they didn't touch the ball. They didn't get close to another hit. It was impossible."

Sitting next to Stone, Chip Caray felt the same way. "What was so amazing about it was how unexpected it was," said Caray. "I remember the day. It was a cold, misty, soggy day at the ballpark. The visibility wasn't particularly good, but very early on we knew Kerry had unbelievable stuff. His slider was breaking two feet, his curveball off the table, his fastball was exploding past hitters."

Ron Santo also felt goose bumps early on. "I've never felt that way before," he said. "That's the first game I've ever seen that the hitters had no chance." High praise from Santo considering that he faced Sandy Koufax when the Dodgers lefty threw a perfect game against the Cubs in 1965.

More surprisingly, the receiver that day was third-string catcher Sandy Martinez, who was working with Wood for the first time. "Scott Servais was our regular catcher. I'm not sure what happened, but Sandy and I were on the same page for a couple of hours." If his other teammates avoided him on the bench for superstition's sake, Wood didn't notice. "I didn't know most of the guys because I'd only been up for a couple of starts."

The victims:

1st–Craig Biggio (swinging), Derek Bell (swinging), Jeff Bagwell (called)

2nd–Jack Howell (swinging), Moises Alou (swinging)

3rd–Brad Ausmus (swinging)

4th–Bagwell (called), Howell (called)

5th–Alou (called), Dave Clark (called), Ricky Gutierrez (called)

6th–Shane Reynolds (called)

7th–Bagwell (swinging), Howell (swinging), Alou (swinging)

8th–Clark (swinging), Gutierrez (swinging), Ausmus (called)

9th–Bill Spiers (swinging), Bell (swinging)

After Derek Bell took a feeble chop to become the 20th victim, the media mob descended on Wood, who was in a daze as he did a postgame interview on WGN-TV. "That's when the chaos started. I was calm and collected during the game. As soon as that last pitch was made, a lot of stuff changed in my life."

"I've seen major league hitters strike out a lot, but I've never seen them miss curveballs and sliders and fastballs by as much as they missed the ball that Kerry delivered that day," said Stone. "It was one of the most overpowering, one of the most dominant, games I had ever seen."

Wood became only the second pitcher in history to strike out as many men as his age (17-year-old Bob Feller also turned the trick for Cleveland). He had a great laugh later that year with the Astros' Derek Bell. "He [Bell] made the last out, and we went back to Houston later in the season," said Wood. "He came up to me and said he wanted me to get it, and I called him on it. He said he wanted me to get it, and that's why he was swinging like that. I thought that was pretty funny. Bagwell, Biggio, and those guys, I respect what those guys have done in the game. When you respect the game, the veteran players tend to have a little respect for you. Those guys were great. Looking back on it, that was a pretty good lineup. At the time you don't think about it. I was young enough and dumb enough not to know what I was doing. I'm glad I'll be able to show my son that tape."

CUBS FANS' PASSION

"I think it boggles a lot of people's minds, especially fans of the other teams. It's amazing. It's an amazing place. The Cubs fans are definitely different from any other place I've been. Obviously, the organization and the teams have gotten better the last four or five years, but when I first came in we didn't have the best teams. We were struggling, but we were sold out every day. Win, lose, or draw, Cubs fans are the best fans. They love their Cub players, they love the atmosphere, they love coming to Wrigley Field, and as players, we love it too. It's an awesome feeling to be able to come out and come here to work each day." —Kerry Wood

The celebration is on after the Cubs win in Pittsburgh to clinch the 1984 Eastern Division title.

WRIGLEY FIELD

"You know what? I love just the ins and outs of the clubhouse. Going behind the scenes. The history in the stadium is obviously tremendous. Knowing that Fergie Jenkins, Billy Williams, Santo played here—roamin' the halls of the same stadium as these guys. It's a special place, it really is. I guess my favorite place obviously would be out there on the mound pitching, but I like the ins and outs of the clubhouse and the concourse, the whole thing."

WGN-TV

"I remember watching WGN coming home from school. I'd catch the last four innings of the game, and I was in Texas. WGN obviously helps the recognition of this team where we have national exposure that a lot of teams don't have. That plays a big part of the loyalty of the fans. Certain parts of the season, for the day games, we're the only game on. People watch us, and it's nationwide, so we've got a huge following."

PLAYING FOR THE CUBS

"You can never imagine. It never crosses your mind how special that it is. They [the fans] take you in and you become one of their own. They live and die with you. You handle it the right way and they will stick with you. Some guys don't. They have become very passionate. Their expectations have raised quite a bit since 2003, and that's great. It's definitely past due. These Cubs fans and Cub Nation deserve a winner."

THE '84 CLINCHER

After 39 years in the desert of second-division finishes, Cubs fans finally reached a small but welcome portion of the Promised Land in 1984 in the unlikely location of Three Rivers Stadium in Pittsburgh. There the Cubs clinched the Eastern Division title and set off a celebration that gave us a glimpse of how crazy things might get when the team finally wins that elusive world championship.

A five-game losing streak the previous week had the Cubs faithful in a nervous mood, but the team rebounded to sweep a doubleheader in St. Louis to set up a possible clincher on Monday, September 24, in Pittsburgh. A meager crowd of 5,472 was on hand, most of them Chicago fans who'd made the trek to witness history. In the booth, Harry Caray seemed determined to read the names of every single one of them as the game started. Harry was joined by a special guest, Jack Brickhouse, who was the VIP guest announcer on WGN for the night.

Ryne Sandberg didn't find out until that morning how special the game was. "I had to learn what a magic number was because I didn't have any experience with what a magic number meant. I knew that there were about 10 games left, but, 'What's the magic number, what do they mean by that?' So I went to Ron Cey and Larry Bowa, and they had to explain it. 'Oh, okay, so if we win tonight, that clinches it.' That's how naïve I was at 24 years old. We clinched that night, and that was one of the biggest thrills in my career."

>>

"We all had so much confidence."

—Rick Sutcliffe

>>

Rick Sutcliffe was given the start that night, a day earlier than scheduled so he would be available if the Cubs needed him under catastrophic circumstances for the season's final weekend. Despite the nervousness of the preceding days as whispers of another collapse surrounded the team, Sutcliffe had a feeling that the Cubs' moment was finally at hand. "I remember walking to the bullpen that night," said Sutcliffe. "There was a huge sign that said, '39 Years of Suffering Are Enough.' I went up to the guy, and I'm not one of those guys that is cocky or whatever. As I walked in, I said, 'Is that your sign?' He said, 'Yeah,' and I handed him the ball I warmed up with and said, 'We're going to end it tonight.' We all had so much confidence."

Gary Matthews, one of six Cubs to drive in 80 or more runs for the year, singled in Ryne Sandberg in the top of the first, and the Cubs were in business. "I remember it like it was yesterday with Sandberg on first," said Matthews. "He was taking off and running. I hit a ball in the gap to score Ryno, and I ended up getting the game-winning hit that night. It was finally getting the monkey off your back, so to speak. To be able to clinch it, and to be able to have the games that we played in St. Louis prior to that, was great. A lot of fans came up, I remember, to Pittsburgh. It was just bedlam. It was really nice, and I'm sure the city of Chicago must have gone just crazy."

The Cubs added a run in the second when Sutcliffe helped his own cause with an RBI single to make the lead 2–0. Keith Moreland bunted for a hit in the third, and Sandberg scored on a throwing error to put the margin at three. After the Pirates nicked Sutcliffe for a run following a Joe Orsulak triple, the Cubs came right back with an insurance run in the fifth to sooth their anxious manager.

"As a player, I was never real nervous," said Jim Frey. "As a manager, I was never real nervous. Sometimes I'd be nervous before the game or after the game or whatever, but during the game I never was. That game I was nervous. Because all of a sudden we had a lead and now, how are we going to hold on? A lot of athletes don't want to admit it, but there's a lot of anxiety in winning. Especially if you get up early, you don't want to blow it. Well, there was some anxiety there. We got a two-run lead, and I remember that we had a man on third, a man on first, a one- or two-run lead, and they played the infield back. It was a slow groundball by Davis, and we got that extra run, which was like gold to me. That extra run was like gold! I said, 'Now we've got a couple more innings, and let's hang on.' And we hung on. That was quite an exciting evening."

Despite not having his best fastball, Sutcliffe was masterful, facing only one man over the limit going into the ninth inning. He quickly retired the first two hitters, and with the crowd roaring, Larry Bowa took a moment to tell his double-play partner to hang on for the ride. "I remember looking at Ryno and telling him, 'One more and you're gonna find out what I've been talking about all year,'" said Bowa.

The last batter of the night was Orsulak, who had both hits off Sutcliffe on the night but had been picked off to end the sixth inning. With the count 1–2, Orsulak had no chance because home-plate umpire Lee Weyer may also have been caught up in the moment. "I remember Jody Davis giving him a sign for a fastball away," said Stone. "You had a feeling that for the significance of that game, if Jody had set up by the dugout, the umpire was going to call strike three because that pitch was a foot-and-a-half off the outside corner, and he rang him up." Davis pumped his fist, hugged Sutcliffe, and the party was on.

One of the lasting images of the night was Frey stuffing his hat down the front of his jersey as he raced to join the celebration on the mound. "That's because of what happened when I was with the Orioles," Frey said. "We'd won a few times, and every time we'd win and people would come on the field, the one thing the young men would do is steal hats, and I didn't want them stealing my hat. I thought I had a lucky hat, and I didn't want some young kid stealing it. I had seen it in Baltimore and even in Kansas City when we'd won there. Most of the time people don't care about losing their hat, but I wanted my lucky hat."

The team quickly retreated to the locker room where garbage buckets full of champagne bottles were quickly emptied, prompting Harry Caray to note on the air somewhat disapprovingly, "Here we come to the wasteful part of the night, where instead of guzzling it down, they pour it out." By all accounts, there was plenty consumed, as well. Davis knew the Cubs had earned the right to let loose and made sure to do just that. "Sutcliffe had won 13 in a row, and we knew we were going to win it at that point, it was just a matter of when," said Davis. "It was a great night, and it almost seemed like everybody in the ballpark was a Cubs fan. It was great for us to go from the ballpark and back to the hotel and turn on the TV and see all the partying in Chicago. We wish we could have won it here in Chicago, but it just didn't work out that way."

RICK SUTCLIFFE

On June 13, 1984, the surging Cubs stood atop the National League East by a slim margin over the New York Mets, but general manager Dallas Green wasn't satisfied that the team could hold on for the long haul. Later that day, Green pulled the trigger on one of the biggest and gutsiest trades in Cubs history, sending outfielder Mel Hall, top draft pick Joe Carter, and pitchers Don Schulze and Darryl Banks to the Cleveland Indians for pitcher Rick Sutcliffe, catcher Ron Hassey, and relief pitcher George Frazier. As much as the trade helped the Cubs on the field, it was also a powerful public relations move, showing that the organization was serious about winning. In Sutcliffe, the team added a premier starting pitcher, whom Harry Caray quickly dubbed "the Red Baron" and who became a fan favorite for the rest of the decade.

"We knew we had to trade Hall, and we thought we could get a pretty good pitcher," said manager Jim Frey. "But to get somebody of Sutcliffe's quality, Dallas actually took a chance and it worked out for us, at least short-term. Sutcliffe became the Cy Young winner, and we won our division and came within a few outs of going to the World Series, which would have really made it all worthwhile. Carter went on to be a great player, but you have to take those chances."

Chicago Tribune beat writer Fred Mitchell saw an energized Cubs club respond to the trade. "Rick Sutcliffe was only 4–5 with Cleveland when the Cubs obtained him," he said. "Something sort of clicked and he got into a good routine, and he got some good offensive support from the Cubs. I think sometimes just a change of scenery can do it."

Sutcliffe quickly fell in love with his new surroundings. "I remember that my wife's first game ever at Wrigley was the Saturday day game where Ryno basically became known to the nation. He won the MVP that day, not that he didn't continue to do a lot of things the whole year. I'll never forget after the game when I walked out, my wife was just crying with excitement. She goes, 'Are all the games like that here?' We had come from Cleveland, and there were more people at the park that day than we would normally see in a month. It was just amazing, the whole town and what was going on." The next day, June 24, Sutcliffe made a memorable first impression on the fans in his Wrigley Field debut by striking out 14 Cardinals en route to a complete-game shutout that led the Cubs to a sweep of St. Louis.

The bearded redhead went on to post a 16–1 record punctuated by a complete-game win at Pittsburgh in the Cubs' division-clinching game. (Quick, name the only loss. It was in Los Angeles to a kid named Orel Hershiser in Sut's third start as a Cub on June 29 of that year.) After a dominating win in Game 1 of the NLCS against the Padres, Sutcliffe's 15-game winning streak came crashing to an end in San Diego in the deciding Game 5.

He was the runaway winner of the National League Cy Young Award and was Exhibit A for Green's Executive of the Year award. "That year for Sutcliffe was enchanted," said Steve Stone. "Without him, they don't win 96 games and don't sweep to the division."

Sutcliffe was the hottest free agent on the market after the 1984 season, but he had developed a severe case of Cubs fever. "As a kid growing up in Kansas City, Missouri, my dream was to play for the Kansas City Royals," he said. "That was the plan all along. In 1985, I was going to do that, but something happened that magical summer of '84 after the trade. Harry Caray gave me a nickname of 'the Red Baron.' It was just so much more than being a pitcher on a baseball team. You truly felt that you were part of a family, and it was an honor to go back there for seven more years."

A hamstring injury in 1985 led to a succession of other injuries that prevented Sut from a repeat of his dream season. Arm problems followed, but he continued to make every effort to take his turn in the rotation. There were times when he seemed to take an eon between pitches, but he likes to joke that "I was just walking around out there waiting for my arm to quit hurting so I could throw the next pitch."

Rick Sutcliffe went 16–1 for the 1984 Cubs and was christened the "Red Baron."

He remained the unquestioned leader of the Cubs' staff for the rest of his tenure in Chicago. His veteran leadership was instrumental in helping a young team become the surprise champion of the National League East in 1989. With his dedication, Sutcliffe earned the respect and affection of the team's other leader, Andre Dawson. "He was a character," said Dawson. "Well-respected. He would go to bat for you under any circumstance, knowing that when he was out there on the mound he was going to give you an all-out effort and he was going to keep you in the ballgame, allow you to win ballgames. He was one of those guys who, in the clubhouse, had a presence. He was by no stretch of the imagination a small guy. He didn't speak very much, but when he did, it carried volumes."

Sutcliffe now covers baseball nationally for ESPN, but he hasn't scratched his Cubs itch and has recently joined the team for a few weeks in spring training as a volunteer pitching instructor. His dream season assured him a hero's welcome any time he returns to the Windy City. "It's kind of funny, walking around Chicago," he said. "I think a lot of people think I'm still playing. I don't know. I wish I was still able to play."

1984

"The thing that jumps out at me is that we never played a game on the road. I remember going to Dodger Stadium, and I was there, I started with the Dodgers, and the big Red Machine would come to town, but nothing ever happened like what happened in '84 when the Cubs went there. In the seventh inning, Jody Davis comes to hit and the crowd, everywhere in the stadium, starts chanting, 'Jo-dee.' All of a sudden in the eighth when Ryno hits, 'M-V-P!' We may not have hit in the bottom of the ninth, but that year we never played on the road. We always had more fans in the ballpark than the home team did. Nobody could believe that it would actually happen, that we could get into the playoffs. All the things you read, all the things you heard about, the ups and downs during that last month of the season, it was really exciting to finally get to the postseason."

WINNING THE DIVISION IN 1989

"I remember everybody getting hurt the first month of the season, and I remember right after the All-Star Game, Don Zimmer brought Mike Bielecki, Greg Maddux, and myself into his office. He said, 'With you guys on the mound, we got a chance. With anybody else, we lose every game.' He said, 'I'm going to run you out there every third day when I can.' I remember saying right then, 'You can do it to Bielecki and me, but not Maddux. His career is just getting going.' Maddux goes, 'What do you mean? With my arm I can do it. It's not a problem for me.' I knew right then that, you know what, this truly was a team. I'll never forget when we lost in the playoffs to the Giants, Don Zimmer came in and had a meeting. He said, 'Let me tell you something, boys. Most of you don't know my history. When I was in Boston, my family couldn't even come to the game and watch because I was the dumbest manager on the face of the earth. Because of you guys, I'm probably going to be the Manager of the Year. I didn't do anything different. You guys just played harder than any other team in baseball this year.' He was bawling. 'I just want to thank you guys for what happened.' When you look back on that year, Don Zimmer—usually a manager might make the difference in 10 or 15 games in a year, but he might have made the difference in 25 or 30 that year with the way he motivated people, moves he made late during the course of the ballgame, and just bringing people together."

FUN WITH ARNE HARRIS

"He understood the responsibility that he had for the fan and he also understood the respect that he had for the player, and what a guy would go through, what he went through to get there and how difficult it was to stay. When I think of Arne, the first thing I do is laugh and I think back to the days when Harry [Caray] might have been overserved on Rush Street the night before and was struggling, and I'd get a call in the dugout. That doesn't happen now. It doesn't happen anywhere else in baseball, but it would be Arne. He said, 'Sut, I need your help.

The Cubs celebrate the 5–3 victory in the 1998 wild-card game.
(Photo courtesy of AP/Wide World Images.)

The big guy is scuffling, can you come up with something?' That's when I would go over and crawl under the dugout and light somebody's shoelace. I'd send the batboy out to the home-plate umpire to ask for the keys to the batter's box. He'd send him to the second-base umpire, he'd go to third, I mean Harry is tapped in on it, everything is working. I'd take bubble gum and I'd stick it on a baseball after I chewed it, and I'd just kind of reach over beside a guy in the dugout and I'd stick it to the roof. Of course, Arne would be zooming in on the baseball, and after about 30 seconds it would drop. There would be nobody around this guy, and he just got hit in the head with a baseball. Harry would have a ball with that, and of course, he would get back into whatever it was Harry Caray would do, and it ended up being a lot of fun."

WRIGLEY FIELD

"Why is this place special? I don't know if it has anything to do with the ivy or the field or the history or the curses or the goats or anything. I think it has more to do with the 40,000 people showing up every day and having a ball. I've seen Cub-Cardinal series, I've seen important games, and you know what, at the end of the game, you put your arm around the guy and you either congratulate him or he congratulates you. It's truly a place for 40,000 people to go and have a great day." —*Rick Sutcliffe*

SUT THE STORYTELLER

"It's '89, it's a big game, and we had lost two or three in a row, and Zimmer had made some moves that didn't work out. All of a sudden, I go to take the mound in the bottom of the ninth, and Zimmer is yelling to the guys in the dugout because that's where the bullpen was, 'Hey, I want a right-hander up.' He would've had four guys up if he had four mounds. I said, 'Wait a minute. Sit your little fat butt down. You screwed up the last three games. You're not messing this one up. I got it.' I yelled to the bullpen, 'Anybody gets up, you're going to deal with me.' So nobody got up.

I got the first two guys out. Third guy comes up, it's Paul O'Neill. He hits a home run. No big deal: 5–2. The fireworks go off. Ba-boom, ba-boom! Ba-boom, boom, boom. They do a good job of it. The very next pitch, Eric Davis hits it even farther: 5–3. We don't have anybody up in the bullpen. The tying run is in the on-deck circle. Fireworks are going off. Ba-boom, ba-boom, ba-boom, boom, boom, boom. Zimmer points out to Joe Girardi to go talk to me. Joe says no. Everybody knew I didn't like anybody on the mound. They try to get Vance Law at third–no. [Shawon] Dunston is saying no. You know Sandberg wasn't coming in. So Billy Connors, our pitching coach, has to come out. When he gets to the mound, I'm yelling at him. I'm saying, 'Get back there! What are you doing?' By the time he gets to the mound, he too is mad. He says, 'I know you're fine. I'm not worried about you winning this game. I'm just here to give the fireworks guy time to reload.' Right in the middle of that, I feel a young punk kid, Mark Grace, blow a snot bubble all over me. Everybody is laughing, and I thought, 'Well, that is pretty funny.' I will close the story with this: I got the next guy out, so we were okay."

THE WILD-CARD GAME

In a year that started with the death of Harry Caray, saw Kerry Wood's 20-strikeout game, provided must-see TV with Sammy Sosa's chase for the home-run record, and nearly ended with Brant Brown's dropped fly ball in Milwaukee, it was only fitting that it took an extra day for the Cubs to define their 1998 season. It came down to a single game, an opportunity for redemption, and a memorable evening known forever as "Wild Night" at Wrigley Field.

On the season's last day, needing a win to clinch at least a tie for the wild-card, the Cubs had stumbled in Houston and lost 4–3 in 11 innings. As the team limped into the clubhouse dazed at seeing the year slip away, word from Denver provided the Cubs with a Lazarus-like comeback. Neifi Perez's home run at Coors Field had given the Colorado Rockies an improbable 9–8 win over San Francisco and left the Giants wondering where a 7–0 lead and punched ticket to the postseason had gone. For the first time since 1980, there would be a game number 163 on the baseball schedule, and thanks to an earlier coin flip, it would be contested at Wrigley Field.

After a season of improbable highs and staggering lows, the atmosphere on the North Side that Monday night was beyond electric. "The single most exciting game in the years that I was broadcasting was game 163," said Steve Stone. "Game 163 I think has to be the most exciting game for any of the teams involved for the simple reason that it's one and done. You play that game, and whoever wins that game goes to the playoffs."

The Cubs organization left no stone unturned in making this a special night, starting with the decision to tap into positive postseason karma by having Michael Jordan throw out the ceremonial first pitch. Jordan's toss to Sammy Sosa was received with a full-throated roar and ratcheted up the already-fevered pitch in the stadium. There were probably more signs that night in Wrigley than ever before for a single game, most of them honoring the memory of Harry Caray, who had died seven months before. Harry was there in more than just spirit thanks to some enterprising fans on Waveland Avenue, who raised an eight-foot balloon in his likeness just beyond the left-field fence, an apparition that has then-Giants manager Dusty Baker shaking his head to this day.

The Cubs gave the assignment of saving their season to veteran right-hander Steve Trachsel, while the Giants countered with Mark Gardner. Neither team managed to break through in the first four innings, but after the Giants went down in the fifth, the Cubs got a boost from a two-time world champion third baseman who had wondered only five weeks before if his time in the majors was at an end.

Gary Gaetti had been cut loose by the Cardinals and, after weighing his options, signed with the Cubs five days later on August 19. His second wind would result in a .320 average and eight big home runs down the stretch, none bigger than the shot that provided the first runs of the night in the fifth inning. After a Henry Rodriguez single, Gaetti reached out for Gardner's belt-high fastball and drove it into the third row of the left-field bleachers, sending the fans there into delirium while 10 feet below them, Giants left fielder Barry Bonds slumped head down into the ivy.

Staked to a 2–0 lead, Trachsel breezed through the sixth inning and saw his cushion double when Matt Mieske's bases-loaded, two-run single in the bottom half of the frame gave the Cubs some breathing room. Mieske's hit would eventually provide the game-winning RBI, which makes for a great trivia question to this day.

Earlier in the day, Trachsel heard various sports outlets predict a high-scoring game because of the Cubs' beat-up pitching staff, and he resolved to not let that happen on his watch. His promise was secure, and he took a no-hitter into the seventh inning, despite yielding six walks and dodging trouble throughout.

Nothing came easy for the Cubs in 1998, and the pattern held true as the Giants rallied in the seventh. After Trachsel retired Charlie Hayes on a liner to second, Brett Mayne ended the no-hitter with a single to right. An ensuing walk chased Trachsel as Matt Karchner came on to face Stan Javier. On the double switch, Orlando Merced was inserted into left field, and proving that the adage "the ball will find you" is especially true in big games, Javier lofted a fly in his direction that hugged the left-field wall. Merced raced over and made a leaping catch that bears an uncanny resemblance to an eerily similar play that Moises Alou wouldn't be able to make five years later. It was the Cubs' night.

Ex-Cub Shawon Dunston singled to load the bases, sending Karchner off and bringing in left-hander Felix Heredia, who faced the daunting task of retiring Bonds. The brooding Giants star had a history of postseason failure at that point in his career, and he added to the misery by grounding to first to let the Cubs off the hook.

Bill Murray led the crowd in an epic rendition of "Take Me Out to the Ballgame" in the seventh inning, followed by a Sosa run on a José Mesa wild pitch to give the Cubs a 5–0 lead after eight. Thumbs across Chicago were poised on champagne corks.

Not so fast. San Francisco touched Terry Mulholland and Kevin Tapani for two runs to open the ninth, forcing manager Jim Riggleman to go back to his bullpen. As he had all season, Riggleman went to Rod Beck with the game on the line, even though he had thrown almost three innings while picking up the loss the day before. Beck's right arm appeared to be hanging by a thread as he took the mound, needing two outs to send the Cubs to the postseason. "The Shooter" inherited Giants runners at first and third, took a deep breath, and attempted to dig down and find some way to pick up his 51st save. After a Jeff Kent force-out at second made it 5–3, Joe Carter, the Cubs' number one draft pick in 1981, stepped to the plate as most of the 39,556 in attendance tried not to think about his home run to win the 1993 World Series. Instead, Carter's last at-bat in the majors was a pop-up to first base.

>>

> ## *"Sometimes you plan for the best, but you never know. We had a great time that year."*
>
> –Sammy Sosa

>>

Stone still marvels at Beck's performance. "He was able to jam Joe Carter on a 79-mile-per-hour fastball," he said. "It was one of those that Joe could have caught and thrown it into the outfield for a base hit, it was so slow. He got it inside on him somehow, and Rod did it with absolute attitude. He knew he was going to get you out. Big arm swing, here it comes, nothing! He had nothing! He did it on just guts."

About 10 feet behind the bag, Mark Grace grabbed Carter's pop-up, cradled his head in his hands, and the celebration was on. "It was great. I caught it, and it was pandemonium," Grace said. "We didn't quit partying for a while. The fans deserved it. I remember I went into the stands, and it was just a big lovefest. It was awesome."

The Cubs mob at the pitcher's mound quickly reconvened in the clubhouse, but it didn't take long for the players to grab a few champagne bottles, head back up the runway, and go out to the field, where none of the standing-room-only throng had left or stopped cheering.

Nobody had more fun on the field than Sosa, who managed to evade the huge cluster of reporters and cameras on the field long enough to pay homage to his right-field bleacher disciples by spraying champagne into the seats. "That was incredible, that was beautiful," said Sosa. "Everybody was wonderful. Sometimes you plan for the best, but you never know. We had a great time that year."

Not everyone on the team got the chance to celebrate. Rookie sensation Kerry Wood had to watch on TV. "I was stuck in Arizona," said Wood, who was on the disabled list as the Cubs tried to get him healthy for the rest of the postseason. "It was tough, knowing the guys for the first time in however long were celebrating, popping champagne, and there I was rehabbing, trying to get ready for the playoffs. That was definitely frustrating for me."

As team president at the time, Andy MacPhail was keenly aware of the impact of being able to clinch a playoff spot at home because the division championships in 1984 and 1989 were won on the road. "Winning at home in front of your home team is really a treat," said MacPhail. "It was really quite a night. Again, what I remember most is the celebration, finally getting into the postseason, players going around the stands and spraying champagne into the crowd, and the crowd loving it. It was a great experience to win just that."

Five days later, the Cubs season would end at Wrigley, swept out of the playoffs in three anticlimactic games by the Atlanta Braves. It didn't matter. For one wild night at Wrigley, the Cubs were champions.

MARK GRACE

When the Cubs started rookie Mark Grace in 1988, he looked to be an unlikely successor to Frank Chance, Phil Cavarretta, and Ernie Banks as a longtime Cubs first baseman, but the 24th-round draft pick would go on to play 1,890 games in his 13 seasons with the team. The left-handed-hitting Grace caught on quickly, batting .314 in his second season as the Cubs caught lightning in a bottle and won the Eastern Division in 1989. His coming-out party was against the Giants, when he hit .647 in the National League Championship Series, the lone bright spot in the Cubs' five-game series loss.

The team foundered after its win in 1989, but not for lack of effort from Grace and his fellow marquee Cubs Andre Dawson and Ryne Sandberg. "We were just guys that came to work every day and did the best we possibly could," said Grace. "We played for some bad teams; there were some great times, but there just wasn't a whole lot of talent there. You wouldn't know from watching us play because, God, we gave it everything we had, every single day. We dove, we slid hard, we took people out, we did everything we possibly could to try to win that baseball game."

Dawson saw Grace break into the majors and became a role model for the young first baseman and knew there was something there. "Mark started out, he replaced Leon Durham in 1988," he said. "He always showed he could handle a bat real well. He worked very diligently defensively and became a very good defensive first baseman. You knew at the plate what you were going to get. He didn't really hit for a lot of power, but he hit for average and he was going to put the ball in play. When he was in the right place in the order, you were going to get production out of him."

Grace's glove may have saved as many runs as he drove in. He holds most Cubs fielding records, including all-time fielding percentage (.995). With a Hall of Fame second baseman next to him, very few ground balls made it through to right field. "Gracie was awesome," said Sandberg. "It got to the point where we covered that right side, we knew where each other was playing. We knew the count, the hitter, we anticipated together. Before every pitch, I'd just take a little peek over to see where he was at, and he would do the same thing, and we would adjust accordingly. We covered that ground pretty well over there. Not too many balls went through that hole. The way that he was able to

pick it at first base, he saved me a couple of errors. Not a ton of errors! I had a few throws slightly off that he picked, and he was a joy to play with."

Why did Cubs fans worship a first baseman who never hit 20 homers or drove in more than 98 runs? Because he was a throwback and was never shy about reminding us of that. He eschewed the use of batting gloves, did whatever he could to get an edge, and was proud of being a ballplayer, not an athlete. Whether it was an exaggerated sigh of relief after surviving one of Shawon Dunston's bullets to first base or using his cleats to dig out a game of tic-tac-toe in Colorado, Gracie's boyish grin let everyone know just how much he loved playing the game. When the game was over, he could be found mingling with the fans at any number of Wrigley Field establishments.

"We called ourselves lunch-pail guys," said Grace. "We would clock in and wear our hard hats and bring our lunch pail and go to work. We would go to work and when the game was over, it was time to have a good time, and the fans certainly saw that. I didn't travel with a posse. I didn't need bodyguards. I was one of the Chicagoans. I was one of the Chicago faithful that, 'You know what? Let's go have some food and a couple of beverages and talk about things.'"

"Gracie got the most out of his talent," said Joe Girardi, who broke into the majors with the Cubs at the same time as Grace. "He wasn't a guy that was going to hit a lot of home runs, but he found a way to drive in runs. He had a lot of confidence in what he needed to do and how he needed to do it. He didn't try to do something that he wasn't capable of, and I think that's why Mark Grace was such a good player."

Grace was also a favorite teammate who never forgot how Rick Sutcliffe and Sandberg taught him the ropes and didn't hesitate to look out for younger players, especially those rookies who struck out 20 batters in a game. "I'm thankful for that," Kerry Wood said. "Guys come up here, and you are a fish out of water. It's the equivalent of going from junior high to high school. You're the little guy again. It's scary when you come up here and you don't know. I

Mark Grace and Sammy Sosa anchored the middle of the Cubs lineup during the '90s.

was 20 at the time, I didn't know anybody. I've watched these guys on TV; you're in awe in the clubhouse. He took me under his wing and really made me feel like I belonged up here. I think we all have that question whether we're good enough to be here when you're called up and scared if you don't do well, you'll be sent back down without the chance to come back up, so he was definitely my positive influence and, believe it or not, he actually kept me out of trouble."

Grace led the National League in hits during the 1990s, an exotic statistic to be sure, but one of which he is proud. His last years in Wrigley Field were marked by yearly contract squabbles, but when the Cubs declined to offer him a contract for 2001, Grace had the last laugh by winning a World Series with the Arizona Diamondbacks. He keyed their Game 7 rally by leading off the ninth inning with a soft single up the middle against Yankees closer Mariano Rivera after a typically gutsy at-bat. Like the man himself, it wasn't pretty, but it got the job done.

CUBS FANS

"There's nothing like it in the National League. Certainly not. The Yankees and Red Sox come to mind in the American League, a love affair and a nation of fans, and it's the same thing with the Chicago Cubs. It's a love affair. It's absolutely insane, that's what it is, but in a great way. I was lucky to be a part of their adoration for 13 years, and I look back on my days in Chicago and I wish they never ended. I couldn't wait to get to the ballpark every day to not only play the game of baseball at the professional level, but to play in front of the most adoring, the most faithful fans that I could ever imagine."

WRIGLEY FIELD

"There's just so many nuances to Wrigley Field that really don't come in to play. Which way the wind is blowing makes such a difference here. The longest grass, infield grass and outfield grass, so the ball just doesn't go anywhere on the ground. The manual scoreboard. The rooftops. There's just so many things that go on here at Wrigley Field that don't go on anywhere else. You just realize the people that have watched games here and brought their families. You talk about probably three and four generations of families have been coming to this ballpark and been lovin' the Cubs, and a century's worth of ballplayers have been playing right out there on that field. It kind of gives you the chills just thinking about it that way."

PLAYING IN THE FIRST NIGHT GAME

"It rained. It rained, and wouldn't you know it, of course, because God didn't want lights at Wrigley Field. Morganna the Kissing Bandit came out and kissed Ryno. I was on deck, and I was jealous because I wanted her to come and kiss me. And then the rains came and it was washed away, so we did it again the next night against the New York Mets and we ended up winning that game. Mike Bielecki pitched for us and Sid Fernandez pitched for the New York Mets, and I ended up getting the first base hit. It was awfully cool. That ball is in the Hall of Fame. Should be in my house, but it's not. No, it's in the Hall of Fame, and that's where it should be."

TEAMMATE GREG MADDUX

"Greg was great. He was a second-round pick for the Cubs. Little bitty guy, you know; he had a good fastball. Dick Pole, an old coach of ours here, taught him a change-up and taught him, 'You don't have to throw hard, kid. You can take a little bit off and just hit your spots.' Next thing you know, Greg Maddux is, for about a 10- to 12-year run, the best pitcher in baseball. It was unfortunate that his heyday was with the Atlanta Braves. It should have been here. It was butchered by the regime that was in charge then. Unfortunately, I think it cost the Chicago Cubs postseason play not having him here for that great run."

THE 1998 WILD-CARD TEAM

"Ninety-eight was an unbelievable year. We were thinking we'd be around .500, and you know, back in the '80s and '90s, let's not kid ourselves, .500 was pretty good for those teams. We ended up winning the wild-card, and it was a great ride that year." —*Mark Grace*

GRACIE'S VERSION OF THE FIREWORKS STORY

"Billy Connors was our pitching coach. Sutcliffe gave up a long ball to Paul O'Neill in Cincinnati, and Cincinnati shot off fireworks after a home run. So the fireworks went off–boom, boom, boom. The next batter was Eric Davis. He hit one a country mile. Boom, boom, boom, boom, again. Billy Connors was walking out to the mound, and Sutcliffe was yelling at him, and I was walking, too. Sutcliffe was yelling at me, too, 'Get off my mound, you blankety-blank blanks.' Finally, Billy Connors said, 'Rick, I know you've got everything under control, I just wanted to give that guy running the fireworks a little more time to reload!' I never laughed so hard in my life on a mound. There's not always strategy going on out there on the mound. There's some good stuff going on out there, too."

KEN HOLTZMAN'S NO-HITTER

Was there ever a happier day at Wrigley Field than August 19, 1969? It was a beautiful day for a huge crowd of 41,033. The Cubs were in first place, and the long-awaited return of the World Series appeared to be on the horizon. Throw in a masterpiece on the mound from Ken Holtzman, and the sun may never have shown more brightly on the Friendly Confines than it did that day.

With Cubs fever at epidemic proportions, the Atlanta Braves hit town for what appeared to be a playoff preview between the National League division leaders (1969 was the first year the leagues split into divisions). Left-hander Holtzman took the mound for the Cubs, and it was quickly evident that he was sharp as the Braves went down in order in the first.

Ron Santo lined a three-run homer off knuckleballer Phil Niekro in the Cubs' half of the first to put the Cubs in front 3–0. No one was more surprised than the Cubs third baseman. "That's the only home run I ever hit off Niekro," Santo said. "I always tried different bats with him, but the first inning he threw me a fastball, and I hit a line drive under the wind in the left-field seats." With a three-run lead, Holtzman took charge.

> *"I'm trying to win the game and go nine innings. If I get a no-hitter that's great, but that's not the reason I'm out there."*
>
> —Ken Holtzman

WGN sports editor Jack Rosenberg was in the broadcast booth that day and was quick to point out that Holtzman went through the Braves without overpowering them. "The thing that was ironic was that he pitched a no-hitter with no strikeouts, which was incredible since Holtzman was a strikeout pitcher."

"I didn't have a lot of walks or anything, so I really didn't have to try for a strikeout," Holtzman said. "I just went and threw 99 percent fastballs and tried to move it around a little bit, and they kept hitting the ball at everybody."

In the seventh inning, Hank Aaron appeared to end the celebration when he hit a Holtzman fastball to left field. By all accounts, the ball was gone. "There goes the no-hitter," intoned Jack Brickhouse mournfully in the booth. What happened next is one of Wrigley Field's most joyous mysteries.

"I had pitched long enough to recognize the crack of the bat and the trajectory," Holtzman said. "When you throw a pitch like that, especially to a guy like Hank Aaron…okay, well, now the score is 3–1."

Like everyone else in the ballpark, Cubs left fielder Billy Williams assumed that it was out of the park. "Actually, when the ball was hit, my first reaction was to give up on it. I happened to look around, and I looked at the flag in center field, and the wind was blowing in hard, so I gave it a try. Lo and behold, the ball started to come back in because the ball was out of the ballpark. The only way I could catch that ball was to turn sideways." Williams wedged into the ivy in the corner where the wall juts in and reached up to make the catch. The legend in the bleachers holds that as soon as the ball was hit, one of the Bleacher Bums stood up and screamed, "Blow, Bums, blow!" and they were able to push the ball back into the park. However it happened, the no-hitter was still alive.

"I didn't know what to make of it," Holtzman said. "I was concentrating so hard on pitching the game and pitch after pitch and everything like that. I can remember at the time, I said, 'You know, there's something special going on in this game, and I can't explain it.' You just go ahead and pitch, but when that happened, I thought maybe it's one of those days, I don't know."

Holtzman quickly retired Felipe Alou and Felix Millan to open the ninth inning, and now all that stood between him and the no-hitter was Hank Aaron. Aaron fouled off two 3–2 pitches. On the air, Brickhouse was marveling at Holtzman's willingness to challenge the Braves' slugger with first base open. "That's the way we thought," Holtzman explained. "I'm trying to win the game and go nine innings. If I get a no-hitter that's great, but that's not the reason I'm out there."

On the next pitch, Aaron grounded sharply to second baseman Glenn Beckert, who trapped it carefully before throwing on to first for the out. As the crowd roared, Santo leaped into Holtzman's arms as the rest of the Cubs headed to the mound to mob their teammate.

Beckert has endured more than his share of ribbing from his teammates over the years over that last out, but he insists he didn't bobble the ball, but just wanted to be careful. "When I went down, I wanted to make real sure that ball wasn't going through because Hank Aaron wasn't really running that good. All I had to do was get it out. I analyzed this—over all the years I played against Hank Aaron, he only hit me two ground balls, and that was the last one. He pulled everything. I was telling them, 'Be ready, Ronnie, he's coming your way. C'mon, Kess, you can do it.' Then he hit me the ball."

The man of the hour isn't so sure and still enjoys having a laugh at Beckert's expense. "I don't think he wanted that ball hit to him," Holtzman laughed. "He kind of double-clutched at it a couple of times. Finally, he put his glove on it and, knowing Beck, I was lucky he didn't throw it into the fourth row. He was only 20 feet away from Ernie, but he got it over there. You're right, to this day, he says, 'I had it all the time. I had plenty of time.' Baloney, he was nervous, and I knew it for many, many years, and I never let him forget that he was nervous in that game."

With Holtzman's victory, the Cubs were a season-high 32 games over .500, and their lead over the Mets in the East Division was eight games. The collapse that followed in September has been well-documented, but for that sunny day in August, all things seemed possible in the Cubs world.

Holtzman would go on to throw another no-hitter for the Cubs in 1971 at Cincinnati, and in the off-season, the Cubs granted his trade request. He was sent to Oakland for Rick Monday. Holtzman lost a possible third no-hitter with the A's when ex-Cub Billy North slipped and fell on a routine fly ball, but he had plenty of other chances to celebrate in Oakland. He won three World Series with the A's, spent time with the Orioles and Yankees (but did not pitch in three postseasons there), then retired in 1979 after two last seasons in the bullpen with the Cubs. ●

Throwing almost all fastballs, Ken Holtzman no-hit the Atlanta Braves in 1969 without getting a strikeout. (Photo courtesy of Getty Images.)

The Hope

>>>

"Remember, Red, hope is a good thing, maybe the best of things, and no good thing ever dies."
—Andy Dufresne, *The Shawshank Redemption*

"Live and be happy, beloved children of my heart, and never forget that until the day comes when God will deign to reveal the future to man, all human wisdom is contained in these words: *wait and hope!*"
—*The Count of Monte Cristo*

Is hope a drug we need to go off of? Or is it keeping us alive? What's the harm in believing?"
—Carrie Bradshaw, *Sex and the City*

Sex and the City? What in the world? Forgive me, but it was the first thing I heard when I turned on the TV in a despondent mood after returning from Game 7 of the 2003 NLCS. I like to think the baseball gods were trying to offer me some solace on that awful night, and if it had to come in the form of *Sex and the City,* well, I was so far down that I took it.

One thing anyone who is around the Cubs has in common is a vivid dream, that special fantasy about the glorious October day the Cubs finally break through and win the World Series. We've all thought long and hard about where we will be when it happens, what we will do when it happens, and most of all, how sweet it will be when it happens. It's all about the day there is finally joy in Mudville.

JOHN MCDONOUGH

"I think everybody wants to be in on it. I use that term 'in on it' by saying when this happens, we all have envisioned what that's going to look like. I'm going to go on record as saying, in my mind, I see this as a fly ball to center field.

Our center fielder catches it here at Wrigley Field, and the Cubs win the World Series. Everybody has a different view, a different dream of what this is all about. Really, we're not on the corner of Clark and Addison, we're on the corner of Hopes and Dreams."

BOB DERNIER

"I see a big long parade. I plan on being in one of those cars, back a little bit, but I'll be in one of those cars. We'll all celebrate a great day. I just know that it's coming soon."

JIM TIANIS, WGN CAMERAMAN

"When they get to the Series, the Cubs are going to be down seven, eight, nine to nothing in the ninth inning. Then they're going to score some runs, and it will be 9–7, the bases will be loaded, and someone is going to hit a bases-loaded triple. I see a Cub sliding into home as the tag is being applied, they're going to call him safe, and Chicago is going to go up for grabs. Boy, would I love to see that!"

BURT HOOTON

"You might have every Cubs fans in the country converge on the city just to be a part of it. Even when I played, all I heard about was 1945, which was the last time they were in the Series, and I was thinking then if we could just win a World Series, this town would go nuts. Just think how many more fans there are now than there were 35 years ago."

ERNIE BANKS

"It's a very important thing for the Cubs to win, more than any other team because of the love and interest of the people who follow this team. The team is a generational team. The fathers came out, and now the kids, and then their kids. It's

Built in 1914, Wrigley Field has been home to the Cubs for more than 90 years and is the second oldest ballpark in America.

generational, and they grow and move to other cities and parts of the world and they still love their team. Ironically, the Cubs colors are red, white, and blue, so it's more of an American team with the American spirit, the spirit of never giving up, staying positive, holding on to enthusiasm, and working hard."

ED HARTIG, CUBS HISTORIAN

"When they beat the Braves in '03 to win their first post-season series since 1908, I grabbed my Cubs flag and ran out of my house and ran up and down the street waving my flag. I wasn't the only one. I can't imagine what's going to happen when the Cubs win a World Series. I'm not even going to try, I'm just going to enjoy it when it happens."

GLENN BECKERT

"I hope I'm still on the right side of the grass. I'll be at the game somehow, some way. I'm just hoping and praying that it happens. It was a lot easier being a player than it is being a fan. As a fan, you can't do anything. You can't make a play, you can't hit the ball—it's tough."

JEFF GARLIN

"I'll be here. Or I'll be in whatever city, Seattle, New York—Anaheim would be very convenient, actually. I will be wherever it is. That's the fact. I will be there. I don't fantasize. In my gut, I feel like we will do it in my lifetime, but many people have said that before me who are no longer with us anymore. So I hope and I pray and I feel good about the current team, so we'll see. I know I'll be wherever it is."

JODY DAVIS

"I think when we win the World Series at Wrigley Field they just need to have the bulldozers there. The fans would carry off most of the ballpark, and it would be a vacant lot by daylight. They could just start building a new park the next day."

ANDY PAFKO

"It's hard to believe what would transpire here. I hope I live long enough to see it. I'll be there and the first in line to get a ticket. I played in a World Series, and I'll relive those days again."

MARK GRACE

"It would be like Mrs. O'Leary's cow kicked the lantern again. It would be another Great Chicago Fire, but it would burn with joy and adulation. It wouldn't be rioting, it would be just dancing in the streets. I think Chicago Cubs fans would just fiddle while it burned. I would be right here. I would be right here enjoying it."

BONNIE HUNT

"I'd love to be at the ballpark with my mom. I would love to be there. The game would be tied with bases loaded because that's typical for a Cubs fan. You have to keep thinking, "Oh no, oh no, oh no." We have to have a lot of that "oh no" moment, I think, to make it a sincere Cubs World Series victory. Bases loaded, a homer is hit, and the place goes nuts. I'm not too picky, and I always believe this is the year."

ERIC KARROS

"It can't be a four-game sweep or anything easy. That's would not be right. I'd love to see them do it with a comeback, fans on the edge of their seats, riding on that roller-coaster seventh game, with the Cubs winning when Steve Bartman reaches out to snatch a ball that is ruled a home run so he is the hero."

GARY MATTHEWS

"I am sincerely pulling for them and want them to have good years. I have so many friends here. The day that it does happen, I think everybody in the stands here are going to see the ghosts get up and fly away."

JACK ROSENBERG

"Every night's gonna be like Saturday night.

"How does it happen? I think it will happen when someone comes out of the bushes. Someone they never had counted on who suddenly has one of the most incredible years that any player could have. One that none of us thought could ever do it catches lightning in a bottle, and that's how they're going to do it."

RYNE SANDBERG

"I had just a small taste of it in the playoff seasons. I can't wait. I have no idea what that's going to be like. It's going to be big. It's going to be big here in Chicago, and it's going to be big throughout the United States. I just want to be part of it, and hopefully I will be part of it."

FRED MITCHELL, *CHICAGO TRIBUNE*

"During my *Tribune* career, I've witnessed the Bears winning the Super Bowl and I've seen the Bulls win six NBA titles, but I think if and when the Cubs ever win a World Series here, it would surpass any of those championships in terms of the reaction, not just here in Chicago, not just in the United States, but I think internationally it would represent such a huge accomplishment knowing that it has been since 1908 that the Cubs have won. The long-suffering Cubs fan acknowledgment will come to an end, and it will be interesting to see what fans will do after such a remarkable thing happens."

MIKE KRUKOW

"I always felt that I wanted to be on that team that finally won it because when that happens it's going to be like the pope coming to Chicago, it's going to be unbelievable. All those guys on that team, they'll all be canonized that same day. Bases loaded, down by three, full count. Two outs. Soriano hits a long drive out to center, and Steve Bartman catches the ball. Home run, Cubs win, and that's how it ends. They win the World Series, and they carry Bartman

around the infield and he hangs on to that ball forever and he never sells it. That's how it should end."

GREG MADDUX

"I think it would be one of the greatest championships in all of sports when it happens. Take the other four sports along with it, and if the Cubs ever win the World Series, it's going to be better than anything ever won before."

PAT KELLY, BUDWEISER HOUSE

"For the Cubs to win the World Series would be unbelievable. I sure hope it happens in my lifetime. Hey, maybe somebody will hit a home run that lands in our yard!"

JIM FREY

"I'd love to see it happen because there are so many people over the years who have done what they could do to try and do it. When you start talking about 90 years or 100 years, it's hard to conceive that a team, an organization could go that long. This will be the celebration of all celebrations in Chicago, I would think, and I'd like to be there for it."

SAMMY SOSA

"You've got to keep fighting, keep fighting. One day they will do it."

RICK FUHS, SCOREBOARD OPERATOR

"I'd like to punch out that last out and see the Cubs win that World Series. I think they would shut the whole city down for a week if the Cubs ever won it. We just have to wish and hope that someday we will win it."

KEN HOLTZMAN

"We used to daydream about it and think what would happen if we could just do it once. When it finally happens, the city is going to release a lot of pent-up frustration, have

"It's going to be better than anything won before."
—Greg Maddux

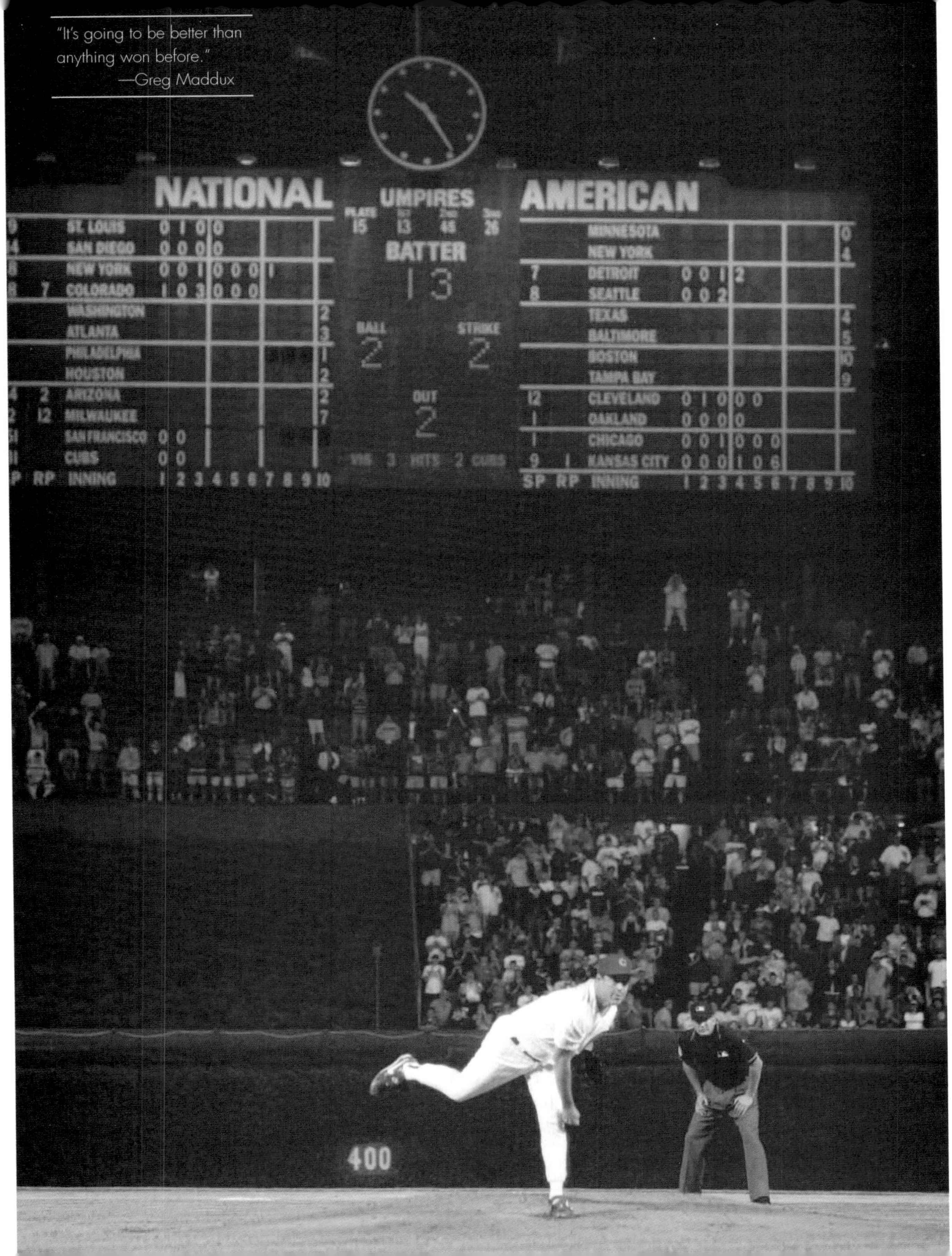

a wild celebration, and everybody is going to get to feel good. I hope I live to see that."

ANDY MACPHAIL

"I'd like to see it happen sooner rather than later like everybody else. In '03 I started to think about this, looking at the crowds outside the ballpark, that if we did win, somebody was going to have to parachute some supplies in to us because there was no way we were going to be able to leave that ballpark for about a week or two. So I was hoping there would be enough left from the concessions people because you weren't going anywhere for a while, and you really wouldn't have it any other way."

JIMMY FARRELL, UMPIRES' ATTENDANT

"The Cubs fans would come from all over just to be here and watch it in the taverns or a nightclub someplace. It would be amazing. Mayor Daley wouldn't know what to do. He'd say, 'Gosh darn it, they did it.'"

LARRY BOWA

"I would like to just be around when it happens. They are going to have their day in the sun. It would be a lot of fun to be in the city when that happens."

BILLY WILLIAMS

"You don't know whether the team will keep the mystique. I know the people will party because it's been 100 years since they got the chance to do it. There will be 40,000 in the park, and not long after, 600,000 will say they were there! That day will come, though, and the fans that will be here, and the fans that have supported this club for so many years are going to rejoice."

LEN KASPER

"Just win it! It doesn't matter how they do it, but I have a feeling if the Cubs do win it, it's going to be in Game 7 of the World Series. There might be an error, there may be fan interference in the fifth inning, but the Cubs will finally

overcome that and win it. That would be the perfect ending to the story."

BILL BUCKNER

"It's going to be pretty cool. It's going to happen. You hope they catch a break at some point. I don't care how it happens, as long as it does. It would be cool if they played the Red Sox, even though that would have meant more a few years ago because you knew one streak would have to end. A lot of the teams that haven't won in a long time have done it, so it needs to be the Cubs' turn."

JOE GIRARDI

"I'd like to see it happen in the seventh game and see them win it in their last at-bat because I think it would be the ultimate for the fans who are on the edge of their seat. I didn't really realize the importance of baseball and WGN to the older generation until I had an aunt who told me she watches every day. My mother grew up in a family of farmers, and they listened to the radio every day to the Cubs games because they were out in the fields. You realize how important it is during the course of the day to so many people's lives, and I think it would just be the ultimate for the Cubs to win in a seventh game."

FRED WASHINGTON, SCOREBOARD OPERATOR

"I cannot envision the joy that I would feel that we made it to a World Series in my lifetime. Every game, win or lose, I have to put a won or a lost flag on top of the scoreboard. To put up the *W* in the World Series, that's the ultimate."

RON SANTO

"I know I'm optimistic every year. I don't know what I would do. I really don't know. I sure hope it happens before I leave this earth, that's for sure."

Fred Washington shows off his less-than-glamorous work space in the scoreboard.

VIN SCULLY

"Someone said to me, 'How long do you want to keep doing this stuff,' and I said, 'You know, I'd kind of like to do it until the Cubs play the Red Sox in the World Series.' Well you know, a couple of years ago, it got awfully close, and I started to wish I could take that back. Maybe that would be perfect, if the Cubs played the Red Sox, but I'm sure if you are a Cubs fan, if you've followed them all these years, you don't care who they play, just make it. I really hope they do one day."

RICK SUTCLIFFE

"I don't know how to put into words what it would mean. I know personally what it would mean for me. It would be an opportunity for the fans who thought we were going to get it in '84 and '89 to finally have it. Just like everything else, it's got to come down to Game 7, and I don't know if we strike out a guy or hit a homer. It seems to me the walk-off homer is the thing right now, so let's have it end in Game 7 with a walk-off homer."

RICK MONDAY

"Having played five years in Chicago, I don't care where I am, if I am able to travel, I'm going to go to Chicago because that is going to be one helluva party."

TOM HELLMAN, CLUBHOUSE MANAGER

"I fantasize about it every day because that's what we're all here for, is to win a World Series because when we do, it's going to be the greatest party in the world."

LEE SMITH

"It's crazy. I've wanted that so much for this city and the fans, but I don't think I'd like to be in Chicago when it happens. I think the city might fall! For the fans and the organization itself, to get out there and be a part of something like that, it is unbelievable. I would love to see that for the city."

KERRY WOOD

"It's a great stadium, a great atmosphere, and I can't imagine playing anywhere else. You better have some extra police enforcement because it's gonna be a helluva party."

JOHN SAMPSON, ENGINE 78 FIREFIGHTER

"You know what? You might as well make it a no-hitter because if you're going to go out, really go out. I used to be a pitcher, so I enjoy the no-hitters and stuff. Make it a no-hitter when the Cubs win it, just to put that exclamation point on it. That would be kind of nice."

ANDRE DAWSON

"Oh my God, it's going to be crazy. That's something I hope I'm around to see because I want to be here in Wrigley Field when it happens."

JIMMY BUFFETT

"If it happens, I'll come back and play a concert for free. I made that promise a long time ago and I didn't do it and a lot of people accuse me of doing it because I thought it would never happen, but that's not the way I think. I'll be back!"

RANDY HUNDLEY

"The only fantasizing for me is to be on the field and be a player. That's what I always dreamed about. That's what I always shared with Todd. Come here and help this ballclub win, and there will be nothing like it. That's where I would want to be, is on the field. Of course, I can't be now, but I would sure like to be in the ballpark somewhere because it will be a wild time. We're going to celebrate it for months and months and months. It's not going to be here and gone in a couple of weeks. We're going to celebrate for a long time."

BOB BRENLY

"Wow! Seal all the exits, and just fill the place up with champagne and dive off the roof into the bubbly. I think

that would be a fitting celebration for the Cubs' first World Series in 100 years, and I'll have my snorkel ready."

FERGUSON JENKINS

"This city will go crazy. I thought they had the great shot in 2003. I just think what the city and the Cubs fans need is for the Cubs and the North Side to win one time and to prove they have a great organization here."

DERREK LEE

"Do you think about it? Yes. Yes, all the time. All off-season, every day. We talk about it in the clubhouse all the time. This city would just go crazy to win here, so that's what we're striving for, and it's definitely a motivating factor."

>>

"This city will go crazy."

—Ferguson Jenkins

>>

STEVE STONE

"If it was just deserts, what would happen is the bases would be loaded in the final game, with the Cubs up one run and a line drive would hit right off the mound, one that usually goes into center field, and it's going to deflect right back to the catcher. He's going to step on the plate for the force-out, and the Cubs are going win the World Series."

For me, thanks to some inclement weather and inexplicable network scheduling, it's an unheard-of World Series day game at Wrigley Field. The shadows cross the pitcher's mound in the top of the ninth as the Cubs nurse a one-run lead. With one out, the runners at first and second take a lead, and there is a one-out ground ball to short. The flip goes to second, then quickly over to first for a coming-full-circle Tinker-to-Evers-to-Chance double play, and the wait is finally over. As the players mob each other on the field, I take a photo of my father out of my pocket for a quick glance of thanks, hug my sons, who are sitting with me, then reach under my seat for the bottle of champagne I've managed to sneak in (you have to put that press pass to good use). I'll pop the cork and join in the greatest roar in Chicago history. After the bedlam on the field subsides a bit, I shift my gaze to the top of that beautiful green scoreboard and watch Fred Washington raise a white flag emblazoned with the ultimate *W*. The next day, I will go downtown with the WGN crew, and we will televise the most joyous parade you could ever imagine. I can't wait. ●